*Betty Crocker*

# the big book
# pies & tarts

Houghton Mifflin Harcourt
Boston • New York • 2013

## General Mills

Food Content and Relationship Marketing Director: Geoff Johnson

Food Content Marketing Manager: Susan Klobuchar

Editors: Diane Carlson, Grace Wells

Kitchen Manager: Ann Stuart

Food Editor: Andrea Bidwell

Recipe Development and Testing: Betty Crocker Kitchens

Photography: General Mills Photography Studios and Image Library

Photographer: Andy Swarbrick

Photography Assistant: Erin Smith

Food Stylists: Carol Grones, Nancy Johnson

Food Styling Assistants: Patty Gabbert, Benjamin Plante

## Houghton Mifflin Harcourt

Publisher: Natalie Chapman

Editorial Director: Cindy Kitchel

Executive Editor: Anne Ficklen

Associate Editor: Heather Dabah

Managing Editor: Marina Padakis

Production Editor: Jamie Selzer

Art Director and Interior Design: Tai Blanche

Cover Design: Suzanne Sunwoo

Interior Layout: Holly Wittenberg

Production Manager: Kevin Watt

This book is printed on acid-free paper. ∞

Library of Congress Cataloging-in-Publication Data:

Crocker, Betty
  Betty Crocker's the big book of pies and tarts / Betty Crocker
          p. cm.
  Includes index.
  ISBN: 978-1-118-43216-7 (pbk.); 978-0-544-17832-8 (ebk.)
  1. Pies  II. Tarts  III. Title  IV. Title: Betty Crocker, the big book of pies and tarts.
  TX773.C738 2013
  641.86/52
                                2012034408

641.8652

The Betty Crocker Kitchens seal guarantees success in your kitchen. Every recipe has been tested in America's Most Trusted Kitchens™ to meet our high standards of reliability, easy preparation and great taste.

FIND MORE GREAT IDEAS AT
*BettyCrocker*.com

For consistent baking results, the Betty Crocker Kitchens recommend Gold Medal® Flour.

Manufactured in the United States of America

DOC 10 9 8 7 6 5 4 3 2 1

Cover Photos: Top (left to right): Cheesy Bacon-Tomato Pie (page 320); Blueberry Pie (page 50); Cherry-Filled Heart-Shaped Pies (page 140); Pumpkin Pie (page 216)

Bottom (left to right): Fudgy Brownie Pie with Caramel Sauce (page 232); Jeweled Cranberry Apricot Tart (page 242)

# Dear Friends,

What could be more loved than a luscious freshly made pie? Folks immediately can tell when a pie is homemade just from the tender, flaky crust—so it's definitely a worthy endeavor. But don't let making a pie intimidate you—with all of our easy methods gathered here, you can make beautiful, delicious pies that will knock the socks off of anything that comes premade from a bakery or grocery store!

In this lovely *Big Book of Pies and Tarts* cookbook, we are sharing all of our best recipes and tips so you can make pie crust that will bring rave reviews any time you make a pie. But if you prefer just a bit of convenience, start with refrigerated pie crust and fill with any of our delicious fillings—no one will know the difference except you!

Just how many types of pie will you find here? You'll be delighted with oodles of fruit pies, an assortment of creamy and chilled pies plus many tarts and mini pies. But that's not all—look for fabulous treats for the holidays—and when you want a hearty main dish, check out the savory selection of dinner pies included.

Let some new flavor combinations excite your taste buds too, like Apple-Pomegranate Slab Pie, Bourbon-Chocolate-Pecan Mini Pies or Muffin Tin Taco Pies. Or perk up your holiday meals with traditionally inspired pies such as Roasted Sweet Potato Pie, Caramel-Apple-Ginger Crostata or Browned Butter Pecan Pie.

Our savory dinner pies will surprise and delight all diners! Look for options that include Mini Bacon Chicken Pot Pies, Potato-Onion-Bacon Slab Pie or Rustic Meat and Potato Pie. There are so many choices; you could have pie nearly every day of the year. Okay, that might be a tad excessive, but we're so excited to bring you this dazzling book of pies that you might just start dreaming about them . . . we do!

Sincerely,
*Betty Crocker*

# contents

Easy as Pie  6

**Fruit Pies 12**

**Creamy &
Chilled Pies 74**

**Tarts & Mini Pies 132**

**Holiday Pies 202**

**Savory Pies 252**

Metric Conversion Guide 326

Index 327

# Easy as Pie

Baking your favorite pie is as easy as 1-2-3 when you know how. And with the selection of tips here, you'll soon be making scrumptious pies like a pro! So go ahead and start baking—but be warned—luscious homemade pies bring oohs and aahs. . . and also requests for seconds!

## Choosing Pie Plates

Use a heat-resistant glass pie plate or dull aluminum pie pan. Shiny or disposable pie pans reflect heat and prevent crusts from browning. Dark pans absorb heat, causing overbrowning. Nonstick pans can cause an unfilled crust to shrink excessively.

- *Use the size* pie plate or pan called for in the recipe.
- No need to grease the pie plate or pan—the fat content in the pastry makes it unnecessary.

## Freezing Pie Pastry

Unbaked and baked pie pastry (without filling) can be frozen for up to 3 months.

- For rounds of pastry dough, wrap tightly in plastic wrap and freeze. Thaw in refrigerator before rolling and filling.
- For unbaked pastry dough in a pie plate or pan, wrap tightly in foil or place in a freezer plastic bag. There's no need to thaw before baking.
- For baked pastry crust in a pie plate or pan, wrap tightly in foil or place in a freezer plastic bag. Thaw before using.

## Baking Pies and Tarts

- Seal pastry so juices cannot escape from edge of pie, and cut slits in top to let steam escape (and to keep pastry from getting soggy).
- Cover edge of crust with pie shield ring or strips of foil to prevent overbrowning.
- Prevent juices that escape from burning on bottom of oven by placing a pan lined with foil or a silicone baking mat on oven rack below pie.
- Bake until crust is golden brown and juice bubbles through slits in top crust.

## Freezing Filled Pies

| UNBAKED PIES |
| --- |
| **FREEZE:** Fruit pies up to 2 months (don't slit top crust) |
| **BAKE:** At 425°F for 15 minutes (slit top crust before baking). Reduce temperature to 375°F and bake 30 to 45 minutes or until juice begins to bubble through slits in crust. |

| BAKED PIES |
| --- |
| **FREEZE:** Fruit, pumpkin, pecan pies up to 2 months. Cool before freezing. (Do not freeze custard, cream or meringue topped pies as they may become watery when thawed.) |
| **THAW:** Unwrap pie and heat at 325°F for 45 minutes or until center is warm. |

## Cooling Pies and Tarts

- Place baked dessert pies and tarts on a cooling rack (to help prevent the bottom crust from getting soggy) for at least 2 hours before cutting.
- Refrigerate cream and custard pies after cooling.
- Cool main-dish pies and quiches for about 10 minutes before serving.

## Cutting/Serving Pies and Tarts

Cut cooled pies and tarts with a sharp, thin-bladed knife. For meringue or ice cream pies, try dipping the knife in warm water before cutting. Use a pie cutter or wedge-shaped spatula to remove individual slices.

## Storing Baked Pies and Tarts

Fruit pies and tarts can be stored at room temperature up to 2 days. All pies containing eggs, dairy products or meat (including custard or cream pies, quiches and main-dish pies) must be stored in the refrigerator for no more than 2 days. Be sure to store as directed in the recipe.

# making pie pastry

What sets great pies apart from the mediocre? The secret lies in having flaky, tender pie crust as a base for your fabulous filling. Here you'll find basic pastry recipes and learn how to make your pastry turn out great, every time.

## One-Crust Pastry

Use this recipe to make any pie or tart. You can bake the pastry before filling for a variety of cooked or fresh fillings, or fill and then bake. Individual recipes will indicate which method to use and how to bake.

**8 servings • PREP TIME: 20 Minutes • START TO FINISH: 1 Hour 5 Minutes**

| | |
|---|---|
| 1 | cup plus 1 tablespoon all-purpose flour |
| ½ | teaspoon salt |
| ⅓ | cup cold shortening |
| 3 | to 5 tablespoons ice-cold water |

**1** In medium bowl, mix flour and salt. Cut in shortening, using pastry blender or fork, until mixture forms coarse crumbs the size of small peas. Sprinkle with the water, 1 tablespoon at a time, tossing with fork until all flour is moistened and pastry almost leaves side of bowl (1 to 2 teaspoons more water can be added if necessary).

**2** Gather pastry into a ball. Shape into flattened round on lightly floured surface. Wrap flattened round in plastic wrap; refrigerate 45 minutes or until dough is firm and cold, yet pliable. This makes the shortening slightly firm, which helps make the baked pastry flaky. If refrigerated longer, let pastry soften slightly at room temperature before rolling.

**3** Using floured rolling pin, roll pastry on lightly floured surface (or pastry board with floured pastry cloth) into round 2 inches larger than upside-down 9-inch glass pie plate or 3 inches larger than 10- or 11-inch tart pan. Fold pastry into fourths and place in pie plate, or roll pastry loosely around rolling pin and transfer to pie plate or tart pan. Unfold or unroll pastry and ease into plate or pan, pressing firmly against bottom and side and being careful not to stretch pastry, which will cause it to shrink when baked.

**4** For pie, trim overhanging edge of pastry 1 inch from rim of pie plate. Fold edge under to form standing rim; flute edges (see Decorative Crust Ideas, page 10). For tart, trim overhanging edge of pastry even with top of tart pan. Fill and bake as directed in desired pie or tart recipe.

**1 Serving:** Calories 140; Total Fat 9g (Saturated Fat 2g, Trans Fat 0g); Cholesterol 0mg; Sodium 150mg; Total Carbohydrate 13g (Dietary Fiber 0g); Protein 1g **Exchanges:** 1 Starch, 1½ Fat **Carbohydrate Choices:** 1

**Butter Crust** Substitute cold butter, cut into ½-inch pieces, for half of the shortening.

# Two-Crust Pastry

Use this recipe for any pie where the filling is cooked between two crusts, such as a fruit pie. For convenience, you could also use just half of the pastry dough for a one-crust pie and freeze the other round of pastry, wrapped tightly in plastic wrap, for another pie.

**8 servings • PREP TIME: 20 Minutes •
START TO FINISH: 1 Hour 5 Minutes**

- 2 cups plus 2 tablespoons all-purpose flour
- 1 teaspoon salt
- ⅔ cup cold shortening
- 6 to 8 tablespoons ice-cold water

**1** In medium bowl, mix flour and salt. Cut in shortening, using pastry blender or fork, until mixture forms coarse crumbs the size of small peas. Sprinkle with the water, 1 tablespoon at a time, tossing with fork until all flour is moistened and pastry almost leaves side of bowl (1 to 2 teaspoons more water can be added if necessary).

**2** Gather pastry into a ball. Divide pastry in half and shape into 2 rounds on lightly floured surface. Wrap flattened rounds in plastic wrap; refrigerate 45 minutes or until dough is firm and cold. This makes the shortening slightly firm, which helps make the baked pastry flaky. If refrigerated longer, let pastry soften slightly at room temperature before rolling.

**3** Using floured rolling pin, roll 1 round of pastry on lightly floured surface (or pastry board with floured pastry cloth) into round 2 inches larger than upside-down 9-inch glass pie plate. Fold pastry into fourths and place in pie plate, or roll pastry loosely around rolling pin and transfer to pie plate. Unfold or unroll pastry and ease into plate, pressing firmly against bottom and side and being careful not to stretch pastry, which will cause it to shrink when baked.

**4** Spoon desired filling into bottom crust. Trim overhanging edge of bottom crust ½ inch from rim of plate.

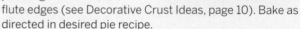

**5** Roll second round out. Fold into fourths and place over filling, or roll loosely around rolling pin and place over filling. Unfold or unroll pastry over filling. Cut slits in pastry so steam can escape.

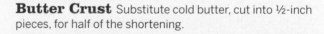

**6** Trim overhanging edge of top pastry 1 inch from rim of plate. Fold edge of top crust under bottom crust, pressing on rim to seal; flute edges (see Decorative Crust Ideas, page 10). Bake as directed in desired pie recipe.

**1 Serving:** Calories 280; Total Fat 18g (Saturated Fat 3g, Trans Fat 0g); Cholesterol 0mg; Sodium 300mg; Total Carbohydrate 26g (Dietary Fiber 0g); Protein 2g **Exchanges:** 1½ Starch, 2 Fat **Carbohydrate Choices:** 2

**Butter Crust** Substitute cold butter, cut into ½-inch pieces, for half of the shortening.

## Making Pie Crust in a Food Processor

**1** Measure 3 tablespoons ice-cold water for One-Crust Pie Pastry or 6 tablespoons ice-cold water for Two-Crust Pie Pastry into liquid measuring cup; set aside.

**2** Place flour, salt and shortening in food processor. Cover and process, using quick on-and-off motions, until particles are the size of small peas.

**3** With food processor running, pour water all at once through feed tube just until dough leaves side of bowl (dough should not form a ball). Continue as directed in step 2 of pastry recipes.

**Bake pie crust until light brown and place on cooling rack to cool.**

# baking methods for pie crust

For many pies (such as apple pie and pecan pie), the filling is added to the unbaked pastry, so the crust and filling bake together. For other pies, the crust is either partially baked before filling is added (to help prevent the crust from becoming soggy from wet filling) or completely baked before filling is added (when the filling does not need to be baked). Each individual recipe will indicate which crust method is used.

## Partially Baked One-Crust Pie

Use this method, if recipe directs, for one-crust pies and tarts that are partially baked before filling is added to prevent bottom crust from becoming soggy.

**1** Heat oven to 425°F. Carefully line pastry with a double thickness of foil, gently pressing foil to bottom and side of pastry. Let foil extend over edge to prevent excessive browning.

**2** Bake 10 minutes; carefully remove foil and bake 2 to 4 minutes longer or until pastry just begins to brown and has become set. If crust bubbles, gently push bubbles down with back of wooden spoon.

**3** Fill and bake as directed in pie or tart recipe, changing oven temperature if necessary.

## Baked One-Crust Pie

Use this method, if recipe directs, for one-crust pies and tarts that are baked completely before filling is added.

**1** Heat oven to 450°F. For pie, trim overhanging edge of pastry 1 inch from rim of pie plate. For tart, trim overhanging edge of pastry even with top of tart pan. Prick bottom and side of pastry thoroughly with fork.

**2** Bake 8 to 10 minutes or until light brown; cool on cooling rack.

## Baked Individual Pie Crusts and Tart Shells

Make pastry as directed for One-Crust Pastry (page 7)—except roll pastry into 13-inch round. Cut into 8 (4½-inch) rounds, rerolling pastry scraps if necessary.

**1** Heat oven to 450°F. Fit rounds over backs of regular-size muffin cups or 6-oz custard cups, making pleats so pastry will fit snugly against the cups. (If using individual pie pans or tart pans, cut pastry rounds 1 inch larger than upside-down pans; fit into pans.) Prick pastry thoroughly with fork to prevent puffing. Place on cookie sheet.

**2** Bake 8 to 10 minutes or until light brown; cool before removing from cups. Fill each shell with ⅓ to ½ cup of your favorite filling, pudding, fresh fruit or ice cream.

### Decorative Cutouts

**For an extra-pretty pie, make decorative cutouts on the top of a two-crust pie. Use a small cookie cutter to cut shapes from the top crust before placing it on the filling. Place cutouts on top of the pie crust, attaching with a little cold water. Sprinkle with coarse sugar.**

# decorative crust ideas

Like a little pie bling? Here's a variety of decorative crust ideas, from creating a pretty pie edge to a beautiful and easy lattice top for you to adorn your favorite pie or tart with.

## Fluted Edges

Fluting the edge of a crust not only adds a decorative touch but also helps keep the filling from bubbling over. Start by forming a stand-up rim of pastry that is even thickness on edge of pie plate, pressing edges together. This seals the pastry and makes fluting easier.

### Scalloped Edge

Place thumb and index finger about 1 inch apart on outside of raised edge. With other index finger, push pastry toward outside to form scalloped edge.

### Rope or Pinched Edge
Place side of thumb on pastry rim at angle. Pinch pastry by pressing knuckle of index finger down into pastry toward thumb.

### Forked or Herringbone Edge
Dip fork tines in flour, then press fork diagonally onto edge without pressing through pastry. Rotate tines 90 degrees and press next to first set of marks. Continue around edge of pastry rotating tines back and forth.

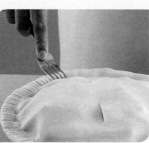

## Lattice Top Crusts

A lattice top crust adds a nice touch to a two-crust pie, letting the filling peek through. For an easy "wow," try one of these methods for the top pastry of your pie. Using a pastry wheel adds a decorative touch to a lattice crust.

### Easy Lattice Top

Make pastry for Two-Crust Pastry, except trim overhanging edge of bottom crust 1 inch from rim of plate. Place filling in crust. After rolling pastry for top crust, cut into ½-inch-wide strips. Place half of strips about ½ inch apart on filling.

Place remaining strips ½ inch apart crosswise over first strips. Trim strips even with edge of overhanging crust. Fold edge up, forming high, stand-up ridge; flute edge as desired.

### Classic Lattice Top
Make pastry for Two-Crust Pastry, except trim overhanging edge of bottom crust 1 inch from rim of plate. Place filling in crust. After rolling pastry for top crust, cut into ½-inch-wide strips. Place half of strips about ½ inch apart on filling. Weave remaining

strips over and under first strips. Trim strips even with edge of overhanging crust. Fold edge up, forming high, stand-up ridge; flute edge as desired.

# Easy Buttermilk Pastry

This pastry is extra easy to roll and handle, and the baked crust is very flaky.

**Two 9-inch crusts (8 servings each) • PREP TIME: 15 Minutes • START TO FINISH: 25 Minutes**

- 2 cups all-purpose flour
- 1 teaspoon salt
- ⅔ cup cold shortening
- 3 tablespoons cold butter
- ⅓ cup buttermilk
- 2 teaspoons vegetable oil

**1** In medium bowl, mix flour and salt. Cut in shortening and butter, using pastry blender or fork, until mixture forms coarse crumbs the size of small peas. Mix in buttermilk and oil with fork until all flour is moistened and pastry leaves side of bowl. Divide in half; shape each half into a ball. If making one-crust pie, wrap second ball of pastry and freeze for later use.

**2** Roll pastry and place in pie plate or pan as directed in Step 3 of One-Crust Pastry (page 7). Fill and bake as directed in pie recipe. Or to bake before filling is added, heat oven to 425°F. Prick bottom and side of pastry thoroughly with fork. Bake 8 to 10 minutes or until light brown; cool on cooling rack.

**1 Serving (For One Crust):** Calories 160; Total Fat 11g (Saturated Fat 3.5g; Trans Fat 1.5g); Cholesterol 5mg; Sodium 170mg; Total Carbohydrate 12g (Dietary Fiber 0g); Protein 2g **Exchanges:** 1 Starch, 2 Fat **Carbohydrate Choices:** 1

# Easy Nut Crust

**One 9-inch crust (8 servings) • PREP TIME: 10 Minutes • START TO FINISH: 20 Minutes**

- 1 cup all-purpose flour
- ½ cup butter, softened
- ¼ cup finely chopped nuts

**1** In medium bowl, mix all ingredients until soft dough forms. Using lightly floured fingers, press firmly and evenly against bottom and side of ungreased 9-inch glass pie plate.

**2** Fill and bake as directed in pie recipe. Or to bake before filling is added, heat oven to 425°F. Bake 7 to 8 minutes or until light brown; cool on cooling rack.

**1 Serving:** Calories 190; Total Fat 14g (Saturated Fat 8g; Trans Fat 0g); Cholesterol 30mg; Sodium 80mg; Total Carbohydrate 12g (Dietary Fiber 0g); Protein 2g **Exchanges:** 1 Starch, 2½ Fat **Carbohydrate Choices:** 1

# Press-in-the-Pan Pastry

No rolling is needed for this crust!

**One 9-inch crust (8 servings) • PREP TIME: 10 Minutes • START TO FINISH: 25 Minutes**

- 1⅓ cups all-purpose flour
- ½ teaspoon salt
- ⅓ cup vegetable oil
- 2 tablespoons ice-cold water

Caramel-Chocolate Pie Supreme (page 82) with Press-in-the-Pan Pastry

**1** In medium bowl, stir flour, salt and oil until all flour is moistened. Sprinkle with cold water, 1 tablespoon at a time, tossing with fork until all water is absorbed. Gather pastry into a ball. Press firmly and evenly against bottom and up side of ungreased 9-inch glass pie plate; flute.

**2** Fill and bake as directed in pie recipe. Or to bake before filling is added, heat oven to 425°F. Prick bottom and side of pastry thoroughly with fork. Bake 10 to 12 minutes or until light brown; cool on cooling rack.

**1 Serving:** Calories 150; Total Fat 9g (Saturated Fat 1.5g; Trans Fat 0g); Cholesterol 0mg; Sodium 150mg; Total Carbohydrate 16g (Dietary Fiber 0g); Protein 2g **Exchanges:** 1 Starch, 1½ Fat **Carbohydrate Choices:** 1

# Graham Cracker Crust

**One 9-inch crust (8 servings) • PREP TIME: 10 Minutes • START TO FINISH: 20 Minutes**

- 1½ cups finely crushed regular or cinnamon graham crackers (24 squares)
- ⅓ cup butter, melted
- 3 tablespoons sugar

**1** Heat oven to 350°F. In medium bowl, stir all ingredients until well mixed. Press mixture firmly and evenly against bottom and side of ungreased 9-inch glass pie plate.

**2** Bake about 10 minutes or until light brown; cool on cooling rack. Fill as directed in pie recipe.

**1 Serving:** Calories 160; Total Fat 9g (Saturated Fat 5g; Trans Fat 0g); Cholesterol 20mg; Sodium 150mg; Total Carbohydrate 17g (Dietary Fiber 0g); Protein 1g **Exchanges:** ½ Starch, ½ Other Carbohydrate, 2 Fat **Carbohydrate Choices:** 1

**Chocolate, Vanilla or Gingersnap Crumb Crust** Substitute 1½ cups finely crushed chocolate wafer cookies (24 cookies), vanilla wafer cookies (35 cookies) or gingersnaps (30 cookies) for the graham crackers. Decrease butter to ¼ cup; omit sugar.

Gingered Apricot Pie
(page 70)

# fruit pies

# Classic Apple Pie

**8 servings • PREP TIME: 30 Minutes • START TO FINISH: 3 Hours 20 Minutes**

Two-Crust Pastry (page 8)
or 1 box Pillsbury® refrigerated
pie crusts, softened as directed
on box

½ cup sugar

¼ cup all-purpose flour

¾ teaspoon ground cinnamon

¼ teaspoon ground nutmeg

Dash salt

6 cups thinly sliced peeled
tart apples (6 medium)

2 tablespoons cold butter,
if desired

2 teaspoons water

1 tablespoon sugar

**1** Heat oven to 425°F. Place 1 pastry round or pie crust in 9-inch glass pie plate.

**2** In large bowl, mix ½ cup sugar, the flour, cinnamon, nutmeg and salt. Stir in apples. Spoon into pastry-lined plate. Cut butter into small pieces; sprinkle over apples.

**3** Cover with second pastry or crust; seal and flute. Cut slits in several places in top crust. Brush crust with water; sprinkle with 1 tablespoon sugar. Cover crust edge with pie crust shield ring or strips of foil to prevent excessive browning.

**4** Bake 40 to 50 minutes or until crust is golden brown and juice begins to bubble through slits in crust, removing foil during last 15 minutes. Cool on cooling rack at least 2 hours before serving.

**1 Serving:** Calories 420; Total Fat 21g (Saturated Fat 7g; Trans Fat 2g); Cholesterol 10mg; Sodium 330mg; Total Carbohydrate 53g (Dietary Fiber 3g); Protein 4g **Exchanges:** 1½ Starch, 2 Fruit, 4 Fat **Carbohydrate Choices:** 3½

**French Apple Pie** Heat oven to 400°F. Spoon apple mixture into pastry-lined plate. Omit butter, 2 teaspoons water and 1 tablespoon sugar. In small bowl, mix 1 cup all-purpose flour and ½ cup packed brown sugar. Cut in ½ cup cold butter with fork until crumbly. Sprinkle over apple mixture. Bake 35 to 40 minutes or until golden brown. Cover top with foil during last 10 to 15 minutes of baking, if necessary, to prevent excessive browning. Serve warm.

## Sweet Success Tip

Once you've had homemade apple pie, nothing else will ever compare. What sets it apart is a tender, flaky crust made by hand or if you're pinched for time, try using refrigerated pie crust for convenience.

# Nutty RazApple Pie

**8 servings • PREP TIME: 30 Minutes • START TO FINISH: 5 Hours 30 Minutes**

## CRUST

- 1 box Pillsbury refrigerated pie crusts, softened as directed on box
- 1 egg white, slightly beaten
- 2 tablespoons cold unsalted butter

## FILLING

- 2 tablespoons lemon juice
- 5 cups thinly sliced peeled apples (such as Golden Delicious, McIntosh and Granny Smith; about 5 medium)
- ⅔ cup sugar
- ½ teaspoon ground cinnamon
- ¼ teaspoon ground nutmeg
- 2 teaspoons pearl tapioca
- 2 tablespoons cornstarch
  Dash salt
- ½ pint (1 cup) fresh raspberries
- 1 tablespoon amaretto
- 2 tablespoons cold unsalted butter

## TOPPING

- 1 egg yolk
- 1 teaspoon water
- 1 tablespoon sliced almonds
- 1 tablespoon sugar
- ¼ teaspoon ground cinnamon

**1** Heat oven to 375°F. Unroll and press 1 pie crust in bottom and up side of 9-inch glass pie plate. Brush crust with beaten egg white. Cut 2 tablespoons butter into small pieces; sprinkle over bottom of crust.

**2** In medium bowl, sprinkle lemon juice over apples. In small bowl, mix ⅔ cup sugar, ½ teaspoon cinnamon, the nutmeg, tapioca, cornstarch and salt. Sprinkle over apples; gently toss. Spoon mixture into crust-lined plate, mounding slightly in center. Sprinkle amaretto evenly over filling. Cut 2 tablespoons butter into small pieces; sprinkle over filling.

**3** Brush top edges of dough with beaten egg white. Top with second crust. Fold top layer of dough under edge of bottom layer and press edges together to seal; flute edges as desired.

**4** In small bowl, beat egg yolk and water. Brush lightly over top crust. Arrange almonds on top. In small bowl, mix 1 tablespoon sugar and ¼ teaspoon cinnamon; sprinkle over top crust and almonds. Cut slits in several places in top crust. Place pie on middle oven rack; place sheet of foil on rack below pie in case of spillover.

**5** Bake 50 to 60 minutes or until crust is golden brown. Cool completely on cooling rack, about 4 hours, before serving. Store covered at room temperature up to 24 hours or refrigerate up to 4 days.

**Marilyn Robinson from Walsenberg, Colorado, entered this winning recipe at the 2010 Colorado State Fair Pie Contest.**

**1 Serving:** Calories 410; Total Fat 19g (Saturated Fat 9g; Trans Fat 0g); Cholesterol 50mg; Sodium 310mg; Total Carbohydrate 57g (Dietary Fiber 3g); Protein 3g **Exchanges:** 1 Starch, 1 Fruit, 2 Other Carbohydrate, 3½ Fat **Carbohydrate Choices:** 4

## Sweet Success Tip
**If you don't like amaretto, substitute apple juice or water in its place.**

# Apple-Raspberry Crumb Pie

**8 servings** • **PREP TIME:** 15 Minutes • **START TO FINISH:** 1 Hour 35 Minutes

## CRUST

1 Pillsbury refrigerated pie crust, softened as directed on box

## FILLING

3 cups thinly sliced peeled cooking apples (3 medium)

½ cup sugar

2 tablespoons all-purpose flour

½ teaspoon ground cinnamon

2 cups fresh or frozen (thawed and drained) raspberries

½ cup cubed or crumbled almond paste (from 7- or 8-oz package)

## TOPPING

½ cup all-purpose flour

¼ cup sugar

¼ cup cold butter

½ cup sliced almonds

**1** Heat oven to 350°F. Place pie crust in 9-inch glass pie plate as directed on box for One-Crust Filled Pie.

**2** In large bowl, toss apples, ½ cup sugar, 2 tablespoons flour and the cinnamon. Spoon into crust-lined plate. Sprinkle with raspberries and almond paste.

**3** In medium bowl, mix ½ cup flour and ¼ cup sugar. Cut in butter, using pastry blender or fork until particles are size of small peas. Stir in almonds. Sprinkle evenly over filling.

**4** Bake 1 hour to 1 hour 20 minutes, covering crust edge with pie crust shield ring or strips of foil after about 30 minutes, until apples are tender in center and topping is golden brown. Serve warm or cool.

**1 Serving:** Calories 420; Total Fat 20g (Saturated Fat 7g; Trans Fat 0g); Cholesterol 20mg; Sodium 150mg; Total Carbohydrate 57g (Dietary Fiber 4g); Protein 4g **Exchanges:** 1 Starch, 3 Other Carbohydrate, 4 Fat **Carbohydrate Choices:** 4

## Sweet Success Tips

You can make the pie several hours before serving. To warm it up, microwave slices on individual microwavable plates on High for about 10 seconds.

Look for almond paste near the baking chocolate and nuts. Check the label to make sure it lists almonds as the first ingredient.

# Apple-Blackberry Pie

**8 servings** • **PREP TIME: 20 Minutes** • **START TO FINISH: 4 Hours 30 Minutes**

1 box Pillsbury refrigerated pie crusts, softened as directed on box
4 cups thinly sliced peeled tart apples (about 4 medium)
2 cups fresh blackberries
½ cup packed brown sugar
4½ teaspoons cornstarch
½ teaspoon ground cinnamon
¼ teaspoon ground nutmeg

**1** Heat oven to 375°F. Make pie crusts as directed on box for Two-Crust Pie using 9-inch glass pie plate.

**2** In large bowl, stir together apples and blackberries. In small bowl, mix brown sugar, cornstarch, cinnamon and nutmeg. Sprinkle over fruit; toss to coat. Spoon into crust-lined plate.

**3** Top with second crust; seal and flute. Cut slits in several places in top crust. Cover crust edge with pie shield ring or strips of foil to prevent excessive browning. Place pie on middle oven rack; place sheet of foil on rack below pie in case of spillover.

**4** Bake 50 minutes. Remove foil; bake 15 to 20 minutes longer or until golden brown. Cool on cooling rack at least 3 hours before serving.

Phyllis Hine from Waveland, Indiana, entered this winning recipe at the 2010 Indiana State Fair Pie Contest.

**1 Serving:** Calories 320; Total Fat 12g (Saturated Fat 5g; Trans Fat 0g); Cholesterol 5mg; Sodium 260mg; Total Carbohydrate 49g (Dietary Fiber 2g); Protein 2g **Exchanges:** 1 Starch, 1 Fruit, 1 Other Carbohydrate, 2½ Fat **Carbohydrate Choices:** 3

## Sweet Success Tip

Tart cooking apples, such as Granny Smith, Greening and Haralson, are all good choices for this pie.

# Apple-Blueberry Pie with Strawberry Sauce

**8 servings • PREP TIME: 30 Minutes • START TO FINISH: 3 Hours 30 Minutes**

## PIE

- 5 cups thinly sliced peeled apples (5 medium)
- 2 cups fresh or frozen (thawed) blueberries
- 1 cup sugar
- ½ teaspoon ground cinnamon
- 3 tablespoons quick-cooking tapioca
- 1 box Pillsbury refrigerated pie crusts, softened as directed on box
- 2 tablespoons cold butter
- 1 egg
- 1 teaspoon water

## SAUCE

- 2 cups fresh strawberries, hulled
- ½ cup sugar
- 1 tablespoon sweet Marsala wine or water
- 1 tablespoon cornstarch
- 2 tablespoons water
- ½ cup whipping cream

**1** Heat oven to 400°F. In large bowl, stir together apples, blueberries, 1 cup sugar, the cinnamon and tapioca. Let stand 15 minutes.

**2** Make pie crusts as directed on box for Two-Crust Pie using 9-inch glass pie plate. Spoon apple mixture into crust-lined plate. Cut butter into small pieces; sprinkle over filling. Top with second crust; seal and flute. Cut slits in several places in top crust. In small bowl, beat egg and 1 teaspoon water; brush over top crust.

**3** Bake 15 minutes. Cover crust edge with pie crust shield ring or strips of foil to prevent excessive browning; reduce oven temperature to 350°F. Bake 40 to 45 minutes longer or until apples are tender. Cool on cooling rack at least 2 hours before serving.

**4** Meanwhile, in 1-quart saucepan, crush enough strawberries to make ⅓ cup. Stir in ½ cup sugar and the wine. Heat to boiling over medium heat. Dissolve cornstarch in 2 tablespoons water; stir into strawberry mixture. Boil 2 minutes, stirring constantly. Remove from heat; cool to room temperature. Stir in whipping cream. Slice remaining strawberries; stir into sauce. Refrigerate until serving time. Top individual slices of pie with sauce.

Paula M. Reed of Cantonsville, Maryland, won first place for this recipe at the 2004 Maryland State Fair. She went on to place in the national Pillsbury Refrigerated Pie Crust Pie Baking Championship.

**1 Serving:** Calories 530; Total Fat 20g (Saturated Fat 10g; Trans Fat 0g); Cholesterol 55mg; Sodium 290mg; Total Carbohydrate 83g (Dietary Fiber 2g); Protein 3g **Exchanges:** 1½ Starch, 1 Fruit, 3 Other Carbohydrate, 4 Fat **Carbohydrate Choices:** 5½

## Sweet Success Tip

Adjust the level of sugar according to how sweet your apples are. If you're using a very sweet variety of apple, you can decrease the sugar to ¾ cup.

# Caramel-Toffee-Apple Pie with Pecans

8 servings • PREP TIME: 55 Minutes • START TO FINISH: 3 Hours 30 Minutes

## FILLING

6 cups sliced peeled apples (mixed varieties, such as 4 Gala and 2 Granny Smith; about 6 medium)

¾ cup granulated sugar

1 tablespoon plus 2 teaspoons cornstarch

1 tablespoon butter

¾ teaspoon ground cinnamon

½ teaspoon ground nutmeg

1 snack-size container (4 oz) cinnamon applesauce

Juice of ½ medium lemon (about 2 tablespoons)

½ cup toffee caramel dip

## CRUST

1 box Pillsbury refrigerated pie crusts, softened as directed on box

½ cup chopped pecans

1 egg

4½ teaspoons half-and-half or milk

2 tablespoons white decorator sugar crystals, if desired

**1** Heat oven to 400°F. In 4-quart saucepan, cook all filling ingredients except caramel dip over medium heat about 5 minutes, stirring occasionally, until butter melts and mixture develops "juice."

**2** Unroll 1 crust; smooth crust with hands. Sprinkle ¼ cup of the pecans on crust, leaving 1½ inches around edge. Using rolling pin, press pecans into crust without them breaking through other side of crust. Run spatula under crust; place pecan side up in 9-inch glass pie plate.

**3** Spoon half of filling mixture into crust. Spoon and spread caramel dip evenly over top. Spoon other half of filling mixture on top. Unroll second crust; smooth crust with hands. Sprinkle remaining ¼ cup pecans on crust, leaving 1½ inches around edge. Using rolling pin, carefully press pecans into crust without breaking through other side of crust. Place crust, pecan side up, over top of filling. Seal edge and flute.

**4** In small bowl, beat egg and half-and-half with fork; lightly brush over entire crust, including fluted edge, brushing gently on areas that have pecans. Sprinkle evenly with sugar crystals. Cut 2 slits in top crust. Line cookie sheet with foil; place pie on cookie sheet.

**5** Bake 20 minutes. Reduce oven temperature to 350°F. Bake 40 to 45 minutes longer or until crust is golden brown and juice begins to bubble through slits in crust. Cool on cooling rack at least 1 hour 30 minutes before serving.

Kelly Bunting of Canton, Michigan, won first place for this recipe at the 2005 Michigan State Fair. She went on to win second place in the national Pillsbury Refrigerated Pie Crust Pie Baking Championship.

**1 Serving:** Calories 390; Total Fat 14g (Saturated Fat 4.5g; Trans Fat 0g); Cholesterol 35mg; Sodium 220mg; Total Carbohydrate 64g (Dietary Fiber 3g); Protein 3g **Exchanges:** 1 Starch, 1 Fruit, 2½ Other Carbohydrate, 2½ Fat **Carbohydrate Choices:** 4

## Sweet Success Tip

When adding the caramel dip over the filling in step 3, use one teaspoon to measure and another teaspoon to scrape the dip out of the spoon.

# Pear Caramel-Apple Praline Pie

**8 servings • PREP TIME: 40 Minutes • START TO FINISH: 5 Hours 35 Minutes**

## CRUST

- 1 box Pillsbury refrigerated pie crusts, softened as directed on box

## FILLING

- ½ cup granulated sugar
- ¼ cup all-purpose flour
- ½ teaspoon ground nutmeg
- ½ teaspoon ground cinnamon
  Dash salt
- 2 cups thinly sliced peeled pears (2 medium)
- 2 cups thinly sliced peeled apples (2 medium)
- 1 tablespoon lemon juice
- 2 tablespoons cold butter

## PRALINE MIXTURE AND TOPPING

- ¾ cup old-fashioned oats
- ¼ cup packed brown sugar
- 1 tablespoon all-purpose flour
- ¼ cup cold butter
- 18 caramels, unwrapped
- 5 tablespoons milk
- ¼ cup chopped pecans
- 1 teaspoon milk, if desired
- 2 teaspoons sugar, if desired

**1** Heat oven to 375°F. Make pie crusts as directed on box for Two-Crust Pie using 9-inch glass pie plate.

**2** In large bowl, mix granulated sugar, ¼ cup flour, the nutmeg, cinnamon and salt. Add pears, apples and lemon juice; toss to coat. Spoon into crust-lined plate. Cut 2 tablespoons butter into small pieces; sprinkle over filling.

**3** In small bowl, mix oats, brown sugar and 1 tablespoon flour. Cut in ¼ cup butter, using pastry blender or fork, until mixture is crumbly. Sprinkle over fruit.

**4** In 1-quart saucepan, heat caramels and 5 tablespoons milk over low heat until caramels are melted. Stir until smooth; add pecans. Drizzle over praline mixture. Top with second crust; seal and flute. Cut slits in several places in top crust. Brush crust with milk and sprinkle with granulated sugar. Cover crust edge with pie shield ring or strips of foil to prevent excessive browning. Place pie on middle oven rack; place sheet of foil on rack under pie in case of spillover.

**5** Bake 45 to 55 minutes or until crust is golden brown and juice begins to bubble through slits in crust. Cool completely on cooling rack, about 4 hours, before serving.

**Beth Campbell from Belleville, Wisconsin, entered this blue ribbon–winning recipe at the 2010 Wisconsin State Fair.**

**1 Serving:** Calories 570; Total Fat 26g (Saturated Fat 11g; Trans Fat 0g); Cholesterol 30mg; Sodium 430mg; Total Carbohydrate 80g (Dietary Fiber 3g); Protein 5g **Exchanges:** 1½ Starch, ½ Fruit, 3½ Other Carbohydrate, 5 Fat **Carbohydrate Choices:** 5

# Apple-Pear Praline Pie

8 servings · PREP TIME: 30 Minutes · START TO FINISH: 3 Hours 40 Minutes

6 cups sliced peeled Granny Smith apples (6 medium)

3 cups thinly sliced peeled pears (3 medium)

¾ cup granulated sugar

¼ cup all-purpose flour

¼ cup ground cinnamon

¼ teaspoon salt

1 box Pillsbury refrigerated pie crusts, softened as directed on box

1 tablespoon all-purpose flour

2 tablespoons cold butter

1 bag (8 oz) toffee bits (1½ cups)

½ cup butter

1 cup packed brown sugar

¼ cup half-and-half

1 cup chopped pecans

**1** Heat oven to 350°F. In large bowl, gently toss apples, pears, granulated sugar, ¼ cup flour, the cinnamon and salt. Let stand 15 minutes.

**2** Place 1 pie crust in 9½-inch glass deep-dish pie plate; sprinkle lightly with 1 tablespoon flour. Spoon apple mixture into crust-lined plate. Cut 2 tablespoons butter into small pieces; sprinkle over filling. Top with ½ cup of the toffee bits. Top with second crust; seal and flute. Cut slits in several places in top crust.

**3** Bake 50 to 55 minutes or until golden brown.

**4** In 1-quart saucepan, melt ½ cup butter over low heat. Stir in brown sugar and half-and-half. Heat to boiling, stirring constantly. Remove from heat; stir in pecans. Spread sauce over top of hot pie; sprinkle with remaining 1 cup toffee bits. Cool on cooling rack at least 2 hours before serving.

**1 Serving:** Calories 840; Total Fat 44g (Saturated Fat 19g; Trans Fat 1g); Cholesterol 55mg; Sodium 530mg; Total Carbohydrate 109g (Dietary Fiber 6g); Protein 3g **Exchanges:** 1 Starch, 1 Fruit, 5 Other Carbohydrate, 8½ Fat **Carbohydrate Choices:** 7

## Sweet Success Tip

For the best results and flavor, purchase pears that are still firm to the touch—they should yield to gentle pressure.

# Orange Juice–Apple Pie

**8 servings** • **PREP TIME: 20 Minutes** • **START TO FINISH: 3 Hours 45 Minutes**

1 box Pillsbury refrigerated pie crusts, softened as directed on box

5 medium Granny Smith apples, peeled, cut into small pieces

¾ cup sugar

5 tablespoons butter

¼ cup frozen orange juice concentrate, thawed

4½ teaspoons cornstarch

Dash salt

**1** Heat oven to 450°F. Place 1 pie crust in 9-inch glass pie plate; press firmly against bottom and side of plate.

**2** In large bowl, stir together remaining ingredients. Spoon into crust-lined plate. Top with second crust; seal and flute. Cut slits in several places in top crust.

**3** Bake 10 minutes. Reduce oven temperature to 350°F. Bake 45 minutes longer or until crust is golden brown and juice begins to bubble through slits in crust. Cool on cooling rack 30 minutes. Refrigerate 2 hours before serving.

**1 Serving:** Calories 420; Total Fat 19g (Saturated Fat 10g; Trans Fat 0g); Cholesterol 25mg; Sodium 350mg; Total Carbohydrate 60g (Dietary Fiber 1g); Protein 0g **Exchanges:** 1 Fruit, 3 Other Carbohydrate, 4 Fat **Carbohydrate Choices:** 4

## Sweet Success Tip

For a decorative touch, use a small cookie cutter with serrated edges to cut holes in the top crust, rather than cutting slits with a knife.

# Apple Cheesecake Pie

**8 servings** • **PREP TIME:** 35 Minutes • **START TO FINISH:** 8 Hours 20 Minutes

## CRUST

1 box Pillsbury refrigerated pie crusts, softened as directed on box

## FILLING

2 packages (8 oz each) cream cheese, softened
½ cup granulated sugar
1 teaspoon vanilla
1 teaspoon almond extract
2 eggs
8 cups thinly sliced peeled apples (5 large)
1½ teaspoons lemon juice
2 tablespoons packed brown sugar
4 teaspoons cornstarch
1½ teaspoons ground cinnamon

## TOPPING

1 egg white
1 tablespoon water
1 teaspoon granulated sugar
½ teaspoon ground cinnamon

**1** Heat oven to 400°F. Make pie crusts as directed on box for Two-Crust Pie using 9-inch glass pie plate.

**2** In large bowl, beat cream cheese, ½ cup granulated sugar, the vanilla and almond extract with electric mixer on high speed until smooth. Beat in eggs, scraping bowl occasionally. Pour into crust-lined plate. In another large bowl, toss apples and lemon juice to coat; stir in brown sugar, cornstarch and 1½ teaspoons cinnamon. Spoon apple mixture over cream cheese layer.

**3** Unroll second crust on lightly floured work surface. With 2- to 2½-inch apple-shaped cookie cutter, cut out apple shapes. Reroll scraps and cut out additional apple shapes. Using pancake turner, gently arrange apple shapes on top of pie to cover most of filling.

**4** In small bowl, beat egg white and water until blended. Brush over apple shapes. In another small bowl, mix 1 teaspoon granulated sugar and ½ teaspoon cinnamon; sprinkle over apple shapes.

**5** Line cookie sheet with foil. Cover pie with sheet of foil to prevent excessive browning; place pie on cookie sheet. Bake 20 minutes. Remove foil; bake 20 to 25 minutes longer or until crust is golden brown. Cool 1 hour on cooling rack. Refrigerate at least 6 hours or overnight. Serve cold. Store in refrigerator.

Kim Wroten of Walkersville, Maryland, won the Pillsbury Refrigerated Pie Crust Pie Baking Championship at the 2009 Maryland State Fair with this recipe.

**1 Serving:** Calories 560; Total Fat 33g (Saturated Fat 10g; Trans Fat 0.5g); Cholesterol 120mg; Sodium 490mg; Total Carbohydrate 59g (Dietary Fiber 2g); Protein 5g **Exchanges:** 1½ Starch, ½ Fruit, 2 Other Carbohydrate, 6½ Fat **Carbohydrate Choices:** 4

## Sweet Success Tip

**Try making this luscious pie with a classic lattice top crust in lieu of the apple-shape cutouts.**

# Apple Slab Pie

**24 servings • PREP TIME: 20 Minutes • START TO FINISH: 2 Hours 15 Minutes**

1   box Pillsbury refrigerated pie crusts, softened as directed on box
1   cup granulated sugar
3   tablespoons all-purpose flour
1   teaspoon ground cinnamon
¼   teaspoon ground nutmeg
¼   teaspoon salt
4½  teaspoons lemon juice
9   cups thinly sliced peeled apples (9 medium)
1   cup powdered sugar
2   tablespoons milk

**1** Heat oven to 450°F. Unroll pie crusts and stack one on top of the other on lightly floured surface. Roll to 17×12-inch rectangle. Fit crust into 15×10×1-inch pan, pressing into corners. Fold extra pastry crust under, even with edges of pan; seal edges.

**2** In large bowl, mix granulated sugar, flour, cinnamon, nutmeg, salt and lemon juice. Add apples; toss to coat. Spoon into crust-lined pan.

**3** Bake 33 to 38 minutes or until crust is golden brown and filling is bubbly. Cool on cooling rack 45 minutes.

**4** In small bowl, mix powdered sugar and milk until well blended. Drizzle over pie. Allow glaze to set before serving, about 30 minutes.

**1 Serving:** Calories 150; Total Fat 4g (Saturated Fat 1.5g; Trans Fat 0g); Cholesterol 0mg; Sodium 110mg; Total Carbohydrate 28g (Dietary Fiber 0g); Protein 0g **Exchanges:** 2 Other Carbohydrate, 1 Fat **Carbohydrate Choices:** 2

## Sweet Success Tip

**Need to make dessert for a potluck or other large gathering? This is the perfect pie for that type of occasion—it's easy to put together and serves a crowd.**

# Apple-Pomegranate Slab Pie

**16 servings** • **PREP TIME: 45 Minutes** • **START TO FINISH: 2 Hours 10 Minutes**

## CRUST

Two-Crust Pastry (page 8)
or 1 box Pillsbury refrigerated
pie crusts, softened as directed
on box

## FILLING

12 cups thinly sliced peeled
    tart apples (about 4 lb)
1⅓ cups sugar
1 teaspoon ground cardamom
    or cinnamon
½ teaspoon salt
2 teaspoons grated orange peel
1 teaspoon vanilla
½ cup cornstarch
    Juice of 2 oranges (about
    ½ cup)
1 cup pomegranate seeds

## GLAZE

3 tablespoons whipping cream
2 tablespoons sugar

**1** Heat oven to 400°F. On well-floured surface, roll 1 pastry round or pie crust to 16×12-inch rectangle. Roll pastry onto rolling pin; unroll into 15×10×1-inch pan. Press pastry in bottom and up sides of pan.

**2** In large bowl, toss apples, 1⅓ cups sugar, the cardamom, salt, orange peel and vanilla. In small bowl, mix cornstarch and orange juice. Add to fruit mixture; stir to combine. Spoon filling evenly into pastry-lined pan. Scatter pomegranate seeds over filling.

**3** On well-floured surface, roll second pastry or pie crust to 15×11-inch rectangle. Place over filling. Fold top crust over bottom crust to seal, crimping edge slightly with fingers. With small knife, cut slits or decorative shapes in top crust. Brush top crust with whipping cream; sprinkle with 2 tablespoons sugar.

**4** Bake 35 to 40 minutes or until crust is golden brown and juice begins to bubble through slits in crust. Cool on cooling rack at least 45 minutes before serving. Serve warm or cool.

**1 Serving:** Calories 290; Total Fat 10g (Saturated Fat 3g; Trans Fat 0g); Cholesterol 0mg; Sodium 220mg; Total Carbohydrate 48g (Dietary Fiber 2g); Protein 2g **Exchanges:** ½ Starch, ½ Fruit, 2 Other Carbohydrate, 2 Fat **Carbohydrate Choices:** 3

## Sweet Success Tips

You'll need 1 pomegranate to get 1 cup seeds for this recipe. If a fresh pomegranate is not available, substitute sweetened dried cranberries in pomegranate juice.

The crust can be prepared a day ahead and refrigerated. Let it stand at room temperature to soften slightly before rolling.

# Apple Dumplings

**6 dumplings • PREP TIME: 55 Minutes • START TO FINISH: 1 Hour 35 Minutes**

Two-Crust Pastry (page 8) or 1 box Pillsbury refrigerated pie crusts, softened as directed on box

6 small cooking apples (such as Golden Delicious, Braeburn or Rome), about 3 inches in diameter✱

3 tablespoons raisins, dried cranberries or dried cherries, if desired

3 tablespoons chopped nuts, if desired

2½ cups packed brown sugar

1⅓ cups water

2 tablespoons butter, softened

¼ teaspoon ground cinnamon

Cream or Sweetened Whipped Cream (page 80), if desired

**1** Heat oven to 425°F. Make pastry as directed—except roll two-thirds of pastry into 14-inch square; cut into 4 (7-inch) squares. Roll remaining pastry into 14×7-inch rectangle; cut into 2 (7-inch) squares. If using refrigerated pie crusts, roll each crust into 21×7-inch rectangle and cut each into 3 (7-inch) squares.

**2** Peel and core apples; place 1 apple on each pastry square. Mix raisins and nuts; spoon into apples. Moisten corners of pastry squares. Bring 2 opposite corners up over apple and pinch together. Repeat with remaining corners, and pinch edges of pastry to seal.

**3** Place dumplings in ungreased 13×9-inch (3-quart) glass baking dish. In 2-quart saucepan, heat brown sugar, water, butter and cinnamon to boiling over high heat, stirring frequently. Carefully pour syrup around dumplings.

**4** Bake about 40 minutes, spooning syrup over dumplings 2 or 3 times, until crust is golden and apples are tender when pierced with small knife or toothpick. Serve warm or cool with cream.

✱ Dough squares will not be large enough to seal larger apples.

**1 Dumpling:** Calories 680; Total Fat 32g (Saturated Fat 9g; Trans Fat 5g); Cholesterol 10mg; Sodium 450mg; Total Carbohydrate 94g (Dietary Fiber 4g); Protein 5g **Exchanges:** 2 Starch, 4 Other Carbohydrate, 6 Fat **Carbohydrate Choices:** 6

## Sweet Success Tip

For lighter dumplings that weight in at 320 calories and 5 grams of fat each, try this—omit the Two-Crust Pastry. Place 6 sheets (18×14 inches) of frozen, thawed phyllo dough on cutting board. Cut into 14-inch square. Discard remaining strips of phyllo. Divide square into 3 stacks of 2 sheets each. Set aside one stack; cover remaining stacks with plastic wrap and then a damp towel to prevent drying. Spray top of uncovered stack with butter-flavored cooking spray. Fold in half; spray top. Cut in half, forming 2 squares. Repeat with remaining stacks to form a total of 6 squares, covering standing squares as directed above until each dumpling is assembled. Continue as directed in step 2, omitting nuts.

# Elegant Pear Custard Pie

**12 servings  •  PREP TIME:  1 Hour  •  START TO FINISH:  6 Hours 10 Minutes**

## POACHED PEARS

- 1 cup sugar
- 1 cup water
- 1 cup pear vodka
- ½ cup elderflower liqueur
- 1 vanilla bean
- 3 lb Bosc or Bartlett pears, peeled, cut in half

## CRUST

One-Crust Pastry (page 7) or 1 Pillsbury refrigerated pie crust, softened as directed on box

## CUSTARD

- ½ cup whipping cream
- ¼ cup reserved poaching liquid
- ¼ cup sugar
  Dash salt
- 4½ teaspoons cornstarch
- 1 whole egg
- 1 egg yolk
- ½ teaspoon vanilla

## GLAZE

- 1 tablespoon reserved poaching liquid

**1** In 4-quart saucepan, stir 1 cup sugar, the water, vodka and liqueur. Cut slit down center of vanilla bean; scrape out seeds. Discard bean; add seeds to mixture in saucepan. Heat to boiling over medium-high heat; add pears. Reduce heat to low. Cover loosely; simmer 25 to 45 minutes or until pears are tender. (Poaching time will vary depending on ripeness of pears.) Remove from heat. Let pears cool in liquid 1 hour.

**2** Meanwhile, heat oven to 425°F. Place pastry or pie crust in 9-inch glass pie plate. Bake as directed for Partially Baked One-Crust Pie (page 9). Cool crust 10 minutes. Reduce oven temperature to 350°F.

**3** Remove pears from liquid to cutting board. Strain poaching liquid through mesh strainer; set liquid aside. Thinly slice pears; arrange in layers in decorative pattern in partially baked crust.

**4** In large bowl, beat all custard ingredients with whisk just until combined. Slowly pour over pears. Carefully place pie in oven (pie plate will be full). Cover crust edge with pie shield ring or strips of foil to prevent excessive browning. Place sheet of foil on rack below pie in case of spillover.

**5** Bake 1 hour 10 minutes or until knife inserted in center comes out clean. Brush top of pie with 1 tablespoon reserved poaching liquid. Cool on cooling rack 1 hour. Refrigerate 2 hours or until completely cool.

**1 Serving:** Calories 310; Total Fat 10g (Saturated Fat 4g; Trans Fat 0g); Cholesterol 45mg; Sodium 125mg; Total Carbohydrate 48g (Dietary Fiber 3g); Protein 2g **Exchanges:** 1 Starch, ½ Fruit, 1½ Other Carbohydrate, 2 Fat **Carbohydrate Choices:** 3

## Sweet Success Tips

**Pear nectar can be substituted for both the vodka and elderflower liqueur.**

**Don't throw away the extra poaching liquid. It is delicious! Create an easy yet fancy dessert by topping vanilla ice cream with fresh raspberries and drizzling with the poaching liquid.**

# Spiced Gingered Pear Pie

**8 servings** • PREP TIME: **25 Minutes** • START TO FINISH: **1 Hour 40 Minutes**

## CRUST

1 box Pillsbury refrigerated pie crusts, softened as directed on box

## FILLING

½ cup packed light brown sugar

¼ cup granulated sugar

2 tablespoons cornstarch

3 tablespoons finely chopped crystallized ginger

1 teaspoon finely grated lemon peel

6 cups thinly sliced peeled pears (about 6 medium)

1 tablespoon cold butter

## TOPPING

1 tablespoon water

4 teaspoons granulated sugar

**1** Heat oven to 425°F. Make pie crusts as directed on box for Two-Crust Pie using 9-inch glass pie plate.

**2** In large bowl, mix brown sugar, ¼ cup granulated sugar and the cornstarch. Stir in ginger and lemon peel. Add pears; toss gently. Spoon into crust-lined plate. Cut butter into small pieces; sprinkle over filling.

**3** Top with second crust; seal and flute. Cut slits or shapes in several places in top crust. Brush crust with water; sprinkle with 4 teaspoons granulated sugar.

**4** Bake 40 to 45 minutes or until pears are tender and crust is golden brown. After 15 to 20 minutes of baking, cover crust edge with pie shield ring or strips of foil to prevent excessive browning. Cool on cooling rack at least 30 minutes before serving. Store covered in refrigerator.

**1 Serving:** Calories 380; Total Fat 14g (Saturated Fat 6g; Trans Fat 0g); Cholesterol 10mg; Sodium 280mg; Total Carbohydrate 62g (Dietary Fiber 2g); Protein 2g **Exchanges:** 1 Starch, 3 Other Carbohydrate, 2½ Fat **Carbohydrate Choices:** 4

## Sweet Success Tips

Ripe Anjou or Bosc pears work well for pies; choose fruit that is fragrant and slightly soft to the touch.

Serve this pie warm with a scoop of vanilla ice cream drizzled with caramel sauce.

# Dutch Pear Pie

**8 servings** • **PREP TIME: 20 Minutes** • **START TO FINISH: 1 Hour 40 Minutes**

## CRUST

1 Pillsbury refrigerated pie crust, softened as directed on box

## FILLING

1 cup sour cream
½ cup granulated sugar
1 tablespoon all-purpose flour
1 teaspoon vanilla
1 egg, beaten
3 cups coarsely chopped peeled pears (3 to 4 medium)

## CRUMB TOPPING

1 cup all-purpose flour
½ cup packed brown sugar
½ cup butter or margarine

**1** Heat oven to 425°F. Place pie crust in 9-inch glass pie plate. Bake as directed for Partially Baked One-Crust Pie (page 9).

**2** Meanwhile, in medium bowl, mix all filling ingredients. Pour into warm partially baked crust.

**3** In medium bowl, mix all topping ingredients with pastry blender or fork until mixture looks like fine crumbs; sprinkle topping evenly over filling.

**4** Reduce oven temperature to 350°F. Bake 40 to 50 minutes or until top is light golden brown. After 30 minutes of baking, cover top of pie with foil to prevent excessive browning. Cool on cooling rack at least 30 minutes before serving. Store in refrigerator.

**1 Serving:** Calories 480; Total Fat 24g (Saturated Fat 13g; Trans Fat 0.5g); Cholesterol 75mg; Sodium 250mg; Total Carbohydrate 61g (Dietary Fiber 2g); Protein 4g **Exchanges:** 2 Starch, 2 Other Carbohydrate, 4½ Fat **Carbohydrate Choices:** 4

## Sweet Success Tip

Purchase pears ahead of time to ensure ripeness. To speed ripening, place pears in a paper or plastic bag at room temperature for several days. Pears are ready when they yield slightly when pressed.

# Cherry Pie

**8 servings • PREP TIME: 40 Minutes • START TO FINISH: 3 Hours 25 Minutes**

Two-Crust Pastry (page 8) or 1 box Pillsbury refrigerated pie crusts, softened as directed on box

1⅓ cups sugar

½ cup all-purpose flour

6 cups fresh sour cherries, pitted

2 tablespoons cold butter, if desired

**1** Heat oven to 425°F. Place 1 pastry round or pie crust in 9-inch glass pie plate.

**2** In large bowl, mix sugar and flour. Stir in cherries. Spoon into pastry-lined plate. Cut butter into small pieces; sprinkle over cherries.

**3** Cover with top pastry or second crust, or top with lattice crust (see Lattice Top Crusts, page 10); seal and flute. If not using lattice crust, cut slits in several places in top crust. Cover edge with pie crust shield ring or strips of foil to prevent excessive browning.

**4** Bake 35 to 45 minutes or until crust is golden brown and juice begins to bubble through slits in crust, removing foil during last 15 minutes. Cool on cooling rack at least 2 hours before serving.

**1 Serving:** Calories 540; Total Fat 22g (Saturated Fat 5g; Trans Fat 3.5g); Cholesterol 0mg; Sodium 300mg; Total Carbohydrate 81g (Dietary Fiber 4g); Protein 5g **Exchanges:** 2 Starch, 1 Fruit, 2 Other Carbohydrate, 4 Fat **Carbohydrate Choices:** 5½

**Quick Cherry Pie** Substitute 6 cups frozen unsweetened pitted tart red cherries, thawed and drained, or 3 cans (14.5 oz each) pitted tart red cherries, drained, for the fresh cherries.

## Sweet Success Tip

The two types of cherries, sweet and sour, are great for different uses. Sour cherries—also called pie cherries, tart cherries or tart red cherries—make wonderful pies. Sweet cherries are great for eating fresh, but are not used as often for pies.

# Amaretto Sweet Cherry Pie

**8 servings** • **PREP TIME: 25 Minutes** • **START TO FINISH: 3 Hours 30 Minutes**

1 cup sugar

¼ cup quick-cooking tapioca

⅛ teaspoon salt

4 cups halved pitted fresh or frozen (do not thaw) dark sweet cherries

¼ cup amaretto

1 box Pillsbury refrigerated pie crusts, softened as directed on box

⅓ cup butter toffee–glazed sliced almonds

1½ tablespoons cold butter

1 egg

1 tablespoon water

**1** Heat oven to 400°F. In large bowl, mix sugar, tapioca and salt; stir in cherries and amaretto. Let stand 15 minutes.

**2** Make pie crusts as directed on box for Two-Crust Pie using 9-inch glass pie plate. Spoon cherry mixture into crust-lined plate. Sprinkle with almonds. Cut butter into small pieces; sprinkle over filling. Top with second crust; seal and flute. Cut slits in several places in top crust.

**3** In small bowl, beat egg and water until blended; brush over top crust. Line cookie sheet with foil; place pie on cookie sheet. Cover crust edge with pie shield ring or strips of foil to prevent excessive browning.

**4** Bake 30 minutes. Remove foil; bake 15 to 20 minutes longer or until golden brown. Cool on cooling rack at least 2 hours before serving.

**Juliana Black of Garland, Texas, won the Pillsbury Refrigerated Pie Crust Pie Baking Championship at the 2009 State Fair of Texas with this recipe.**

**1 Serving:** Calories 450; Total Fat 16g (Saturated Fat 7g; Trans Fat 0g); Cholesterol 35mg; Sodium 340mg; Total Carbohydrate 72g (Dietary Fiber 2g); Protein 2g **Exchanges:** 1 Starch, 1½ Fruit, 2½ Other Carbohydrate, 3 Fat **Carbohydrate Choices:** 5

## Sweet Success Tip

For layered flavor, fold a dash of amaretto or a teaspoon of almond extract into whipped cream or whipped topping and serve it with this pie.

# ABC (Almond Bing Cherry) Pie

**8 servings** · **PREP TIME: 35 Minutes** · **START TO FINISH: 3 Hours 35 Minutes**

1 box Pillsbury refrigerated pie crusts, softened as directed on box

4 cups halved pitted fresh or frozen (partially thawed) dark sweet cherries

1 tablespoon lemon juice

½ teaspoon almond extract

¾ cup sugar

3 tablespoons cornstarch

1 tablespoon cold butter

2 tablespoons milk

2 tablespoons sugar

¼ cup sliced almonds

**1** Heat oven to 350°F. Make pie crusts as directed on box for Two-Crust Pie using 9-inch glass pie plate.

**2** In large bowl, stir cherries, lemon juice and almond extract. In small bowl, mix ¾ cup sugar and the cornstarch; stir into cherries. Spoon into crust-lined plate. Cut butter into small pieces; sprinkle over filling.

**3** To make lattice top, cut second crust into ½-inch-wide strips with pastry cutter. Place half of the strips across filling in pie plate. Weave remaining strips with first strips to form lattice. Trim ends of strips even with edge of bottom crust. Fold trimmed edge of bottom crust over ends of strips, forming a high stand-up rim; seal and flute.

**4** In small saucepan, heat milk, 2 tablespoons sugar and the almonds to boiling; reduce heat to medium. Cook 2 minutes, stirring constantly. Brush mixture over lattice strips.

**5** Bake 20 minutes; cover crust edge with pie crust shield ring or strips of foil to prevent excessive browning. Bake 30 to 40 minutes longer or until golden brown. Cool on cooling rack at least 2 hours before serving.

**Lola Nebel of Cambridge, Minnesota, won the Pillsbury Refrigerated Pie Crust Pie Baking Championship at the 2009 Minnesota State Fair with this recipe.**

**1 Serving:** Calories 410; Total Fat 15g (Saturated Fat 6g; Trans Fat 0g); Cholesterol 10mg; Sodium 290mg; Total Carbohydrate 66g (Dietary Fiber 2g); Protein 2g **Exchanges:** 1 Starch, 1 Fruit, 2½ Other Carbohydrate, 3 Fat **Carbohydrate Choices:** 4½

## Sweet Success Tip

**For an easy lattice top, place second half of pastry strips crosswise across first strips instead of weaving them. Trim, seal and flute as directed in the recipe.**

# Sparkling Cherry Pie

**8 servings** • **PREP TIME: 35 Minutes** • **START TO FINISH: 3 Hours 35 Minutes**

| | |
|---|---|
| 4 | cups pitted fresh or frozen (thawed) sour red cherries |
| 1⅓ | cups sugar |
| ¼ | cup quick-cooking tapioca |
| 1 | tablespoon all-purpose flour |
| | Dash salt |
| ¼ | teaspoon almond extract |
| 1 | box Pillsbury refrigerated pie crusts, softened as directed on box |
| 1 | tablespoon cold butter |
| 1 | teaspoon milk |
| 1 | teaspoon sugar |

**1** Heat oven to 400°F. In large bowl, mix cherries, 1⅓ cups sugar, the tapioca, flour, salt and almond extract. Let stand 10 minutes.

**2** Make pie crusts as directed on box for Two-Crust Pie using 9-inch glass pie plate. Spoon cherry mixture into crust-lined plate. Cut butter into small pieces; sprinkle over filling.

**3** Top with second crust; seal and flute. Cut slits in several places in top crust. Brush crust with milk; sprinkle with 1 teaspoon sugar.

**4** Bake 20 minutes; cover crust edge with pie shield ring or strips of foil to prevent excessive browning. Reduce oven temperature to 350°F; bake 40 minutes longer or until crust is golden brown and filling is bubbly. Cool on cooling rack at least 2 hours before serving.

Marianne Carlson of Jefferson, Iowa, won the Pillsbury Refrigerated Pie Crust Pie Baking Championship at the 2009 Iowa State Fair with this recipe.

**1 Serving:** Calories 420; Total Fat 14g (Saturated Fat 6g; Trans Fat 0g); Cholesterol 10mg; Sodium 310mg; Total Carbohydrate 72g (Dietary Fiber 1g); Protein 1g **Exchanges:** 1 Starch, 1½ Fruit, 2½ Other Carbohydrate, 2½ Fat **Carbohydrate Choices:** 5

## Sweet Success Tip

**Look for the pie crust shield ring at kitchen specialty stores—it's a handy tool to have for covering the crust edge instead of using foil strips.**

# Starstruck Raspberry-Almond Pie

**8 servings** • **PREP TIME: 50 Minutes** • **START TO FINISH: 4 Hours 45 Minutes**

## CRUST

Two-Crust Pastry (page 8)
or 1 box Pillsbury refrigerated
pie crusts, softened as directed
on box

## ALMOND LAYER

½ cup whole blanched almonds
2 tablespoons butter
¼ cup granulated sugar
2 teaspoons all-purpose flour
1 egg
½ teaspoon almond extract

## BERRY LAYER

1 cup granulated sugar
5 tablespoons cornstarch
1 tablespoon grated orange peel
5 cups fresh or frozen (thawed)
raspberries
1 egg
1 tablespoon whipping cream
2 tablespoons coarse sugar or
sanding sugar

**1** Heat oven to 400°F. Place 1 pastry round or pie crust in 9-inch glass pie plate; flute edges. On lightly floured surface, roll second pastry or pie crust to 13-inch round. With 1½-inch star cookie cutter, cut out 45 stars; set aside.

**2** Place almonds in food processor. Cover; process until finely chopped. Add butter, ¼ cup granulated sugar and the flour; process until blended. Add 1 egg and the almond extract; process until blended. Spread mixture evenly in pastry-lined plate.

**3** In large bowl, mix 1 cup granulated sugar, the cornstarch and orange peel. Add raspberries; toss gently. Spoon berry mixture evenly over almond layer. In small bowl, beat 1 egg and the whipping cream. Arrange stars in circular pattern on top of filling (with tips touching), covering entire surface. Brush rim and stars with egg mixture; sprinkle with coarse sugar.

**4** Place cookie sheet on rack below pie in case of spillover. Bake 10 minutes. Cover crust edge with pie shield ring or strips of foil to prevent excessive browning. Bake 40 to 45 minutes longer or until crust is golden brown and juices are bubbly. (If crust becomes too brown, cover entire crust with foil.) Cool on cooling rack at least 3 hours before serving.

**1 Serving:** Calories 580; Total Fat 28g (Saturated Fat 7g; Trans Fat 0g); Cholesterol 55mg; Sodium 340mg; Total Carbohydrate 76g (Dietary Fiber 7g); Protein 8g **Exchanges:** 2½ Starch, 1 Fruit, 1½ Other Carbohydrate, 5½ Fat **Carbohydrate Choices:** 5

## Sweet Success Tip

**We've used stars to decorate this pie but different cookie cutters can be used to celebrate different events!**

# Cherry-Strawberry Pie

**8 servings** • **PREP TIME: 25 Minutes** • **START TO FINISH: 3 Hours 15 Minutes**

1 box Pillsbury refrigerated pie crusts, softened as directed on box

1 egg white, slightly beaten

¾ cup sugar

2 tablespoons quick-cooking tapioca

2 tablespoons cornstarch

¼ teaspoon salt

1 bag (16 oz) frozen red cherries, thawed, drained and juice reserved

1 box (10 oz) frozen strawberries in light syrup, thawed, drained and syrup reserved

1 tablespoon lemon juice

2 tablespoons cold butter

**1**  Heat oven to 400°F. Unroll 1 pie crust in 9-inch glass pie plate; brush with beaten egg white.

**2**  In 2-quart saucepan, mix sugar, tapioca, cornstarch and salt. Stir in reserved cherry juice and strawberry syrup. Heat over medium heat 5 to 10 minutes, stirring frequently, until juice becomes thick and boils. Remove from heat. Stir in cherries, strawberries and lemon juice. Pour into crust-lined plate. Cut butter into small pieces; sprinkle over filling.

**3**  Top with second crust; seal and flute. Cut slits in several places in top crust.

**4**  Bake 45 to 50 minutes or until crust is golden brown and juice begins to bubble through slits in crust. Cool on cooling rack at least 2 hours before serving. Store in refrigerator.

**1 Serving:** Calories 400; Total Fat 18g (Saturated Fat 7g; Trans Fat 0g); Cholesterol 45mg; Sodium 330mg; Total Carbohydrate 59g (Dietary Fiber 1g); Protein 1g **Exchanges:** 4 Other Carbohydrate, 3½ Fat **Carbohydrate Choices:** 4

## Sweet Success Tip

For a pretty finishing touch, garnish the pie with maraschino cherries and fresh strawberries.

# Cherry–Red Raspberry Pie

**8 servings** • **PREP TIME: 20 Minutes** • **START TO FINISH: 4 Hours 20 Minutes**

2 cups fresh red raspberries
1 cup pitted sour cherries
1½ cups sugar
2 tablespoons quick-cooking tapioca
1 teaspoon lemon juice
1 box Pillsbury refrigerated pie crusts, softened as directed on box
2 tablespoons cold butter
1 tablespoon milk
1 teaspoon sugar

**1** In large bowl, gently toss raspberries and cherries. Add 1½ cups sugar, the tapioca and lemon juice; mix well. Let stand 1 hour.

**2** Heat oven to 400°F. Place 1 pie crust in 9-inch glass pie plate. Spoon fruit mixture into crust-lined plate. Cut butter into small pieces; sprinkle over filling.

**3** Cut second crust into 1-inch-wide strips with pastry cutter. Place 5 to 7 strips across filling. Place remaining strips crosswise over first strips. Seal and flute edges. Brush crust with milk; sprinkle with 1 teaspoon sugar. Cover crust edge with pie shield ring or strips of foil to prevent excessive browning.

**4** Bake 15 minutes. Reduce oven temperature to 350°F; bake 40 to 45 minutes longer, removing foil after 10 minutes, until filling is bubbly and crust is golden brown. Cool on cooling rack at least 2 hours before serving.

**1 Serving:** Calories 270; Total Fat 9g (Saturated Fat 4.5g; Trans Fat 0g); Cholesterol 10mg; Sodium 160mg; Total Carbohydrate 46g (Dietary Fiber 2g); Protein 0g **Exchanges:** 3 Other Carbohydrate, 2 Fat **Carbohydrate Choices:** 3

## Sweet Success Tip

**Brushing the top crust with milk and sprinkling with sugar results in a crisp and crunchy sweet crust—and gives the perfect pie shop look!**

# Cherry-Berry Sweetheart Pie

**8 servings** • **PREP TIME: 30 Minutes** • **START TO FINISH: 3 Hours 10 Minutes**

1 box Pillsbury refrigerated pie crusts, softened as directed on box

2 cups pitted fresh or frozen (partially thawed) dark sweet cherries

2 cups fresh or frozen (do not thaw) raspberries

¾ cup granulated sugar

2 tablespoons all-purpose flour

2 tablespoons quick-cooking tapioca

¼ teaspoon salt

½ teaspoon almond extract

¾ cup all-purpose flour

½ cup granulated sugar

½ cup cold butter

1 tablespoon coarse sugar

**1** Heat oven to 425°F. Make pie crusts as directed on box for Two-Crust Pie using 9-inch glass pie plate.

**2** In large bowl, mix cherries, raspberries, ¾ cup granulated sugar, 2 tablespoons flour, the tapioca, salt and almond extract. Spoon into crust-lined plate.

**3** Unroll second crust on work surface. With floured 2-inch heart-shaped cookie cutter, cut about 16 hearts from crust.

**4** In small bowl, mix ¾ cup flour and ½ cup granulated sugar. Cut in butter, using pastry blender or fork, until mixture looks like fine crumbs; sprinkle over filling. Place heart cutouts over crumbs. Sprinkle coarse sugar on top.

**5** Bake 15 minutes; cover crust edge with pie crust shield ring or strips of foil to prevent excessive browning. Bake 15 to 25 minutes longer or until golden brown. Cool on cooling rack at least 2 hours before serving.

Jeff Case of Mattydale, New York, won the Pillsbury Refrigerated Pie Crust Pie Baking Championship at the 2009 New York State Fair with this recipe.

**1 Serving:** Calories 540; Total Fat 24g (Saturated Fat 12g; Trans Fat 0g); Cholesterol 35mg; Sodium 440mg; Total Carbohydrate 79g (Dietary Fiber 3g); Protein 2g **Exchanges:** 1 Starch, 1½ Fruit, 3 Other Carbohydrate, 4½ Fat **Carbohydrate Choices:** 5

## Sweet Success Tip

For an extra touch, add a couple drops of red food color and almond extract to whipped topping; spoon onto slices before serving.

# Cherry-Blueberry Pie

**8 servings** · **PREP TIME: 25 Minutes** · **START TO FINISH: 3 Hours 20 Minutes**

### CRUST

1 box Pillsbury refrigerated pie crusts, softened as directed on box

### FILLING

½ cup sugar
2 tablespoons cornstarch
¼ teaspoon ground cinnamon
1 can (21 oz) cherry pie filling
1½ cups fresh blueberries

### EGG GLAZE

1 egg white
1 teaspoon water
2 teaspoons sugar

**1** Heat oven to 425°F. Make pie crusts as directed on box for Two-Crust Pie using 9-inch glass pie plate.

**2** In large bowl, mix ½ cup sugar, the cornstarch and cinnamon. Stir in pie filling and blueberries. Spoon into crust-lined plate. To make lattice top, cut second crust into ½-inch-wide strips with pastry cutter. Arrange strips in lattice design over filling. Seal and flute.

**3** In small bowl, beat egg white and water with fork until blended; brush over top crust (discard any remaining egg white mixture). Sprinkle with 2 teaspoons sugar. Cover crust edge with strips of foil to prevent excessive browning.

**4** Bake 45 to 55 minutes or until crust is golden brown, removing foil during last 15 minutes. Cool on cooling rack at least 2 hours before serving. Store covered in refrigerator.

**1 Serving:** Calories 340; Total Fat 14g (Saturated Fat 5g; Trans Fat 0g); Cholesterol 5mg; Sodium 230mg; Total Carbohydrate 53g (Dietary Fiber 1g); Protein 1g **Exchanges:** ½ Starch, 3 Other Carbohydrate, 2½ Fat **Carbohydrate Choices:** 3½

## Sweet Success Tip

Raspberries are also good in this pie in place of blueberries. If fresh berries aren't available, you can use frozen instead.

# Blueberry Pie

**8 servings • PREP TIME: 20 Minutes • START TO FINISH: 3 Hours 5 Minutes**

Two-Crust Pastry (page 8)
or 1 box Pillsbury refrigerated
pie crusts, softened as directed
on box

1¼  cups sugar

½  cup cornstarch

½  teaspoon ground cinnamon,
   if desired

6  cups fresh or frozen (thawed
   and drained) blueberries

1  tablespoon lemon juice

1  tablespoon cold butter,
   if desired

**1**  Heat oven to 425°F. Place 1 pastry round or pie crust in 9-inch glass pie plate.

**2**  In large bowl, mix sugar, cornstarch and cinnamon. Stir in blueberries. Spoon into pastry-lined plate. Sprinkle with lemon juice. Cut butter into small pieces; sprinkle over blueberries.

**3**  Top with second pastry or crust, or make lattice top (see Lattice Top Crusts, page 10); seal and flute. If not using lattice top, cut slits in top crust. Cover crust edge with pie crust shield ring or strips of foil to prevent excessive browning.

**4**  Bake 35 to 45 minutes or until crust is golden brown and juice begins to bubble through slits in crust, removing foil during last 15 minutes. Cool on cooling rack at least 2 hours before serving.

**1 Serving:** Calories 410; Total Fat 19g (Saturated Fat 4.5g; Trans Fat 3g); Cholesterol 0mg; Sodium 270mg; Total Carbohydrate 57g (Dietary Fiber 4g); Protein 4g **Exchanges:** 1 Starch, 1 Fruit, 2 Other Carbohydrate, 3½ Fat **Carbohydrate Choices:** 4

**Blueberry-Peach Pie** Substitute 2½ cups sliced peeled fresh peaches for 4 cups of the blueberries; omit lemon juice. Place blueberries in pastry-lined plate; sprinkle with half of the sugar mixture. Top with peaches; sprinkle with remaining sugar mixture. Continue as directed in step 3.

## Sweet Success Tip
**Blackberries, boysenberries, loganberries or raspberries can be substituted for the blueberries; just omit the lemon juice.**

# Fresh Blueberry Pie

**8 servings • PREP TIME: 40 Minutes • START TO FINISH: 3 Hours 40 Minutes**

1 box Pillsbury refrigerated pie crusts, softened as directed on box
¾ cup sugar
3 tablespoons cornstarch
1 cup water
4 cups fresh blueberries
½ teaspoon ground cinnamon
½ teaspoon grated lemon peel
1 tablespoon fresh lemon juice

**1** Heat oven to 450°F. Make 1 pie crust as directed on box for One-Crust Baked Shell; cool. Roll out second crust on lightly floured surface; with small cookie cutter, cut out decorative shapes for top of pie. Place cutouts on ungreased cookie sheet. Bake 7 minutes; cool.

**2** Meanwhile, in 2-quart saucepan, mix sugar and cornstarch. Gradually stir in water. Cook over medium heat about 10 minutes, stirring frequently, until clear. Add 1½ cups of the blueberries. Reduce heat to low. Cover; cook about 10 minutes longer until mixture is thickened and bubbly. Stir in cinnamon, lemon peel and lemon juice. Stir in remaining 2½ cups blueberries.

**3** Pour filling into cooled baked shell. Arrange cutouts on top of pie. Let stand until set, about 3 hours, before serving.

Rebecca Tenckinck from Warwick, New York, won first place with this recipe at the 2010 New York State Fair Pie Contest.

**1 Serving:** Calories 340; Total Fat 12g (Saturated Fat 5g; Trans Fat 0g); Cholesterol 5mg; Sodium 260mg; Total Carbohydrate 56g (Dietary Fiber 2g); Protein 2g **Exchanges:** 1 Starch, 1 Fruit, 1½ Other Carbohydrate, 2½ Fat **Carbohydrate Choices:** 4

## Sweet Success Tip

Using a star-shaped cookie cutter for the cutouts on top of the pie makes this a perfect dessert for the Fourth of July! Use any cutter of your choice to suit the holiday or occasion.

## Showstopping Top Crusts

**Add a bit of pastry-shop glitz with one of these simple top crust treatments *before* baking✻:**

**Shiny Crust:** Brush crust with milk.

**Sugary Crust:** Brush crust lightly with water or milk; sprinkle with granulated sugar or with coarse sugar crystals.

**Glazed Crust:** Brush crust lightly with beaten egg or egg yolk mixed with a teaspoon of water.

**Or try this treatment *after* baking:**

**Glaze for Baked Pie Crust:** In small bowl, mix ½ cup powdered sugar, 2 to 3 teaspoons milk, orange juice or lemon juice and, if desired, 2 teaspoons grated orange or lemon peel. Brush or drizzle over warm baked pie crust (but do not let glaze run over edge of the pie).

✻ These pastry treatments may make the pie brown more quickly. If this happens, lay a sheet of foil loosely over the top of the pie to slow the browning.

# Blueberry-Apple-Peach Pie

8 servings · PREP TIME: 40 Minutes · START TO FINISH: 3 Hours 50 Minutes

## CRUST

- 1 box Pillsbury refrigerated pie crusts, softened as directed on box

## FILLING

- 6 cups sliced peeled apples
- 3 cups sliced peeled fresh peaches or 1 can (29 oz) sliced peaches, drained
- 1 tablespoon lemon juice
- ¾ cup granulated sugar
- ½ cup pie filling enhancer (thickener)
- 1 tablespoon cornstarch
- ½ teaspoon salt
- ½ teaspoon ground cinnamon
- 1 cup fresh or frozen (partially thawed) blueberries
- ½ teaspoon vanilla

## CRUMB TOPPING

- 1 cup all-purpose flour
- ⅔ cup packed brown sugar
- ½ cup old-fashioned oats
- ½ teaspoon ground cinnamon
- ¼ teaspoon salt
- ½ cup cold unsalted butter
- ½ teaspoon milk
- 2 tablespoons coarse sugar

**1** Heat oven to 400°F. Make pie crusts as directed on box for Two-Crust Pie using 9½-inch deep-dish glass pie plate.

**2** In large bowl, toss apples and peaches with lemon juice. In small bowl, mix ¾ cup granulated sugar, the pie filling enhancer, cornstarch, ½ teaspoon salt and ½ teaspoon cinnamon. Sprinkle over apples and peaches; toss to mix well. Gently stir in blueberries and vanilla. Spoon into crust-lined plate.

**3** In medium bowl, mix flour, brown sugar, oats, ½ teaspoon cinnamon and ¼ teaspoon salt. Cut in butter, using pastry blender or fork, until mixture looks like fine crumbs. Sprinkle topping over filling; press down lightly.

**4** Cut second crust into ½-inch-wide strips with pastry cutter. Place half of the strips across filling in pie plate. Weave remaining strips with first strips to form lattice. Trim ends of strips even with edge of bottom crust. Fold trimmed edge of bottom crust over ends of strips, forming a high stand-up rim; seal and flute. Brush lattice strips with milk; sprinkle with coarse sugar.

**5** Cover pie with sheet of foil to prevent excessive browning; bake 30 minutes. Remove foil; reduce oven temperature to 350°F. Bake 35 to 40 minutes longer or until top is golden brown. Cool on cooling rack at least 2 hours before serving.

Jennifer Klingler of Hamburg, Pennsylvania, won the Pillsbury Refrigerated Pie Crust Pie Baking Championship at the 2009 Allentown (PA) Fair with this recipe.

**1 Serving:** Calories 670; Total Fat 24g (Saturated Fat 12g; Trans Fat 0g); Cholesterol 35mg; Sodium 510mg; Total Carbohydrate 110g (Dietary Fiber 3g); Protein 3g **Exchanges:** 1 Starch, 2½ Fruit, 4 Other Carbohydrate, 4½ Fat **Carbohydrate Choices:** 7

## Sweet Success Tip

For an easy serving "wow," drizzle each dessert plate with blueberry pancake syrup before adding a slice of this delicious mixed-fruit pie.

# Raz-Black-Blue Pie

**8 servings** • **PREP TIME: 35 Minutes** • **START TO FINISH: 3 Hours 40 Minutes**

3 cups fresh or frozen (partially thawed) blackberries

2 cups fresh or frozen (partially thawed) raspberries

1½ cups fresh or frozen (partially thawed) blueberries

1½ cups sugar

¼ cup quick-cooking tapioca

¼ teaspoon salt

1 tablespoon lemon juice

1 box Pillsbury refrigerated pie crusts, softened as directed on box

½ teaspoon flour

2 tablespoons cold butter

1 egg white, beaten

2 tablespoons coarse sugar

**1** Heat oven to 450°F. In large bowl, mix berries, sugar, tapioca, salt and lemon juice. Let stand 15 minutes.

**2** Meanwhile, unroll 1 pie crust on work surface. Sprinkle both sides lightly with flour; place in 9-inch glass pie plate. Press firmly against side and bottom. Spoon berry mixture into crust-lined plate. Cut butter into small pieces; sprinkle over filling.

**3** Cut second crust into 1-inch-wide strips with pastry cutter. Place half of strips across filling in pie plate. Weave remaining strips with first strips to form lattice. Trim ends of strips even with edge of bottom crust; seal and flute. Brush with egg white; sprinkle with coarse sugar.

**4** Place pie on middle oven rack; place sheet of foil on rack below pie in case of spillover. Bake 15 minutes. Reduce oven temperature to 350°F. Cover crust edge with pie crust shield ring or strips of foil to prevent excessive browning; bake 40 to 50 minutes or until golden brown. Cool on cooling rack at least 2 hours before serving.

**Tamera Battle of Tacoma, Washington, won the Pillsbury Refrigerated Pie Crust Pie Baking Championship at the 2009 Western Washington Fair with this recipe.**

**1 Serving:** Calories 470; Total Fat 15g (Saturated Fat 7g; Trans Fat 0g); Cholesterol 15mg; Sodium 380mg; Total Carbohydrate 80g (Dietary Fiber 5g); Protein 2g **Exchanges:** 1 Starch, 1½ Fruit, 3 Other Carbohydrate, 3 Fat **Carbohydrate Choices:** 5

## Sweet Success Tip

For a special touch, drizzle warmed blueberry pancake syrup over the top of each slice just before serving.

# Wild Berry Pie

**8 servings • PREP TIME: 30 Minutes • START TO FINISH: 4 Hours 25 Minutes**

1   box Pillsbury refrigerated pie crusts
1   tablespoon sour cream
1½  quarts wild berries (such as black raspberries, blackberries, black mulberries, blueberries, red huckleberries, black huckleberries or strawberries)
1   cup sugar
6   tablespoons cornstarch
1   teaspoon lemon juice
1   teaspoon milk, if desired
2   teaspoons sugar, if desired

**1**   Heat oven to 400°F. Remove pie crusts from box, but leave in pouches. Microwave 20 seconds in pouches to soften. Remove crusts from pouches; mix sour cream into dough using hands. Divide dough in half. On lightly floured surface, roll out thin. Place 1 crust in 9-inch glass pie plate.

**2**   In large bowl, mix berries, 1 cup sugar and cornstarch. Add lemon juice. Spoon into crust-lined plate.

**3**   Top with second crust; seal and flute. Cut slits in several places in top crust. Brush with milk and sprinkle with additional sugar. Place pie on middle oven rack; place sheet of foil on rack below pie in case of spillover.

**4**   Bake 45 to 55 minutes or until crust is golden brown and filling is bubbly. Cool on cooling rack at least 3 hours before serving.

Christy Lynn Larson from Clarinda, Iowa, entered this winning recipe at the 2010 Iowa State Fair Pie Contest.

**1 Serving:** Calories 390; Total Fat 13g (Saturated Fat 5g; Trans Fat 0g); Cholesterol 10mg; Sodium 260mg; Total Carbohydrate 67g (Dietary Fiber 3g); Protein 2g **Exchanges:** 2½ Starch, 2 Other Carbohydrate, 2 Fat **Carbohydrate Choices:** 4½

## Sweet Success Tip

If using wild berries such as huckleberries or mulberries, you may want to increase the sugar slightly due to their tartness.

# Grape Pie

**8 servings** • **PREP TIME: 35 Minutes** • **START TO FINISH: 3 Hours 15 Minutes**

## CRUST

- 1 box Pillsbury refrigerated pie crusts, softened as directed on box
- ½ teaspoon all-purpose flour

## FILLING

- 4 cups red seedless grapes
- 1 cup granulated sugar
- ½ cup packed brown sugar
- ½ teaspoon salt
- 3 tablespoons butter
- 2 tablespoons honey
- 1 teaspoon vanilla
- 1 teaspoon lemon juice
- ¼ cup all-purpose flour

## TOPPING

- 1½ cups old-fashioned oats
- ¾ cup packed brown sugar
- ½ cup butter, softened
- 1 teaspoon vanilla
- 1 egg, beaten

**1** Heat oven to 425°F. Unroll 1 pie crust on work surface. Sprinkle both sides lightly with flour; place in ungreased 9½-inch glass deep-dish pie plate. Press firmly against bottom and side.

**2** In 4-quart saucepan, stir together all filling ingredients except flour. Cook over medium heat 10 minutes, stirring frequently, until grapes are tender. Remove from heat; stir in ¼ cup flour. Set aside.

**3** In medium bowl, mix oats, ¾ cup brown sugar, ½ cup butter and 1 teaspoon vanilla with fork until crumbly. Spoon two-thirds of topping into crust-lined plate. Spoon filling over topping.

**4** Cut second crust into ½-inch-wide strips with pastry cutter. Place half of the strips across filling in pie plate. Weave remaining strips with first strips to form lattice. Trim ends of strips even with edge of bottom crust. Fold trimmed edge of bottom crust over ends of strips, forming a high stand-up rim; seal and flute. Brush lattice strips with egg. Sprinkle remaining one-third of topping over pie.

**5** Cover pie with sheet of foil to prevent excessive browning; bake 20 minutes. Remove foil; bake 15 to 20 minutes longer or until topping is golden brown. Cool on cooling rack at least 2 hours before serving.

**Mardell Costa of Pueblo, Colorado, won the Pillsbury Refrigerated Pie Crust Pie Baking Championship at the 2009 Colorado State Fair with this recipe.**

**1 Serving:** Calories 740; Total Fat 30g (Saturated Fat 15g; Trans Fat 0.5g); Cholesterol 75mg; Sodium 560mg; Total Carbohydrate 114g (Dietary Fiber 2g); Protein 4g **Exchanges:** 2½ Starch, 1½ Fruit, 3½ Other Carbohydrate, 5½ Fat **Carbohydrate Choices:** 7½

## Sweet Success Tip

Perfectly complement this pie with a scoop of French vanilla ice cream on each slice.

# Fresh Strawberry Pie

**8 servings** • **PREP TIME: 40 Minutes** • **START TO FINISH: 4 Hours 35 Minutes**

One-Crust Pastry (page 7)
or 1 Pillsbury refrigerated pie
crust, softened as directed
on box

1½  quarts fresh strawberries,
     hulled

1  cup sugar

2  tablespoons cornstarch

½  cup water

    Red food color, if desired

1  package (3 oz) cream cheese,
    softened

1  teaspoon grated lemon peel

**1**  Heat oven to 450°F. Bake pastry or pie crust as directed for Baked One-Crust Pie (page 9). Cool completely on cooling rack.

**2**  Meanwhile, in small bowl, mash enough strawberries to measure 1 cup. In 2-quart saucepan, mix sugar and cornstarch. Gradually stir in ½ cup water and mashed strawberries (add 1 to 2 drops food color if deeper red color is desired). Cook and stir over medium heat until mixture thickens and boils; boil and stir 1 minute. Remove from heat; cool.

**3**  In small bowl, beat cream cheese and lemon peel until smooth. Spread evenly in baked crust. Quarter or slice remaining strawberries (or leave whole, if desired); arrange over cream cheese layer. Pour cooked strawberry mixture over top. Refrigerate until set, about 3 hours. Store remaining pie in refrigerator.

**1 Serving:** Calories 330; Total Fat 14g (Saturated Fat 4.5g; Trans Fat 0g); Cholesterol 10mg; Sodium 180mg; Total Carbohydrate 48g (Dietary Fiber 2g); Protein 3g **Exchanges:** 1 Starch, ½ Fruit, 1½ Other Carbohydrate, 2½ Fat **Carbohydrate Choices:** 3

## Sweet Success Tip

**For a double strawberry hit, use 3 ounces of strawberry cream cheese spread in place of the regular cream cheese.**

# Summer's Delight Pie

**8 servings** • PREP TIME: 40 Minutes • START TO FINISH: 3 Hours 40 Minutes

## FILLING

| | |
|---|---|
| 1 | tablespoon butter |
| ¾ | cup sliced blanched almonds |
| 5 | large peaches, peeled, sliced |
| 2 | large nectarines, sliced |
| ½ | cup dried cherries |
| ½ | cup granulated sugar |
| ¼ | cup quick-cooking tapioca |
| ½ | teaspoon ground cinnamon |
| ½ | teaspoon vanilla |
| ¼ | teaspoon almond extract |
| 2 | tablespoons butter |
| 1 | tablespoon red cinnamon candies |

## CRUST AND TOPPING

| | |
|---|---|
| 1 | box Pillsbury refrigerated pie crusts, softened as directed on box |
| ¼ | cup sliced blanched almonds |
| ¼ | cup granulated sugar |
| ½ | teaspoon ground cinnamon |
| 2 | teaspoons vanilla sugar |

**1** Heat oven to 350°F. In 10-inch skillet, melt 1 tablespoon butter over medium heat. Add ¾ cup almonds. Cook and stir until almonds are toasted. Remove from skillet to heatproof plate; cool.

**2** In large bowl, mix remaining filling ingredients. Stir in toasted almonds.

**3** Make pie crusts as directed on box for Two-Crust Pie using 9-inch glass pie plate. Spoon peach mixture into crust-lined plate. Unroll second crust on work surface. With 2½- or 3-inch round cookie cutter, cut 1 circle from center of crust. Place remaining crust piece on pie; seal and flute. Cut dough circle into triangles; place around opening in crust to look like sun shape.

**4** In small bowl, mix ¼ cup almonds, ¼ cup granulated sugar and ½ teaspoon cinnamon; spoon into opening in top crust. Sprinkle vanilla sugar over top crust.

**5** Bake 50 to 60 minutes or until deep golden brown. Cool on cooling rack at least 2 hours before serving.

Sandra Trifilo of Glenham, New York, won the Pillsbury Refrigerated Pie Crust Pie Baking Championship at the 2009 Dutchess County (NY) Fair with this recipe.

**1 Serving:** Calories 530; Total Fat 23g (Saturated Fat 8g; Trans Fat 0g); Cholesterol 15mg; Sodium 320mg; Total Carbohydrate 75g (Dietary Fiber 4g); Protein 4g **Exchanges:** 1 Starch, 1½ Fruit, 2½ Other Carbohydrate, 4½ Fat **Carbohydrate Choices:** 5

## Sweet Success Tip

**If fresh peaches and nectarines aren't available, you can use 7 cups frozen sliced peaches, thawed and drained, instead.**

# Rhu-Berry Pie

8 servings • PREP TIME: 25 Minutes • START TO FINISH: 2 Hours 10 Minutes

1 box Pillsbury refrigerated pie crusts, softened as directed on box

2 cups cut-up fresh or frozen rhubarb

2 cups fresh blueberries

¾ cup granulated sugar

¼ cup all-purpose flour

⅛ teaspoon ground nutmeg

Dash salt

2 teaspoons milk

1 tablespoon coarse sugar, if desired

**1** Heat oven to 400°F. Make pie crusts as directed on box for Two-Crust Pie using 9-inch glass pie plate. Trim excess dough from edge of pie plate.

**2** In large bowl, gently toss rhubarb, blueberries, granulated sugar, flour, nutmeg and salt. Spoon into crust-lined plate.

**3** Cut second crust into ½-inch-wide strips with pastry cutter. Place half of the strips across filling in pie plate. Weave remaining strips with first strips to form lattice. Trim ends of strips even with edge of bottom crust. Fold trimmed edge of bottom crust over ends of strips; seal and flute. Brush crust with milk; sprinkle with coarse sugar.

**4** Bake 42 to 46 minutes or until crust is golden brown and filling is bubbly. Cool on cooling rack at least 1 hour before serving.

**1 Serving:** Calories 350; Total Fat 14g (Saturated Fat 5g; Trans Fat 0g); Cholesterol 10mg; Sodium 240mg; Total Carbohydrate 54g (Dietary Fiber 1g); Protein 0g **Exchanges:** 3½ Other Carbohydrate, 3 Fat **Carbohydrate Choices:** 3½

## Sweet Success Tip
Get creative with the crust! Use a small cookie cutter to cut squares, circles or other shapes from the second crust, and arrange in desired design on filling instead of topping with a lattice crust.

# Rhubarb Pie

8 servings • PREP TIME: 25 Minutes • START TO FINISH: 3 Hours 20 Minutes

Two-Crust Pastry (page 8)
or 1 box Pillsbury refrigerated
pie crusts, softened as directed
on box

2 to 2⅓ cups sugar

⅔ cup all-purpose flour

1 teaspoon grated orange peel,
if desired

6 cups chopped (½-inch pieces)
fresh rhubarb

1 tablespoon cold butter,
if desired

**1** Heat oven to 425°F. Place 1 pastry round or pie crust in 9-inch glass pie plate.

**2** In large bowl, mix sugar, flour and orange peel. Stir in rhubarb. Spoon into pastry-lined plate. Cut butter into small pieces; sprinkle over rhubarb.

**3** Cover with top pastry or second crust; seal and flute. Cut slits in several places in top crust. Cover crust edge with pie crust shield ring or strips of foil to prevent excessive browning.

**4** Bake 50 to 55 minutes or until crust is golden brown and juice begins to bubble through slits in crust, removing foil during last 15 minutes. Cool on cooling rack at least 2 hours before serving.

**1 Serving:** Calories 540; Total Fat 21g (Saturated Fat 5g; Trans Fat 3.5g); Cholesterol 0mg; Sodium 300mg; Total Carbohydrate 84g (Dietary Fiber 3g); Protein 5g **Exchanges:** 2 Starch, 1 Fruit, 2½ Other Carbohydrate, 3 Fat **Carbohydrate Choices:** 5½

**Quick Rhubarb Pie** Substitute 2 bags (16 ounces each) frozen unsweetened rhubarb, thawed and drained, for the fresh rhubarb.

**Strawberry-Rhubarb Pie** Substitute 3 cups sliced fresh strawberries for 3 cups of the rhubarb. Use 2 cups sugar.

## Sweet Success Tip

Rhubarb is very tart, so it requires sugar to make it sweet. But you can use the lower amount of sugar for young, thin rhubarb stalks that may be less tart.

# Peach-Rhubarb Pie

8 servings • PREP TIME: 35 Minutes • START TO FINISH: 3 Hours 20 Minutes

## CRUST

1 box Pillsbury refrigerated pie crusts, softened as directed on box

## FILLING

1 cup granulated sugar

¾ cup packed brown sugar

3 tablespoons quick-cooking tapioca

1 teaspoon ground cinnamon

Dash salt

½ cup orange juice

2 cups chopped fresh or frozen (partially thawed) rhubarb

3 medium peaches, peeled and chopped, or 3 cups frozen (partially thawed) sliced peaches, chopped

## TOPPING

1 cup chopped pecans

¾ cup coconut

2 tablespoons packed brown sugar

3 tablespoons butter, melted

**1** Heat oven to 375°F. Make pie crusts as directed on box for Two-Crust Pie using 9-inch glass pie plate.

**2** In small bowl, mix 1 cup granulated sugar, ¾ cup brown sugar, the tapioca, cinnamon, salt and orange juice. Place rhubarb in crust-lined plate; sprinkle with half of the sugar mixture. Top with peaches; sprinkle with remaining sugar mixture. Top with second crust; seal and flute. Cut slits in several places in top crust.

**3** Bake 35 minutes. In small bowl, mix all topping ingredients; sprinkle over top crust. Bake 10 minutes longer or until golden brown. Cool on cooling rack at least 2 hours before serving.

Margaret Miller of Burdett, Kansas, won the Pillsbury Refrigerated Pie Crust Pie Baking Championship at the 2009 Kansas State Fair with this recipe.

**1 Serving:** Calories 640; Total Fat 31g (Saturated Fat 13g; Trans Fat 0g); Cholesterol 15mg; Sodium 340mg; Total Carbohydrate 88g (Dietary Fiber 4g); Protein 2g **Exchanges:** 1 Starch, 1½ Fruit, 3½ Other Carbohydrate, 6 Fat **Carbohydrate Choices:** 6

## Sweet Success Tip

You can use either flaked or shredded coconut in this topping.

# Peach Pie

**8 servings • PREP TIME: 30 Minutes • START TO FINISH: 3 Hours 15 Minutes**

Two-Crust Pastry (page 8) or 1 box Pillsbury refrigerated pie crusts, softened as directed on box

⅔ cup sugar

⅓ cup all-purpose flour

¼ teaspoon ground cinnamon

6 cups sliced peeled peaches (6 to 8 medium)

1 teaspoon lemon juice

1 tablespoon cold butter, if desired

Milk, if desired

Sugar, if desired

**1** Heat oven to 425°F. Place 1 pastry round or pie crust in 9-inch glass pie plate.

**2** In large bowl, mix sugar, flour and cinnamon. Stir in peaches and lemon juice. Spoon into pastry-lined plate. Cut butter into small pieces; sprinkle over peaches.

**3** Cover with top pastry or crust; seal and flute. Cut slits in several places in top crust. Brush crust lightly with milk; sprinkle with sugar. Cover crust edge with pie crust shield ring or strips of foil to prevent excessive browning.

**4** Bake about 45 minutes or until crust is golden brown and juice begins to bubble through slits in crust, removing foil during last 15 minutes. Cool on cooling rack at least 2 hours before serving.

**1 Serving:** Calories 440; Total Fat 21g (Saturated Fat 5g; Trans Fat 3.5g); Cholesterol 0mg; Sodium 300mg; Total Carbohydrate 59g (Dietary Fiber 5g); Protein 5g **Exchanges:** 2 Starch, 1 Fruit, 1 Other Carbohydrate, 3 Fat **Carbohydrate Choices:** 4

**Apricot Pie** Substitute 6 cups fresh apricot halves for the peaches.

## Sweet Success Tip

Save time by using frozen sliced peaches, partially thawed and drained, instead of peeling and slicing fresh peaches. Using frozen peaches also means you can make this mouthwatering pie all year-round!

# Peach Crumble Pie

8 servings • PREP TIME: 35 Minutes • START TO FINISH: 2 Hours 30 Minutes

## CRUST

One-Crust Pastry (page 7) or 1 Pillsbury refrigerated pie crust, softened as directed on box

## FILLING

| | |
|---|---|
| 4 | cups quartered peeled peaches (8 to 10 medium) |
| ½ | cup granulated sugar |
| ½ | teaspoon ground nutmeg |
| 2 | tablespoons whipping cream |
| 1 | egg |

## TOPPING

| | |
|---|---|
| ½ | cup all-purpose flour |
| ¼ | cup packed brown sugar |
| ¼ | teaspoon ground cinnamon |
| ¼ | teaspoon ground nutmeg |
| ¼ | cup butter, softened |

**1** Heat oven to 425°F. Place pastry in 9-inch glass pie plate.

**2** Place peaches in pastry-lined plate. Mix granulated sugar and ½ teaspoon nutmeg; sprinkle over peaches. In small bowl, beat whipping cream and egg with fork or whisk until blended; pour over peaches. In another small bowl, mix all topping ingredients with fork until crumbly; sprinkle over peaches.

**3** Cover crust edge with pie shield ring or strips of foil to prevent excessive browning. Bake 35 to 40 minutes or until top is golden brown, removing foil during last 15 minutes. Cool on cooling rack 30 minutes. Serve warm.

**1 Serving:** Calories 360; Total Fat 18g (Saturated Fat 7g; Trans Fat 2g); Cholesterol 45mg; Sodium 200mg; Total Carbohydrate 46g (Dietary Fiber 2g); Protein 4g **Exchanges:** 1 Starch, ½ Fruit, 1½ Other Carbohydrate, 3½ Fat **Carbohydrate Choices:** 3

## Sweet Success Tip

**Refrigerating the dough before rolling allows the shortening to become slightly firm, which helps make the baked pastry flaky.**

# Peach Slab Pie

**24 servings • PREP TIME: 20 Minutes • START TO FINISH: 2 Hours 15 Minutes**

1   box Pillsbury refrigerated pie crusts, softened as directed on box
¾   cup packed brown sugar
¼   cup cornstarch
2   tablespoons lemon juice
¼   teaspoon salt
9   cups sliced peeled peaches
1   roll (16.5 oz) Pillsbury refrigerated sugar cookies

**1**   Heat oven to 375°F. Unroll pie crusts and stack one on top of the other on lightly floured surface. Roll to 17×12-inch rectangle. Fit crust into 15×10×1-inch pan, pressing into corners. Fold extra pastry under, even with edges of pan; seal edges.

**2**   In large bowl, mix brown sugar, cornstarch, lemon juice and salt. Add peaches; toss to coat. Spoon mixture into crust-lined pan.

**3**   Break cookie dough into coarse crumbs; spoon crumbs evenly over filling.

**4**   Bake 50 to 60 minutes or until crust is golden brown and filling is bubbling. Cool on cooling rack 45 minutes before serving.

**1 Serving:** Calories 210; Total Fat 7g (Saturated Fat 2.5g; Trans Fat 1g); Cholesterol 0mg; Sodium 180mg; Total Carbohydrate 34g (Dietary Fiber 1g); Protein 1g **Exchanges:** ½ Starch, 1½ Other Carbohydrate, 1½ Fat **Carbohydrate Choices:** 2

## Sweet Success Tip

**Frozen sliced peaches, thawed and drained, can be substituted for fresh in this recipe.**

# Plum Peachy Pie

**8 servings** · **PREP TIME: 25 Minutes** · **START TO FINISH: 2 Hours 45 Minutes**

1   box Pillsbury refrigerated pie crusts, softened as directed on box
1   cup sugar
¼   cup cornstarch
1   tablespoon peach-flavored gelatin
4   cups sliced peeled fresh peaches or frozen (thawed) sliced peaches
2   medium red plums, peeled, pitted and thinly sliced
1   tablespoon cold butter
½   teaspoon sugar

**1**   Heat oven to 400°F. Make pie crusts as directed on box for Two-Crust Pie using 9-inch glass pie plate.

**2**   In large bowl, mix 1 cup sugar, the cornstarch and gelatin; stir in peaches. Spoon into crust-lined plate. Top with plum slices. Cut butter into small pieces; sprinkle over filling.

**3**   Top with second crust; seal and flute. Cut slits in several places in top crust. Brush small amount of water over top crust; sprinkle with ½ teaspoon sugar.

**4**   Cover crust edge with pie shield ring or strips of foil to prevent excessive browning. Bake 10 minutes. Reduce oven temperature to 350°F; bake 35 to 40 minutes longer or until crust is golden brown and peaches are tender. Cool on cooling rack at least 1 hour 30 minutes before serving.

Linda Pauls of Buhler, Kansas, won first place with this recipe at the 2006 Kansas State Fair. She went on to place in the national Pillsbury Refrigerated Pie Crust Pie Baking Championship.

**1 Serving:** Calories 390; Total Fat 14g (Saturated Fat 6g; Trans Fat 0g); Cholesterol 10mg; Sodium 280mg; Total Carbohydrate 64g (Dietary Fiber 1g); Protein 2g **Exchanges:** ½ Starch, 1 Fruit, 2½ Other Carbohydrate, 3 Fat **Carbohydrate Choices:** 4

## Sweet Success Tip

Adding peach-flavored gelatin not only bumps up the peach flavor, but also thickens the filling as the pie cools.

# Gingered Apricot Pie

8 servings • PREP TIME: 25 Minutes • START TO FINISH: 2 Hours 40 Minutes

1   box Pillsbury refrigerated pie crusts, softened as directed on box
4   cups sliced peeled apricots
¾   cup granulated sugar
5   tablespoons all-purpose flour
¾   teaspoon ground ginger
½   teaspoon ground cinnamon
1   tablespoon cold butter
2   tablespoons turbinado sugar (raw sugar)

**1** Heat oven to 425°F. Place 1 pie crust in 9-inch glass pie plate. Trim excess dough from edge of plate; reserve excess dough.

**2** In large bowl, mix apricots, granulated sugar, flour, ginger and cinnamon. Spoon into crust-lined plate. Cut butter into small pieces; sprinkle over filling.

**3** Top with second crust; seal and flute. Cut slits in several places in top crust. If desired, use reserved dough to create shapes to decorate top of pie. Lightly brush top crust with water. Sprinkle with turbinado sugar.

**4** Bake 20 minutes. Cover crust edge with pie crust shield ring or strips of foil to prevent excessive browning. Bake 20 to 25 minutes longer or until crust is golden brown and juice begins to bubble through slits in crust. Cool on cooling rack at least 1 hour 30 minutes before serving.

**1 Serving:** Calories 370; Total Fat 14g (Saturated Fat 6g; Trans Fat 0g); Cholesterol 10mg; Sodium 290mg; Total Carbohydrate 59g (Dietary Fiber 2g); Protein 1g **Exchanges:** ½ Starch, 1 Fruit, 2½ Other Carbohydrate, 2½ Fat **Carbohydrate Choices:** 4

## Sweet Success Tip

**Look for the turbinado or raw sugar near the granulated sugar or in the baking section of the grocery store. This specialty sugar has a very delicate molasses flavor—try it in your tea or coffee for a splash of flavor.**

# Mango-Pineapple Pie with Macadamia Lattice Crust

8 servings • PREP TIME: 45 Minutes • START TO FINISH: 3 Hours 5 Minutes

1 box Pillsbury refrigerated pie crusts, softened as directed on box

¾ cup coarsely chopped macadamia nuts

2 cups mango chunks

2 cups chopped fresh pineapple, drained

¾ cup sugar

¼ cup canned cream of coconut (not coconut milk)

3 tablespoons cornstarch

½ teaspoon salt

1 tablespoon butter

3 tablespoons milk

1 tablespoon sugar

**1** Heat oven to 350°F. Place 1 pie crust in 9-inch glass pie plate. Place second pie crust on lightly floured sheet of waxed paper. Using pastry cutter, gently mark lines on crust 1 inch apart for guides for cutting strips. Sprinkle macadamia nuts between lines on crust; use rolling pin to gently press nuts into crust. Cut into strips along lines; set aside.

**2** In 2-quart saucepan, mix mango, pineapple, ¾ cup sugar and the cream of coconut. In small bowl, mix cornstarch and salt; stir into fruit mixture. Cook over medium-low heat until thickened. Stir in butter. Spoon into crust-lined plate.

**3** Place 5 to 7 reserved pie crust strips across filling. Place remaining strips crosswise over tops of first strips. Seal and flute edges. Brush top crust with milk; sprinkle with 1 tablespoon sugar.

**4** Bake 45 to 50 minutes or until golden brown. Cool on cooling rack at least 1 hour 30 minutes before serving.

**1 Serving:** Calories 470; Total Fat 24g (Saturated Fat 10g; Trans Fat 0g); Cholesterol 10mg; Sodium 440mg; Total Carbohydrate 62g (Dietary Fiber 2g); Protein 1g **Exchanges:** ½ Starch, 1 Fruit, 2½ Other Carbohydrate, 5 Fat **Carbohydrate Choices:** 4

## Sweet Success Tip

Look for ripe mangoes to peel and cut up for this tropical pie, or purchase a 24-ounce jar of sliced mango in the produce department's refrigerated section and cut the slices into chunks.

Peanut Butter Ice Cream Pie
(page 124)

# creamy & chilled pies

# Classic French Silk Pie

10 servings • PREP TIME: 20 Minutes • START TO FINISH: 5 Hours

One-Crust Pastry (page 7)
or 1 Pillsbury refrigerated pie
crust, softened as directed
on box

 1 cup butter, softened

1½ cups sugar

 3 teaspoons vanilla

 3 oz unsweetened baking
chocolate, melted, cooled

 5 pasteurized eggs✱

1½ cups Sweetened Whipped
Cream (page 80)

Chocolate curls, if desired
(page 82)

**1** Heat oven to 450°F. Bake pastry or pie crust as directed for Baked
One-Crust Pie (page 9). Cool completely on cooling rack.

**2** In medium bowl, beat butter with electric mixer on medium speed until
creamy. Gradually beat in sugar until light and fluffy and sugar begins to
dissolve, 3 to 5 minutes. Beat in vanilla and chocolate. Add eggs, one at a
time, beating on high speed after each addition until light and fluffy, about
3 minutes. Beat until sugar is completely dissolved. Pour into cooled baked
crust. Refrigerate until set, at least 4 hours.

**3** Spread whipped cream over pie. Garnish with chocolate curls. Store in
refrigerator.

✱Pasteurized eggs are uncooked eggs that have been heat-treated to kill bacteria
which can cause food poisoning and gastrointestinal distress. Because the eggs in
this recipe are not cooked, be sure to use pasteurized eggs. They can be found in
the dairy case at large supermarkets.

**1 Serving:** Calories 420; Total Fat 29g (Saturated Fat 13g; Trans Fat 2g); Cholesterol 35mg; Sodium 250mg;
Total Carbohydrate 35g (Dietary Fiber 2g); Protein 4g **Exchanges:** 1 Starch, 1 Other Carbohydrate, 6 Fat
**Carbohydrate Choices:** 2

**Mocha French Silk Pie** Beat in 1½ teaspoons instant coffee
granules or crystals with the baking chocolate.

## Sweet Success Tip

Do not use margarine or vegetable oil spreads instead of butter in this
recipe because the filling will be curdled instead of smooth and creamy.

# German Chocolate Pie

**10 servings** • **PREP TIME: 20 Minutes** • **START TO FINISH: 5 Hours 10 Minutes**

1   Pillsbury refrigerated pie crust, softened as directed on box

1   package (4 oz) sweet baking chocolate, chopped

¼   cup butter

1   can (12 oz) evaporated milk

1½   cups sugar

2   tablespoons cornstarch

⅛   teaspoon salt

4   egg yolks

½   teaspoon vanilla

¼   teaspoon almond extract

1   cup flaked coconut

1   cup chopped pecans

**1**   Heat oven to 375°F. Place pie crust in 9-inch glass pie plate as directed on box for One-Crust Filled Pie.

**2**   In 1-quart saucepan, heat chocolate and butter over medium-low heat until melted and mixture can be stirred smooth. Remove from heat; gradually stir in milk.

**3**   In medium bowl, mix sugar, cornstarch and salt. In small bowl, mix egg yolks, vanilla and almond extract. Gradually add chocolate mixture to egg mixture, stirring with whisk. Add chocolate–egg yolk mixture to cornstarch mixture, stirring with whisk. Pour filling into crust-lined plate.

**4**   In small bowl, mix coconut and pecans; sprinkle over filling.

**5**   Bake 45 to 50 minutes or until puffed and almost set. Cool on cooling rack at least 4 hours before serving. Store in refrigerator.

**1 Serving:** Calories 510; Total Fat 29g (Saturated Fat 13g; Trans Fat 0g); Cholesterol 95mg; Sodium 240mg; Total Carbohydrate 54g (Dietary Fiber 3g); Protein 7g **Exchanges:** 2½ Starch, 1 Other Carbohydrate, 5½ Fat **Carbohydrate Choices:** 3½

## Sweet Success Tips

The pie may be slightly soft when just out of the oven, but it will set up nicely for slicing once cooled.

Dress up each slice with whipped cream, toasted coconut and chocolate shavings.

# Chocolate-Cashew Pie

**8 servings** · **PREP TIME: 25 Minutes** · **START TO FINISH: 5 Hours 40 Minutes**

1   Pillsbury refrigerated pie crust, softened as directed on box
¾   cup light corn syrup
½   cup sugar
3   tablespoons butter, melted
1   teaspoon vanilla
3   eggs
1   cup semisweet chocolate chips (6 oz)
1   cup cashew halves
10  whole cashews
1   cup whipping cream
2   tablespoons sugar
2   tablespoons unsweetened baking cocoa

**1**  Heat oven to 325°F. Place pie crust in 9-inch glass pie plate as directed on box for One-Crust Filled Pie.

**2**  In large bowl, beat corn syrup, ½ cup sugar, the melted butter, vanilla and eggs with whisk. Reserve 2 tablespoons chocolate chips. Stir remaining chips and the cashew halves into egg mixture. Pour filling into crust-lined plate.

**3**  Place pie on middle oven rack; place sheet of foil on rack below pie in case of spillover. Bake 45 to 55 minutes or until set and golden brown. Cool on cooling rack at least 4 hours before serving.

**4**  Line plate with waxed paper. In small microwavable bowl, microwave reserved 2 tablespoons chocolate chips on High 45 to 60 seconds or until melted. Dip large end of each whole cashew into melted chocolate. Place on plate. Refrigerate 15 to 20 minutes or until set.

**5**  In chilled medium bowl, beat whipping cream, 2 tablespoons sugar and the cocoa with electric mixer on high speed until stiff peaks form. Pipe whipped cream around edge of pie; garnish with chocolate-dipped cashews. Store in refrigerator.

**1 Serving:** Calories 780; Total Fat 45g (Saturated Fat 21g; Trans Fat 0.5g); Cholesterol 130mg; Sodium 350mg; Total Carbohydrate 86g (Dietary Fiber 2g); Protein 9g **Exchanges:** 2½ Starch, 3 Other Carbohydrate, 9 Fat **Carbohydrate Choices:** 6

## Sweet Success Tip

The cocoa adds a nice mild chocolate flavor to the whipped cream but if you prefer it without the chocolate color, omit the cocoa.

# Rich Chocolate Bottom Pie with Hazelnut Crust

8 servings · PREP TIME: 25 Minutes · START TO FINISH: 4 Hours

## CRUST

- 1 cup all-purpose flour
- ½ cup cold butter
- ¼ cup finely chopped hazelnuts (filberts)
- ½ teaspoon ground cinnamon

## FILLING

- 1 cup granulated sugar
- 1 cup light corn syrup
- 2 tablespoons butter, melted
- 2 teaspoons vanilla
- 4 eggs
- ⅛ teaspoon salt
- ¼ cup hazelnut spread with cocoa (from 13-oz jar)

**1** Heat oven to 350°F. In medium bowl, place flour. Cut in ½ cup butter, using pastry blender or fork, until crumbly. Stir in hazelnuts and cinnamon. Gather dough into a ball. Press dough against bottom and side of 9-inch glass pie plate.

**2** In large bowl, beat granulated sugar, corn syrup, 2 tablespoons butter, the vanilla, eggs and salt with electric mixer on medium speed about 1 minute or until well blended. Spoon hazelnut spread over bottom of crust, carefully spreading to cover. Pour filling over hazelnut spread. Place pie plate on cookie sheet in case of spillover.

**3** Bake 60 to 65 minutes or until top is golden brown and filling is almost set (filling will jiggle slightly in center). Cover crust edge with pie shield ring or strips of foil if necessary to prevent excessive browning. Cool on cooling rack 30 minutes. Refrigerate at least 2 hours or overnight before serving.

**4** Top each slice of pie with whipped cream.

**1 Serving:** Calories 620; Total Fat 30g (Saturated Fat 16g; Trans Fat 1g); Cholesterol 160mg; Sodium 230mg; Total Carbohydrate 79g (Dietary Fiber 1g); Protein 6g **Exchanges:** 1 Starch, 4½ Other Carbohydrate, ½ Medium-Fat Meat, 5½ Fat **Carbohydrate Choices:** 5

## Sweet Success Tip

For the best results, refrigerate this amazingly delicious, decadent pie overnight so the filling sets up before cutting.

## Sweetened Whipped Cream

**1½ cups**

- ¾ cup whipping cream
- 2 tablespoons powdered sugar or granulated sugar

In chilled small bowl, beat whipping cream and powdered sugar with electric mixer on low speed until mixture begins to thicken. Gradually increase speed to high and beat just until soft peaks form. To make 1 cup whipped cream, use ½ cup whipping cream and 4 teaspoons sugar.

# Caramel-Chocolate Pie Supreme

**12 servings • PREP TIME: 30 Minutes • START TO FINISH: 2 Hours 55 Minutes**

Easy Nut Crust (page 11)

30 caramels (from 14-oz bag), unwrapped

2 tablespoons butter

2 tablespoons water

½ cup chopped pecans, toasted✽

2 packages (3 oz each) cream cheese, softened

⅓ cup powdered sugar

1 package (4 oz) sweet baking chocolate, chopped

3 tablespoons hot water

1 teaspoon vanilla

2 cups whipping cream

2 tablespoons powdered sugar

Chocolate curls, if desired

**1** Heat oven to 450°F. Make and bake crust as directed. Cool completely on cooling rack.

**2** In 2-quart saucepan, heat caramels, butter and 2 tablespoons water over medium heat, stirring frequently, until caramels are melted. Pour into cooled baked crust. Sprinkle with pecans. Refrigerate about 1 hour or until chilled.

**3** In small bowl, beat cream cheese and ⅓ cup powdered sugar with spoon until smooth. Spread over caramel layer; refrigerate.

**4** Meanwhile, in 1-quart saucepan, heat chocolate and 3 tablespoons hot water over low heat, stirring constantly, until chocolate is melted. Cool to room temperature. Stir in vanilla.

**5** In chilled large bowl, beat whipping cream and 2 tablespoons powdered sugar with electric mixer on low speed until mixture begins to thicken. Gradually increase speed to high and beat until stiff peaks form. Reserve 1½ cups.

**6** Fold chocolate mixture into remaining whipped cream. Spread over cream cheese layer. Garnish with reserved whipped cream and chocolate curls. Cover; refrigerate at least 1 hour until firm but no longer than 48 hours.

**1 Serving:** Calories 520; Total Fat 39g (Saturated Fat 21g; Trans Fat 1g); Cholesterol 85mg; Sodium 190mg; Total Carbohydrate 38g (Dietary Fiber 2g); Protein 6g **Exchanges:** 1½ Starch, 1 Other Carbohydrate, 7½ Fat **Carbohydrate Choices:** 2½

✽To toast pecans, heat oven to 350°F. Spread pecans in ungreased shallow pan. Bake uncovered 6 to 10 minutes, stirring occasionally, until light brown.

## Chocolate Curls

**To make chocolate curls, let a bar of milk or semisweet chocolate stand at room temperature about 15 minutes. Pull a swivel vegetable peeler or thin, sharp knife across the block, using long, thin strokes. Use a toothpick to lift curls and arrange on the dessert.**

# Caramel Cream Pie

**8 servings** • **PREP TIME: 30 Minutes** • **START TO FINISH: 2 Hours 30 Minutes**

Easy Nut Crust (page 11)
⅔ cup sugar
3 cups half-and-half
4 egg yolks
¼ cup cornstarch
¼ teaspoon salt
2 tablespoons butter, softened
1 teaspoon vanilla
1 cup Sweetened Whipped Cream (page 80)

**1** Heat oven to 450°F. Make and bake crust as directed. Cool completely on cooling rack.

**2** Meanwhile, in 2-quart saucepan, heat sugar over medium heat until it begins to melt. Stir until sugar is completely dissolved and becomes deep golden brown to amber colored. Remove from heat; gradually stir in 2¾ cups of the half-and-half (mixture will boil and splatter at first). Heat over low heat, stirring frequently, until any hardened sugar bits dissolve. Remove from heat.

**3** In small bowl, beat egg yolks, cornstarch, salt and remaining ¼ cup half-and-half with fork until well blended. Gradually add egg yolk mixture to half-and-half mixture until well blended, stirring with whisk. Cook and stir over medium heat until mixture thickens and boils. Boil 1 minute, stirring constantly. Remove from heat. Stir in butter and vanilla; cool filling slightly.

**4** Pour warm filling into cooled baked crust. Press plastic wrap on filling to prevent tough layer from forming on top. Refrigerate at least 2 hours or until set. Remove plastic wrap. Spread whipped cream over pie. Store in refrigerator.

**1 Serving:** Calories 500; Total Fat 35g (Saturated Fat 20g; Trans Fat 1g); Cholesterol 195mg; Sodium 220mg; Total Carbohydrate 38g (Dietary Fiber 0g); Protein 6g **Exchanges:** 1 Starch, 1½ Other Carbohydrate, ½ Medium-Fat Meat, 6½ Fat **Carbohydrate Choices:** 2½

## Sweet Success Tip

**Use brown sugar, instead of granulated or powdered sugar, to sweeten the whipped cream and add more caramel flavor.**

# Banana Cream Pie

**8 servings** · **PREP TIME: 30 Minutes** · **START TO FINISH: 3 Hours 10 Minutes**

One-Crust Pastry (page 7),
Easy Buttermilk Pastry
(page 11) or Press-in-the-Pan
Pastry (page 11)

4   egg yolks
⅔   cup sugar
¼   cup cornstarch
½   teaspoon salt
3   cups milk
2   tablespoons butter, softened
2   teaspoons vanilla
2   ripe but firm large bananas
1   cup Sweetened Whipped Cream
    (page 80)

**1** Heat oven to 450°F. Bake pastry as directed for Baked One-Crust Pie (page 9). Cool completely on cooling rack.

**2** In medium bowl, beat egg yolks with fork; set aside. In 2-quart saucepan, mix sugar, cornstarch and salt. Gradually stir in milk. Cook and stir over medium heat until mixture thickens and boils. Boil 1 minute, stirring constantly. Immediately and gradually stir at least half of the hot mixture into egg yolks, then stir back into hot mixture in saucepan. Boil 1 minute, stirring constantly. Remove from heat. Stir in butter and vanilla; cool filling slightly.

**3** Slice bananas into cooled baked crust; pour warm filling over bananas. Press plastic wrap on filling to prevent tough layer from forming on top. Refrigerate at least 2 hours or until set. Remove plastic wrap. Spread whipped cream over pie. Store in refrigerator.

**1 Serving:** Calories 410; Total Fat 22g (Saturated Fat 8g; Trans Fat 2g); Cholesterol 135mg; Sodium 370mg; Total Carbohydrate 46g (Dietary Fiber 1g); Protein 7g **Exchanges:** 1 Starch, 1 Fruit, ½ Other Carbohydrate, ½ Low-Fat Milk, 4½ Fat **Carbohydrate Choices:** 3

**Butterscotch Cream Pie** Substitute dark or light brown sugar for the granulated sugar. Omit bananas.

**Chocolate-Banana Cream Pie** Make Chocolate Cream Pie filling (below). Cool filling slightly. Slice bananas into crust; pour warm filling over bananas. Continue as directed.

**Chocolate Cream Pie** Increase sugar to 1½ cups and cornstarch to ⅓ cup; omit butter and bananas. Stir in 2 ounces unsweetened baking chocolate, chopped, after adding milk.

**Coconut Cream Pie** Increase cornstarch to ⅓ cup. Substitute 1 can (14 ounces) coconut milk (not cream of coconut) and milk to equal 3 cups for the milk. Stir in ¾ cup toasted flaked coconut with the butter. Omit bananas. Refrigerate pie 3 hours until set. Top with whipped cream; sprinkle with ¼ cup toasted flaked coconut.

# Dulce de Leche–Banana Pie

**8 servings • PREP TIME: 35 Minutes • START TO FINISH: 1 Hour 20 Minutes**

One-Crust Pastry (page 7) or 1 Pillsbury refrigerated pie crust, softened as directed on box

1 can (13.4 oz) dulce de leche (caramelized sweetened condensed milk)

3 ripe but firm medium bananas

1 cup whipping cream

¼ cup powdered sugar

½ cup semisweet chocolate chips

1 teaspoon vegetable oil

**1** Heat oven to 450°F. Bake pastry or pie crust as directed for Baked One-Crust Pie (page 9). Cool completely on cooling rack.

**2** Spoon contents of can of dulce de leche into center of cooled baked crust; gently spread to edge. Thinly slice bananas; arrange over dulce de leche.

**3** In chilled medium bowl, beat whipping cream and powdered sugar with electric mixer on high speed until stiff peaks form. Spread over bananas.

**4** In small resealable freezer plastic bag, place chocolate chips and oil; seal bag. Microwave on High 30 to 60 seconds or until softened. Gently squeeze bag until chocolate is smooth; cut off tiny corner of bag. Squeeze bag to pipe melted chocolate over whipped cream. Store in refrigerator.

**1 Serving:** Calories 600; Total Fat 32g (Saturated Fat 12g; Trans Fat 1g); Cholesterol 80mg; Sodium 1710mg; Total Carbohydrate 50g (Dietary Fiber 5g); Protein 29g **Exchanges:** 1½ Starch, 1½ Other Carbohydrate, ½ Vegetable, 1 Medium-Fat Meat, 2 High-Fat Meat, 2 Fat **Carbohydrate Choices:** 3

## Sweet Success Tip

Dulce de leche is a traditional Spanish confection made from milk and is also a popular culinary reference to rich caramel flavors. Look for canned dulce de leche in the Hispanic section of the supermarket.

# Bananas Foster Pie

**8 servings** • **PREP TIME: 30 Minutes** • **START TO FINISH: 3 Hours 40 Minutes**

1  box Pillsbury refrigerated pie crusts, softened as directed on box

1  package (8 oz) cream cheese, softened

1  package (5.3 oz) chèvre (goat) cheese

¼  cup granulated sugar

1  teaspoon vanilla

6  ripe but firm small bananas, sliced

6  tablespoons unsalted butter

¾  cup packed brown sugar

1½  teaspoons ground cinnamon

½  teaspoon ground nutmeg

1  teaspoon rum extract

Milk, if desired

Coarse sugar, if desired

**1** Heat oven to 350°F. Make pie crusts as directed on box for Two-Crust Pie using 9-inch glass pie plate.

**2** In small bowl, beat cream cheese, goat cheese, granulated sugar and vanilla with electric mixer on high speed until smooth. Spread mixture in crust-lined plate; top with banana slices.

**3** In 1-quart saucepan, heat butter, brown sugar, cinnamon and nutmeg over low heat, stirring constantly, until butter is melted and mixture is smooth. Remove from heat; stir in rum extract. Pour over bananas. Top with second crust; seal and flute. Cut slits in several places in top crust. Brush top crust with milk; sprinkle with coarse sugar.

**4** Cover crust edge with strips of foil to prevent excessive browning. Bake 30 minutes. Remove foil; bake 30 to 40 minutes longer or until golden brown. Cool on cooling rack at least 2 hours before serving. Store in refrigerator.

Kandace Kanzler of Louisville, Kentucky, won the Pillsbury Refrigerated Pie Crust Pie Baking Championship at the 2009 Kentucky State Fair with this recipe.

**1 Serving:** Calories 640; Total Fat 36g (Saturated Fat 20g; Trans Fat 1g); Cholesterol 75mg; Sodium 480mg; Total Carbohydrate 70g (Dietary Fiber 2g); Protein 6g **Exchanges:** 2 Starch, 2½ Other Carbohydrate, 7 Fat **Carbohydrate Choices:** 4½

## Sweet Success Tip

**Fold ½ teaspoon of rum extract into frozen (thawed) whipped cream topping to serve on this pie, and garnish with additional banana slices, if desired.**

# Macadamia Nut–Banana Cream Pie

**8 servings** • **PREP TIME: 40 Minutes** • **START TO FINISH: 3 Hours 15 Minutes**

## CRUST

| | |
|---|---|
| 1¼ | cups all-purpose flour |
| ½ | cup macadamia nuts, finely chopped |
| ⅓ | cup butter, softened |
| 2 | tablespoons granulated sugar |
| ½ | teaspoon vanilla |
| 1 | whole egg, beaten |

## FILLING

| | |
|---|---|
| ⅔ | cup granulated sugar |
| ¼ | cup cornstarch |
| ½ | teaspoon salt |
| 3 | cups whole milk |
| 4 | egg yolks |
| 2 | tablespoons butter |
| 3 | teaspoons vanilla |
| 2 | ripe but firm large bananas |

## TOPPING

| | |
|---|---|
| 1 | cup whipping cream |
| 2 | tablespoons powdered sugar or granulated sugar |
| ½ | cup macadamia nuts, coarsely chopped, toasted ✱ |

**1** In medium bowl, beat all crust ingredients with electric mixer on low speed about 1 minute or just until blended. Press mixture on bottom and up side of ungreased 9-inch glass pie plate. Prick bottom and side of crust thoroughly with fork. Refrigerate 30 minutes while preparing filling.

**2** In 2-quart saucepan, mix ⅔ cup sugar, the cornstarch and salt. In large bowl, beat milk and egg yolks with whisk until blended; gradually stir into sugar mixture. Cook over medium-low heat about 15 minutes, stirring constantly, until mixture thickens and boils. Boil 2 minutes, stirring constantly with whisk; remove from heat. Add 2 tablespoons butter and 3 teaspoons vanilla; beat with whisk. Press plastic wrap on filling to prevent tough layer from forming. Cool at room temperature while baking crust.

**3** Heat oven to 400°F. Bake crust 16 to 18 minutes or until edge is golden brown. Cool at room temperature 15 minutes. Slice bananas into crust. Stir filling well; pour evenly over bananas. Press plastic wrap on filling; refrigerate at least 2 hours or until thoroughly chilled.

**4** In chilled small bowl, beat whipping cream and powdered sugar with electric mixer on high speed until soft peaks form; spread over top of pie. Sprinkle with toasted nuts.

✱ To toast macadamia nuts, heat oven to 350°F. Spread nuts in ungreased shallow pan. Bake uncovered 6 to 10 minutes, stirring occasionally, until golden brown.

**1 Serving:** Calories 590; Total Fat 36g (Saturated Fat 17g; Trans Fat 1g); Cholesterol 200mg; Sodium 320mg; Total Carbohydrate 55g (Dietary Fiber 3g); Protein 9g **Exchanges:** 1½ Starch, 2 Other Carbohydrate, ½ High-Fat Meat, 6½ Fat **Carbohydrate Choices:** 3½

**Macadamia Nut–Chocolate-Banana Cream Pie** Add 2 ounces unsweetened baking chocolate, chopped, to the filling with the milk and egg yolks.

## Sweet Success Tip

**Pecans or walnuts can be substituted for the macadamia nuts.**

# Crunchy Crust Blueberry Swirl Pie

**8 servings • PREP TIME: 30 Minutes • START TO FINISH: 3 Hours 30 Minutes**

### CRUST

- ½ cup butter
- ¾ cup all-purpose flour
- ½ cup quick-cooking oats
- ½ cup chopped nuts
- 2 tablespoons sugar

### FILLING AND TOPPING

- 1 box (4-serving size) lemon-flavored gelatin
- ½ cup boiling water
- 1 can (21 oz) blueberry pie filling
- ½ cup sour cream
- Sweetened whipped cream (page 80), if desired

**1** Heat oven to 400°F. Butter 9-inch glass pie plate.

**2** In 2½-quart microwavable bowl, microwave butter uncovered on High 30 seconds, then in 10-second increments, until melted. Stir in flour, oats, nuts and sugar. Press in bottom and up side of pie plate. Bake 11 to 13 minutes or until edges are golden brown. Cool completely on cooling rack.

**3** Meanwhile, in 1½-quart bowl, dissolve gelatin in boiling water. Stir in pie filling. Refrigerate until thickened, about 1 hour.

**4** Pour filling into cooled baked crust. Spoon sour cream by tablespoonfuls on top. Cut through sour cream and lightly fold filling over it, making swirls. Refrigerate 2 hours or until cold. Top individual servings with whipped cream. Store in refrigerator.

Mrs. Richard Furry of La Mesa, California, submitted this recipe in Bake-Off® Contest 23, 1972, and was one of 100 finalists.

**1 Serving:** Calories 380; Total Fat 20g (Saturated Fat 10g; Trans Fat 0.5g); Cholesterol 40mg; Sodium 140mg; Total Carbohydrate 47g (Dietary Fiber 2g); Protein 5g **Exchanges:** 1 Starch, 2 Other Carbohydrate, 4 Fat **Carbohydrate Choices:** 3

## Sweet Success Tip

Make sure to use quick-cooking oats in this recipe. Instant or old-fashioned oats will not work.

# Fresh Berry Custard Pie

**2 pies; 16 servings** · **PREP TIME: 25 Minutes** · **START TO FINISH: 3 Hours 25 Minutes**

## CRUST

1 box Pillsbury refrigerated pie crusts, softened as directed on box
    All-purpose flour

## FILLING

3 cups sugar
½ cup all-purpose flour
4 cups fresh berries (such as blueberries or raspberries)
4 eggs
1 can (12 oz) evaporated milk
1 teaspoon vanilla

## TOPPING

1 cup sugar
⅔ cup all-purpose flour
½ cup cold butter
½ teaspoon vanilla

**1** Heat oven to 350°F. Unroll pie crusts; sprinkle both sides of crusts with flour. Place crusts in 2 (9-inch) glass pie plates.

**2** In large bowl, mix 3 cups sugar and ½ cup flour. Add berries; toss to coat. Divide berry mixture between crust-lined plates. In medium bowl, beat eggs, milk and 1 teaspoon vanilla with whisk; pour evenly over berry mixture.

**3** In another medium bowl, mix 1 cup sugar and ⅔ cup flour. Cut in butter, using pastry blender or fork, until mixture looks like coarse crumbs. Stir in ½ teaspoon vanilla. Sprinkle topping evenly over filling.

**4** Bake about 1 hour or until topping is golden brown. Cool on cooling rack at least 2 hours before serving. Store in refrigerator.

**Lisa Arnold from West Tawakoni, Texas, won first place at the 2010 Texas State Fair with this recipe.**

**1 Serving:** Calories 440; Total Fat 14g (Saturated Fat 7g; Trans Fat 0g); Cholesterol 75mg; Sodium 200mg; Total Carbohydrate 74g (Dietary Fiber 2g); Protein 4g **Exchanges:** 1½ Starch, 3½ Other Carbohydrate, 2½ Fat **Carbohydrate Choices:** 5

## Sweet Success Tip

Sliced fresh strawberries can be used in this pie, but don't use only strawberries. The filling will hold together better if you use a combination of other berries (blueberries, raspberries or even blackberries) with the strawberries (use a total of 4 cups).

# Fresh Blueberry Cheesecake Pie

**8 servings** • **PREP TIME:** 35 Minutes • **START TO FINISH:** 4 Hours 30 Minutes

## CRUST

One-Crust Pastry (page 7)
or 1 Pillsbury refrigerated pie
crust, softened as directed
on box

## FILLING

2 packages (8 oz each) cream
cheese, softened
⅔ cup sugar
1 cup sour cream
2 eggs
1 teaspoon vanilla

## BLUEBERRY TOPPING

½ cup sugar
1 tablespoon cornstarch
½ teaspoon ground cinnamon
¼ cup water
2 tablespoons lemon juice
2 cups fresh blueberries

**1** Heat oven to 425°F. Place pastry or pie crust in 9-inch glass pie plate. Bake as directed for Partially Baked One-Crust Pie (page 9). Cool crust 10 minutes. Reduce oven temperature to 375°F.

**2** In large bowl, beat cream cheese and ⅔ cup sugar with electric mixer on medium speed until light and fluffy. Add sour cream, eggs and vanilla; beat on low speed just until blended. Pour into partially baked crust. Cover crust edge with pie shield ring or strips of foil to prevent excessive browning.

**3** Bake 25 to 30 minutes or until filling is set but center still jiggles slightly when moved. Cool on cooling rack 1 hour.

**4** Meanwhile, in 1½-quart saucepan, mix ½ cup sugar, the cornstarch and cinnamon. Stir in water and lemon juice until smooth. Stir in 1 cup of the blueberries. Heat to boiling over medium-high heat, stirring constantly. Boil 2 minutes or until thickened and most of the blueberries have popped. Stir in remaining 1 cup blueberries. Remove from heat; cool.

**5** Spread cooled blueberry topping over cooled cheesecake. Refrigerate at least 2 hours before serving.

**1 Servings:** Calories 560; Total Fat 35g (Saturated Fat 17g; Trans Fat 1g); Cholesterol 125mg; Sodium 370mg; Total Carbohydrate 52g (Dietary Fiber 1g); Protein 7g **Exchanges:** 2 Starch, ½ Fruit, 1 Other Carbohydrate, 7 Fat **Carbohydrate Choices:** 3½

# Fresh Berry Slab Pie

**24 servings • PREP TIME: 20 Minutes • START TO FINISH: 2 Hours 5 Minutes**

1 box Pillsbury refrigerated pie crusts, softened as directed on box
2 containers (6 oz each) plain fat-free yogurt
2 packages (3 oz each) cream cheese, softened
3 cups sliced fresh strawberries
1½ cups fresh blueberries
1½ cups fresh raspberries
1 cup strawberry glaze

**1** Heat oven to 450°F. Unroll pie crusts and stack one on top of the other on lightly floured surface. Roll to 17×12-inch rectangle. Fit crust into 15×10×1-inch pan, pressing into corners. Fold extra crust under, even with edges of pan; crimp edges. Prick bottom and sides of crust with fork.

**2** Bake 10 to 12 minutes or until golden brown. Cool completely on cooling rack.

**3** In medium bowl, beat yogurt and cream cheese with electric mixer on medium speed until smooth. Spoon into cooled baked crust. Refrigerate about 1 hour or until set.

**4** In large bowl, toss berries and strawberry glaze. Spoon berry mixture over cream cheese layer. Store in refrigerator.

**1 Serving:** Calories 120; Total Fat 7g (Saturated Fat 3g; Trans Fat 0g); Cholesterol 10mg; Sodium 120mg; Total Carbohydrate 13g (Dietary Fiber 1g); Protein 2g **Exchanges:** ½ Starch, ½ Other Carbohydrate, 1 Fat **Carbohydrate Choices:** 1

# Tropical Pineapple, Mango and Cream Pie

**8 servings** • **PREP TIME: 40 Minutes** • **START TO FINISH: 3 Hours 30 Minutes**

## CRUST

- 1 box Pillsbury refrigerated pie crusts, softened as directed on box

## CREAM CHEESE FILLING

- 1 package (8 oz) cream cheese, softened
- ¼ cup sugar
- 1 teaspoon coconut extract
- 1 egg

## FRUIT FILLING

- 2 cups mango chunks
- 2 cups chopped fresh pineapple, drained
- ¾ cup sugar
- ¼ cup canned cream of coconut (not coconut milk)
- 3 tablespoons cornstarch
- ½ teaspoon salt
- 2 tablespoons butter

## TOPPING

- 1 tablespoon milk
- 1 teaspoon sugar
- ¾ cup chopped macadamia nuts

**1** Heat oven to 350°F. Make pie crusts as directed on box for Two-Crust Pie using 9-inch glass pie plate.

**2** In medium bowl, beat all cream cheese filling ingredients with electric mixer on high speed until smooth. Spread in crust-lined plate.

**3** In 2-quart saucepan, mix mango, pineapple, ¾ cup sugar and the cream of coconut. In small bowl, mix cornstarch and salt; stir into fruit mixture. Cook over medium-low heat, stirring constantly, until thickened. Stir in butter until melted. Pour over cream cheese layer.

**4** Top with second crust; seal and flute. Cut slits in several places in top crust. Brush top crust with milk; sprinkle with 1 teaspoon sugar and the macadamia nuts.

**5** Bake 45 to 50 minutes or until golden brown. Cool on cooling rack at least 2 hours before serving. Store in refrigerator.

Paula Pittman of Choctaw, Oklahoma, won the Pillsbury Refrigerated Pie Crust Pie Baking Championship at the 2009 Oklahoma State Fair with this recipe.

**1 Serving:** Calories 610; Total Fat 36g (Saturated Fat 16g; Trans Fat 0g); Cholesterol 70mg; Sodium 550mg; Total Carbohydrate 68g (Dietary Fiber 2g); Protein 4g **Exchanges:** ½ Starch, 1½ Fruit, 2½ Other Carbohydrate, 7 Fat **Carbohydrate Choices:** 4½

## Sweet Success Tip

For a little change of flavor, add ¼ teaspoon of coconut extract to sweetened whipped cream (page 80), then top each slice of pie with a spoonful just before serving.

# Pineapple-Lemon Layered Pie

**8 servings • PREP TIME: 35 Minutes • START TO FINISH: 3 Hours 50 Minutes**

## CRUST

- 1 Pillsbury refrigerated pie crust, softened as directed on box

## BOTTOM LAYER

- 1½ cups granulated sugar
- 6 tablespoons cornstarch
- ¼ teaspoon salt
- ⅓ cup lemon juice
- ½ cup cold water
- 3 egg yolks, well beaten
- 2 tablespoons butter
- 1½ cups boiling water
- 1 teaspoon lemon extract
- 1 teaspoon lemon peel
- 3 drops yellow food color

## MIDDLE LAYER

- 1 cup powdered sugar
- 1 package (8 oz) cream cheese, softened
- 1½ cups whole milk
- 2 boxes (4-serving size each) lemon instant pudding and pie filling mix
- ½ cup drained crushed pineapple (from 8-oz can)
- ½ teaspoon pineapple extract

## TOP LAYER

- 1 cup powdered sugar
- 1 package (8 oz) cream cheese, softened
- 1 teaspoon lemon extract
- 1 container (8 oz) frozen whipped topping, thawed

**1** Heat oven to 450°F. Bake pie crust as directed on box for One-Crust Baked Shell using 9½-inch glass deep-dish pie plate. Cool completely on cooling rack.

**2** Meanwhile, in 3-quart saucepan, mix granulated sugar, cornstarch and salt with whisk. Stir in lemon juice and cold water until blended. Add egg yolks; stir until smooth. Add butter. Gradually stir in boiling water. Heat to boiling over medium heat, stirring constantly. Boil 2 minutes. Remove from heat. Stir in 1 teaspoon lemon extract, the lemon peel and food color. Cool 30 minutes. Pour into cooled baked shell. Refrigerate at least 30 minutes.

**3** In medium bowl, beat 1 cup powdered sugar and 1 (8-oz) package cream cheese with electric mixer on medium speed until smooth. Add milk; stir until well blended. Add pudding mixes; beat 2 minutes or until thickened. Fold in pineapple and pineapple extract. Pour over bottom layer. Refrigerate at least 30 minutes.

**4** In small bowl, beat 1 cup powdered sugar, 1 (3-oz) package cream cheese and 1 teaspoon lemon extract until smooth. Fold in whipped topping. Spread over middle layer. Refrigerate at least 2 hours before serving.

Debra Gruber from Slatington, Pennsylvania, entered this award-winning recipe at the 2010 Pennsylvania State Fair.

**1 Serving:** Calories 900; Total Fat 38g (Saturated Fat 22g; Trans Fat 1g); Cholesterol 155mg; Sodium 850mg; Total Carbohydrate 127g (Dietary Fiber 0g); Protein 12g **Exchanges:** 3 Starch, 5½ Other Carbohydrate, 7½ Fat **Carbohydrate Choices:** 8½

## Sweet Success Tip

**Make sure to chill each layer well so the pie sets up before adding additional layers.**

# Lemon Mascarpone Tart

**12 servings · PREP TIME: 40 Minutes · START TO FINISH: 3 Hours 15 Minutes**

## CRUST

Easy Nut Crust (page 11)

## FILLING

¾ cup mascarpone cheese
(from 8-oz container)
1 cup sugar
2 tablespoons grated lemon peel
⅓ cup lemon juice
2 tablespoons whipping cream
1 teaspoon vanilla
2 whole eggs
1 egg yolk

## TOPPING

1 cup whipping cream
3 tablespoons mascarpone
cheese (from 8-oz container)
2 tablespoons honey
½ teaspoon vanilla

## GARNISH

Grated lemon peel or lemon
peel twists

**1** Prepare crust as directed, using pistachio nuts. Press mixture evenly in bottom and up side of 10-inch tart pan with removable bottom. Refrigerate 30 minutes.

**2** Meanwhile, heat oven to 350°F. In medium bowl, beat ¾ cup mascarpone cheese, the sugar and 2 tablespoons lemon peel with electric mixer on low speed until blended. Add lemon juice, 2 tablespoons whipping cream and 1 teaspoon vanilla; beat until well blended. Add eggs and egg yolk, beating on low speed just until combined. Spread filling evenly in chilled crust. Place sheet of foil on rack below tart in case of spillover.

**3** Bake about 35 minutes or until filling is set but center still jiggles slightly when moved. Cool on cooling rack 1 hour. Refrigerate at least 1 hour.

**4** In chilled large bowl, beat 1 cup whipping cream and 3 tablespoons mascarpone cheese with electric mixer on high speed until soft peaks form. Stir in honey and ½ teaspoon vanilla. Spread over top of tart. Garnish with lemon peel. Remove side of pan before serving.

**1 Serving:** Calories 340; Total Fat 23g (Saturated Fat 13g; Trans Fat 0.5g); Cholesterol 110mg; Sodium 90mg; Total Carbohydrate 29g (Dietary Fiber 0g); Protein 3g **Exchanges:** 1 Starch, 1 Other Carbohydrate, 4½ Fat **Carbohydrate Choices:** 2

## Sweet Success Tip

When measuring honey or other sticky ingredients, such as corn syrup or peanut butter, spray your measuring spoon or cup with cooking spray and the sticky ingredient will slide right out!

# Lemon Meringue Pie

**8 servings** • **PREP TIME: 50 Minutes** • **START TO FINISH: 3 Hours 5 Minutes**

## CRUST

One-Crust Pastry (page 7),
Easy Buttermilk Pastry
(page 11) or Press-in-the-Pan
Pastry (page 11)

## MERINGUE

½  cup sugar
4  teaspoons cornstarch
½  cup cold water
4  egg whites
⅛  teaspoon salt

## FILLING

3  egg yolks
1½  cups sugar
⅓  cup plus 1 tablespoon
   cornstarch
1½  cups water
3  tablespoons butter
2  teaspoons grated lemon peel
½  cup lemon juice
2  drops yellow food color,
   if desired

**1** Heat oven to 425°F. Bake pastry as directed for Baked One-Crust Pie (page 9). Cool completely on cooling rack.

**2** Meanwhile, in 1-quart saucepan, mix ½ cup sugar and 4 teaspoons cornstarch. Stir in ½ cup cold water. Cook and stir over medium heat until mixture thickens and boils. Boil 1 minute, stirring constantly; remove from heat. Cool completely while making filling. (To cool more quickly, place in freezer about 10 minutes.)

**3** In small bowl, beat egg yolks with fork; set aside. In 2-quart saucepan, mix 1½ cups sugar and ⅓ cup plus 1 tablespoon cornstarch. Gradually stir in 1½ cups water. Cook and stir over medium heat until mixture thickens and boils. Boil 1 minute, stirring constantly. Immediately and gradually stir at least half of the hot mixture into egg yolks, then stir back into hot mixture in saucepan. Boil 2 minutes, stirring constantly, until very thick. (Do not boil less than 2 minutes or filling may stay too soft or become runny.) Remove from heat. Stir in butter, lemon peel, lemon juice and food color. Press plastic wrap on filling to prevent tough layer from forming on top.

**4** Heat oven to 350°F. In large bowl, beat egg whites and salt with electric mixer on high speed just until soft peaks begin to form. Very gradually, beat in cooled sugar mixture until stiff peaks form.

**5** Pour hot lemon filling into cooled baked crust. Spoon and spread meringue onto hot filling, carefully sealing meringue to edge of crust to prevent shrinking or weeping.

**6** Bake 12 to 15 minutes or until meringue is light brown. Cool on cooling rack away from drafts 2 hours. Store in refrigerator.

**1 Serving:** Calories 450; Total Fat 17g (Saturated Fat 6g; Trans Fat 1.5g); Cholesterol 95mg; Sodium 250mg; Total Carbohydrate 70g (Dietary Fiber 0g); Protein 5g **Exchanges:** 2 Starch, 2½ Other Carbohydrate, 3 Fat **Carbohydrate Choices:** 4½

## Sweet Success Tip

**To speed up the beating, let the egg whites warm up about 30 minutes to room temperature.**

# Key Lime Pie

**8 servings • PREP TIME: 20 Minutes • START TO FINISH: 2 Hours 55 Minutes**

Graham Cracker Crust
(page 11)

4 egg yolks

2 cans (14 oz each) sweetened
condensed milk (not evaporated)

¾ cup bottled or fresh Key lime
juice or regular lime juice

1 to 2 drops green food color,
if desired

1½ cups Sweetened Whipped
Cream (page 80)

**1** Make crust as directed—except do not bake. Heat oven to 375°F.

**2** In medium bowl, beat egg yolks, condensed milk, lime juice and food color with electric mixer on medium speed about 1 minute or until well blended. Pour filling into unbaked crust.

**3** Bake 14 to 16 minutes or until center is set. Cool on cooling rack 15 minutes. Cover and refrigerate until chilled, at least 2 hours but no longer than 3 days. Spread whipped cream over pie. Store in refrigerator.

**1 Serving:** Calories 430; Total Fat 23g (Saturated Fat 13g; Trans Fat 1g); Cholesterol 165mg; Sodium 230mg; Total Carbohydrate 48g (Dietary Fiber 0g); Protein 7g **Exchanges:** ½ Starch, 2½ Other Carbohydrate, 1 High-Fat Meat, 3 Fat **Carbohydrate Choices:** 3

## Sweet Success Tip

Key limes are smaller and rounder than the more familiar Persian limes and can be difficult to find. The good news is that bottled Key lime juice is available in most large grocery stores.

# Lemon Cream Cheese–Blueberry Pie

**8 servings** • **PREP TIME: 20 Minutes** • **START TO FINISH: 2 Hours 5 Minutes**

## CRUST

1 box Pillsbury refrigerated pie crusts, softened as directed on box

## FILLING

1 package (8 oz) cream cheese, softened

1½ cups milk

1 box (4-serving size) lemon instant pudding and pie filling mix

## TOPPING

1 can (21 oz) blueberry pie filling with more fruit

1 cup frozen whipped topping, thawed

Lemon peel twists or small lemon wedges, if desired

**1** Heat oven to 450°F. Bake pie crust as directed on box for One-Crust Baked Shell using 9-inch glass pie plate. Cool completely on cooling rack.

**2** In small bowl, beat cream cheese with electric mixer on medium speed until fluffy. In medium bowl, beat milk and pudding mix on medium speed until well blended. Add cream cheese; beat until smooth. Spread filling in cooled baked shell. Refrigerate 1 hour.

**3** Top individual servings with blueberry pie filling; garnish with whipped topping and lemon peel. Store in refrigerator.

**1 Serving:** Calories 370; Total Fat 19g (Saturated Fat 10g; Trans Fat 0g); Cholesterol 40mg; Sodium 420mg; Total Carbohydrate 46g (Dietary Fiber 2g); Protein 4g **Exchanges:** 1 Starch, 2 Other Carbohydrate, 3½ Fat **Carbohydrate Choices:** 3

**Chocolate Cream Cheese–Cherry Pie** Substitute chocolate instant pudding for the lemon, and cherry pie filling for the blueberry. Garnish with chocolate curls.

**Butterscotch Cream Cheese–Apple Pie** Substitute butterscotch instant pudding for the lemon, and apple pie filling for the blueberry. Garnish with fresh apple pieces.

## Sweet Success Tip

**This pie can be made a day ahead. Cover and refrigerate it overnight, and top as directed just before serving.**

# Sour Cream–Raisin Pie

8 servings • PREP TIME: 35 Minutes • START TO FINISH: 3 Hours 50 Minutes

## CRUST

1 box Pillsbury refrigerated pie crusts, softened as directed on box

## FILLING

1 cup raisins
1¼ cups water
1 cup sugar
3 tablespoons all-purpose flour
½ teaspoon salt
3 egg yolks
1 cup sour cream
2 tablespoons butter, softened
1 cup chopped walnuts or pecans
1 teaspoon vanilla

## MERINGUE

3 egg whites
½ teaspoon cream of tartar
⅓ cup sugar
1 teaspoon vanilla, if desired

**1** Heat oven to 450°F. Bake pie crust as directed on box for One-Crust Baked Shell using 9-inch glass pie plate. Cool completely on cooling rack. Reduce oven temperature to 350°F.

**2** In 1-quart saucepan, heat raisins and water to boiling. Reduce heat; simmer 5 minutes. Drain; set aside.

**3** In 2-quart saucepan, mix 1 cup sugar, the flour and salt. In medium bowl, beat egg yolks, sour cream and butter. Add to sugar mixture in pan. Cook over low heat about 15 minutes or until thick. Remove from heat. Add drained raisins, nuts and 1 teaspoon vanilla. Pour filling into cooled baked shell.

**4** In large bowl, beat egg whites and cream of tartar with electric mixer on high speed until foamy. Gradually add ⅓ cup sugar, beating until stiff peaks form. Add 1 teaspoon vanilla. Spoon and spread meringue over filling carefully sealing meringue to edge of crust to prevent shrinking or weeping.

**5** Place pie on middle oven rack; place sheet of foil on rack below pie in case of spillover. Bake about 12 minutes or until meringue is lightly browned. Cool completely on cooling rack, about 3 hours. Cover and refrigerate any remaining pie.

Carolyn Wynn from Star City, Arkansas, entered this winning recipe at the 2010 Arkansas State Fair Pie Contest.

**1 Serving:** Calories 630; Total Fat 32g (Saturated Fat 12g; Trans Fat 0g); Cholesterol 105mg; Sodium 480mg; Total Carbohydrate 77g (Dietary Fiber 2g); Protein 7g **Exchanges:** 2½ Starch, 2½ Other Carbohydrate, 6 Fat **Carbohydrate Choices:** 5

## Sweet Success Tip

Dark raisins have been dried in the sun for several weeks, which is how they get their color and shriveled appearance. Golden raisins are more plump and moist than dark ones because they have been treated with sulfur dioxide to prevent darkening.

# Strawberry Marshmallow Pie

**8 servings • PREP TIME: 20 Minutes • START TO FINISH: 9 Hours**

1 box Pillsbury refrigerated pie crusts, softened as directed on box

2 packages (8 oz each) cream cheese, softened

1 jar (13 oz) marshmallow creme

4 cups sliced fresh strawberries

1 container (12 to 14 oz) strawberry glaze

**1** Heat oven to 450°F. Bake 1 pie crust as directed on box for One-Crust Baked Shell using 9-inch glass pie plate. Cool completely on cooling rack.

**2** Meanwhile, unroll second pie crust on work surface. With desired cookie cutters, cut shapes from crust; place on ungreased cookie sheet. Bake 6 to 8 minutes or until light brown. Remove from cookie sheet to cooling rack; cool.

**3** In medium bowl, beat cream cheese with electric mixer on high speed until light and fluffy. Stir in marshmallow creme. In large bowl, mix strawberries and glaze. Reserve 1 cup strawberry mixture; set aside.

**4** Spoon about one-third of the marshmallow mixture into cooled baked shell; top with remaining strawberry mixture and remaining two-thirds marshmallow mixture. Top with 1 cup reserved strawberry mixture.

**5** Arrange baked cutouts over filling. Cover; refrigerate at least 8 hours or until set but not firm. Store in refrigerator.

Joyce Gaddie of Clinton, Tennessee, won the Pillsbury Refrigerated Pie Crust Pie Baking Championship at the 2009 Tennessee Valley Fair with this recipe.

**1 Serving:** Calories 610; Total Fat 32g (Saturated Fat 16g; Trans Fat 0.5g); Cholesterol 65mg; Sodium 500mg; Total Carbohydrate 76g (Dietary Fiber 2g); Protein 4g **Exchanges:** 1½ Starch, ½ Fruit, 3 Other Carbohydrate, 6 Fat **Carbohydrate Choices:** 5

## Sweet Success Tip

To quickly soften cream cheese, use your microwave. Remove the foil wrapper and place the cream cheese in a microwavable bowl. Microwave uncovered on Medium (50%) for 1 to 1½ minutes.

# Strawberry-Pretzel Pie

8 servings • PREP TIME: 45 Minutes • START TO FINISH: 8 Hours 45 Minutes

1 box Pillsbury refrigerated pie crusts, softened as directed on box

1 egg white

1 cup crushed pretzels

1¾ cups sugar

6 tablespoons butter, melted

2 packages (8 oz each) cream cheese, softened

1 container (12 oz) frozen whipped topping, thawed

1 bag (16 oz) frozen unsweetened strawberries, partially thawed, sliced

1 cup boiling water

1 box (8-serving size) strawberry-flavored gelatin

**1** Heat oven to 450°F. Unroll 1 pie crust in 10-inch glass pie plate or 9½-inch glass deep-dish pie plate. Trim outside edge. Prick bottom and side of crust generously with fork. Cut second crust into ¼-inch strips; braid 3 strips at a time. Brush egg white on crust edge; place braid on edge, pushing in slightly.

**2** In small bowl, mix crushed pretzels, ¼ cup of the sugar and the melted butter. Press mixture in bottom of crust-lined plate. Bake 10 to 12 minutes or until golden brown. Cool completely on cooling rack.

**3** In medium bowl, beat cream cheese and remaining 1½ cups sugar with electric mixer on low speed until sugar is dissolved, or mix with spoon. Carefully fold in whipped topping. Reserve 2 cups mixture for garnish; refrigerate until ready to serve. Spread remaining cream cheese–whipped topping mixture in cooled baked crust.

**4** Place flat layer of strawberry slices on top of filling. In medium bowl, mix boiling water and gelatin (with a few ice cubes) to make about 1⅔ cups gelatin. Refrigerate just until slightly thickened; pour over strawberries. Refrigerate 8 hours or overnight.

**5** Pipe reserved 2 cups reserved cream cheese–whipped topping mixture on top of pie.

Judy Tarner from Clinton, Tennessee, entered this winning recipe at the 2010 Tennesse State Fair pie contest.

**1 Serving:** Calories 890; Total Fat 50g (Saturated Fat 29g; Trans Fat 1g); Cholesterol 90mg; Sodium 680mg; Total Carbohydrate 100g (Dietary Fiber 2g); Protein 9g **Exchanges:** 2½ Starch, ½ Fruit, 3½ Other Carbohydrate, 10 Fat **Carbohydrate Choices:** 6½

## Sweet Success Tip

**If you're short on time, this pie can be made without the decorative braided crust edge. Use 1 crust and flute the edge as desired.**

# Grasshopper Pie

8 servings · PREP TIME: 30 Minutes · START TO FINISH: 5 Hours

## CHOCOLATE COOKIE CRUMB CRUST

- 1½ cups finely crushed thin chocolate wafer cookies (24 cookies)
- ¼ cup butter, melted

## FILLING

- ½ cup milk
- 32 large marshmallows (from 10-oz bag)
- ¼ cup green or white crème de menthe
- 3 tablespoons white crème de cacao
- 1½ cups whipping cream
  Few drops green food color, if desired

## GARNISH

- 2 tablespoons reserved crumbs
  Grated semisweet baking chocolate, if desired

**1** Heat oven to 350°F. In medium bowl, stir all crust ingredients until well mixed. Reserve 2 tablespoons crumbs for garnish. Press remaining crumb mixture firmly and evenly against bottom and side of 9-inch glass pie plate. Bake 10 minutes. Cool on cooling rack 15 minutes.

**2** Meanwhile, in 3-quart saucepan, heat milk and marshmallows over low heat, stirring constantly, just until marshmallows are melted. Refrigerate about 20 minutes, stirring occasionally, until mixture mounds slightly when dropped from a spoon. (If mixture becomes too thick, place saucepan in bowl of warm water and stir mixture until proper consistency.) Gradually stir in crème de menthe and crème de cacao.

**3** In chilled large bowl, beat whipping cream with electric mixer on low speed until mixture begins to thicken. Gradually increase speed to high and beat until stiff peaks form. Fold marshmallow mixture into whipped cream. Fold in food color.

**4** Spread filling in cooled baked crust. Sprinkle with reserved crumbs and grated chocolate. Refrigerate about 4 hours or until set. Store in refrigerator.

**1 Serving:** Calories 410; Total Fat 23g (Saturated Fat 13g; Trans Fat 1.5g); Cholesterol 65mg; Sodium 200mg; Total Carbohydrate 46g (Dietary Fiber 0g); Protein 3g **Exchanges:** 1 Starch, 2 Other Carbohydrate, 4½ Fat **Carbohydrate Choices:** 3

**Café Latte Pie** Substitute water for the milk, add 1 tablespoon instant espresso coffee powder or granules with the water. Substitute coffee-flavored liqueur for the crème de menthe and Irish whiskey for the crème de cacao.

**Irish Cream Pie** Substitute ⅓ cup Irish cream liqueur for the crème de menthe and crème de cacao.

# Chai Cream Pie

**8 servings • PREP TIME: 25 Minutes • START TO FINISH: 2 Hours 55 Minutes**

### CRUST

1 Pillsbury refrigerated pie crust, softened as directed on box

### FILLING

1 cup water

1 package (1.1 oz) chai tea latte mix

1 bag (10.5 oz) miniature marshmallows (5½ cups)

1 tablespoon butter

2 tablespoons caramel-flavored sundae syrup

1½ cups whipping cream

¼ cup chopped pecans

Shaved chocolate

**1** Heat oven to 450°F. Bake pie crust as directed on box for One-Crust Baked Shell using 9-inch glass pie plate. Cool completely on cooling rack.

**2** Meanwhile, in 3-quart saucepan, heat water to boiling over high heat. Stir in chai tea mix; reduce heat to low. Using whisk, stir in marshmallows and butter just until marshmallows are melted. Stir in caramel syrup. Refrigerate about 30 minutes or until cool and thickened.

**3** In chilled medium bowl, beat whipping cream with electric mixer on high speed until stiff peaks form. Reserve 1 cup whipped cream; refrigerate until serving time. Fold remaining whipped cream into cooled filling. Pour into cooled baked shell. Sprinkle with pecans. Cover; refrigerate 2 hours or until filling is set.

**4** Garnish with reserved whipped cream and shaved chocolate. Cover and refrigerate any remaining pie.

**1 Serving:** Calories 440; Total Fat 25g (Saturated Fat 12g; Trans Fat 0.5g); Cholesterol 60mg; Sodium 210mg; Total Carbohydrate 51g (Dietary Fiber 0g); Protein 2g **Exchanges:** ½ Starch, 3 Other Carbohydrate, 5 Fat **Carbohydrate Choices:** 3½

## Sweet Success Tip

**Look for the chai tea mix where you find tea at the grocery store—it's full of wonderful fragrant spices!**

# Vodka Lemonade Cocktail Pie

**8 servings  ·  PREP TIME: 15 Minutes  ·  START TO FINISH: 4 Hours**

1   Pillsbury refrigerated pie crust, softened as directed on box

1   pint (2 cups) lemon sherbet, softened

1   container (6 oz) lemon cream pie fat-free yogurt

1   can (12 oz) frozen lemonade concentrate, thawed

¼   cup vodka

Lemon slices, if desired

**1**   Heat oven to 450°F. Bake pie crust as directed on box for One-Crust Baked Shell using 9-inch glass pie plate. Cool completely on cooling rack.

**2**   In medium bowl, mix sherbet, yogurt, lemonade concentrate and vodka until blended. Spoon into cooled baked shell. Freeze uncovered until firm, about 3 hours.

**3**   Remove pie from freezer 10 minutes before cutting. Garnish with lemon slices.

**1 Serving:** Calories 370; Total Fat 13g (Saturated Fat 5g; Trans Fat 0g); Cholesterol 5mg; Sodium 280mg; Total Carbohydrate 56g (Dietary Fiber 0g); Protein 2g **Exchanges:** 1 Starch, 3 Other Carbohydrate, 2½ Fat **Carbohydrate Choices:** 4

## Sweet Success Tip

**It's a cocktail for the fork! This refreshing frozen pie—a delicious version of a favorite summertime drink—is the perfect dessert for a grown-up gathering on a hot summer's night.**

# Mai Tai Cocktail Pie

**8 servings** • **PREP TIME: 15 Minutes** • **START TO FINISH: 4 Hours**

1   Pillsbury refrigerated pie crust, softened as directed on box

1   pint (2 cups) mango sorbet, softened

1   pint (2 cups) coconut sorbet

2   containers (6 oz each) piña colada fat-free yogurt

¼   cup rum

Fresh or refrigerated mango slices, if desired

**1**   Heat oven to 450°F. Bake pie crust as directed on box for One-Crust Baked Shell using 9-inch glass pie plate. Cool completely on cooling rack.

**2**   In large bowl, mix sorbets, yogurt and rum until blended. Spoon filling into cooled baked shell. Freeze uncovered until firm, about 3 hours.

**3**   Remove pie from freezer 10 minutes before cutting. Garnish with mango slices.

**1 Serving:** Calories 410; Total Fat 14g (Saturated Fat 7g; Trans Fat 0g); Cholesterol 10mg; Sodium 290mg; Total Carbohydrate 64g (Dietary Fiber 0g); Protein 3g **Exchanges:** 1 Starch, 3½ Other Carbohydrate, 2½ Fat **Carbohydrate Choices:** 4

## Sweet Success Tip

The tropical flavors in a mai tai cocktail aren't limited to the happy hour glass; try them in this fabulous frozen sorbet pie.

# Strawberry Daiquiri Cocktail Pie

**8 servings** • **PREP TIME: 15 Minutes** • **START TO FINISH: 4 Hours**

1 Pillsbury refrigerated pie crust, softened as directed on box

1 pint (2 cups) strawberry sorbet, softened

2 containers (6 oz each) strawberry fat-free yogurt

1 cup frozen strawberries, thawed, chopped

¼ cup rum

8 whole fresh strawberries

¼ cup sugar

**1** Heat oven to 450°F. Bake pie crust as directed on box for One-Crust Baked Shell using 9-inch glass pie plate. Cool completely on cooling rack.

**2** In medium bowl, mix sorbet, yogurt, chopped strawberries and rum until blended. Spoon into cooled baked shell. Freeze uncovered until firm, about 3 hours.

**3** Remove pie from freezer 10 minutes before cutting. Moisten whole strawberries; roll in sugar. Garnish each slice of pie with 1 sugared strawberry.

**1 Serving:** Calories 380; Total Fat 12g (Saturated Fat 5g; Trans Fat 0g); Cholesterol 10mg; Sodium 290mg; Total Carbohydrate 59g (Dietary Fiber 1g); Protein 3g **Exchanges:** 1 Starch, 3 Other Carbohydrate, 2½ Fat **Carbohydrate Choices:** 4

# Sangria Cocktail Pie

**8 servings** • **PREP TIME: 15 Minutes** • **START TO FINISH: 4 Hours**

1   Pillsbury refrigerated pie crust, softened as directed on box

1   pint (2 cups) raspberry sherbet, softened

2   containers (6 oz each) red raspberry fat-free yogurt

1   cup frozen raspberries, thawed

½   cup sangria

½   cup fresh raspberries, if desired

**1**   Heat oven to 450°F. Bake pie crust as directed on box for One-Crust Baked Shell using 9-inch glass pie plate. Cool completely on cooling rack.

**2**   In medium bowl, mix sherbet, yogurt, thawed raspberries and sangria until blended. Spoon into cooled baked shell. Freeze uncovered until firm, about 3 hours.

**3**   Remove pie from freezer 10 minutes before cutting. Garnish with fresh raspberries.

**1 Serving:** Calories 340; Total Fat 13g (Saturated Fat 6g; Trans Fat 0g); Cholesterol 10mg; Sodium 300mg; Total Carbohydrate 49g (Dietary Fiber 2g); Protein 3g **Exchanges:** 1½ Starch, 1½ Other Carbohydrate, 2½ Fat **Carbohydrate Choices:** 3

# Blueberry-Topped Lemon Ice Cream Pie

8 servings  •  PREP TIME: 10 Minutes  •  START TO FINISH: 5 Hours 35 Minutes

1 vanilla wafer crumb crust (6 oz)
1 pint (2 cups) vanilla ice cream, slightly softened
1 pint (2 cups) lemon sherbet, slightly softened
½ cup fresh or frozen blueberries
¼ cup blueberry preserves
1 tablespoon lemon juice
  Lemon slices, if desired

**1**  Heat oven to 375°F. Bake crumb crust 5 minutes. Cool completely on cooling rack.

**2**  Spread 1 cup of the vanilla ice cream over bottom of cooled baked crust. Freeze 30 minutes. Spread lemon sherbet over ice cream. Freeze 30 minutes. Spread remaining 1 cup ice cream over sherbet. Freeze 4 hours or until firm.

**3**  In small bowl, mix blueberries, preserves and lemon juice. Refrigerate until serving time. Cut pie into slices; serve 1 tablespoon blueberry mixture over each slice. Garnish with lemon slices.

**1 Serving:** Calories 350; Total Fat 16g (Saturated Fat 6g; Trans Fat 3g); Cholesterol 20mg; Sodium 250mg; Total Carbohydrate 48g (Dietary Fiber 3g); Protein 4g **Exchanges:** 1 Starch, 2 Other Carbohydrate, 3 Fat **Carbohydrate Choices:** 3

**Blueberry-Topped Orange Ice Cream Pie** Use orange sherbet and juice instead of lemon sherbet and juice. Garnish with orange slices or grated orange peel.

## Sweet Success Tip
If the ice cream and sherbet begin to melt before you're done assembling the pie, place them—along with the rest of the pie—in the freezer until slightly firm, about 15 minutes.

# Easy Lemonade Pie

8 servings · PREP TIME: 10 Minutes · START TO FINISH: 4 Hours 50 Minutes

Graham Cracker Crust
(page 11)

1 quart (4 cups) vanilla ice cream,
softened

1 can (6 oz) frozen lemonade
concentrate, thawed

Few drops yellow food color,
if desired

Lemon slices or lemon peel
twists, if desired

**1** Heat oven to 350°F. Make and bake crust as directed—except use all of the crumb mixture for crust, not reserving any for topping. Cool on cooling rack 30 minutes.

**2** In large bowl, mix ice cream, lemonade concentrate and food color. Mound mixture in cooled baked crust. Freeze 4 hours or until firm.

**3** Remove pie from freezer a few minutes before cutting. Garnish with lemon slices or peel.

**1 Serving:** Calories 340; Total Fat 17g (Saturated Fat 10g; Trans Fat 0.5g); Cholesterol 50mg; Sodium 200mg; Total Carbohydrate 43g (Dietary Fiber 1g); Protein 3g **Exchanges:** 2½ Other Carbohydrate, ½ Low-Fat Milk, 3 Fat **Carbohydrate Choices:** 3

## Sweet Success Tips

For pink lemonade pie, use pink lemonade concentrate and red food color.

Plan ahead to make 2 pies and keep an extra in the freezer for unexpected guests.

# Peanut Butter Ice Cream Pie

**8 servings** • **PREP TIME: 25 Minutes** • **START TO FINISH: 6 Hours 30 minutes**

## CHOCOLATE COOKIE CRUMB CRUST

1½   cups finely crushed thin chocolate wafer cookies (24 cookies)

¼   cup butter, melted

## FILLING

2   pints (4 cups) peanut butter ice cream

1   pint (2 cups) chocolate or vanilla ice cream

½   cup salted cocktail peanuts

## CHOCOLATE–PEANUT BUTTER SAUCE

1   cup bittersweet or semisweet chocolate chips (6 oz)

¼   cup creamy peanut butter
    Dash salt

¼   cup whipping cream

1   tablespoon light corn syrup

## GARNISH

1   cup chocolate-covered peanuts, coarsely chopped

**1** Heat oven to 350°F. In medium bowl, stir all crust ingredients until well mixed. Press mixture firmly and evenly against bottom and side of 9-inch glass pie plate. Bake 10 minutes. Cool on cooling rack 15 minutes. Freeze 10 minutes. Meanwhile, place both ice creams in refrigerator to soften, about 20 to 30 minutes.

**2** In medium bowl, stir together chocolate chips, peanut butter and salt. In 1-quart saucepan, heat whipping cream and corn syrup over low heat until hot but not boiling. Pour over peanut butter mixture; cover bowl with plastic wrap. Let stand 1 minute; stir until smooth.

**3** Spread ⅓ cup of the chocolate–peanut butter sauce in bottom of chilled crust. Sprinkle with cocktail peanuts. Spoon 3 cups of the peanut butter ice cream over top; spread evenly. Quickly and carefully spread ½ cup chocolate–peanut butter sauce over ice cream (it will start to freeze). With small ice cream scoop or tablespoon, alternate scoops of chocolate ice cream and remaining 1 cup peanut butter ice cream over top, covering pie and achieving bubble look.

**4** Sprinkle chocolate-covered peanuts over top. Drizzle with remaining chocolate–peanut butter sauce. Freeze 5 hours or until firm. Place pie in refrigerator 30 minutes before cutting to soften slightly.

**1 Serving:** Calories 720; Total Fat 43g (Saturated Fat 21g; Trans Fat 1g); Cholesterol 70mg; Sodium 380mg; Total Carbohydrate 69g (Dietary Fiber 5g); Protein 13g **Exchanges:** 1½ Starch, 2½ Other Carbohydrate, 1 Milk, 7 Fat **Carbohydrate Choices:** 4½

## Sweet Success Tip

If the chocolate peanut butter sauce hardens too much while assembling the pie, microwave in 10-second increments until it's softened.

# "Jamocha" Ice Cream Pie

**8 servings • PREP TIME: 20 Minutes • START TO FINISH: 4 Hours 20 Minutes**

### CRUST

- 1 cup all-purpose flour
- ½ cup butter, softened
- 2 teaspoons instant coffee powder or granules

### FILLING

- 2 pints (4 cups) coffee ice cream, slightly softened
- ¾ cup hot fudge topping

### GARNISH, IF DESIRED

Coffee-flavored chocolate candies or chocolate-covered coffee beans

**1** Heat oven to 400°F. In medium bowl, mix all crust ingredients with spoon until dough forms. Press dough firmly and evenly in bottom and up side of 9-inch glass pie plate. Bake 12 to 15 minutes or until light brown. Cool completely on cooling rack.

**2** Spread 2 cups of the ice cream in cooled baked crust. Cover; freeze 1 hour or until firm.

**3** Spread hot fudge topping over ice cream. Carefully spread remaining 2 cups ice cream over topping. Cover; freeze at least 2 hours until firm but no longer than 2 weeks.

**4** Remove pie from freezer about 10 minutes before cutting. Garnish with candies.

**1 Serving:** Calories 410; Total Fat 22g (Saturated Fat 12g; Trans Fat 1g); Cholesterol 65mg; Sodium 230mg; Total Carbohydrate 47g (Dietary Fiber 2g); Protein 6g **Exchanges:** 2 Starch, 1 Other Carbohydrate, 4 Fat **Carbohydrate Choices:** 3

## Sweet Success Tip

**Save time and purchase a convenient 6-ounce chocolate or vanilla wafer crumb crust instead of making and baking the crust.**

# Coffee Ice Cream Pie

**8 servings** • **PREP TIME: 20 Minutes** • **START TO FINISH: 2 Hours 50 Minutes**

## CRUST

1½ cups finely crushed chocolate wafer cookies (24 cookies)

½ cup butter or margarine, softened

¼ cup coconut

3 tablespoons finely chopped cashews or macadamia nuts

## FILLING

1 quart (4 cups) coffee ice cream, slightly softened

## TOPPING

1 cup hot fudge topping, warmed

Whole cashews or macadamia nuts, if desired

**1** In medium bowl, mix all crust ingredients. Press mixture in bottom and up side of 9-inch glass pie plate; refrigerate 15 minutes.

**2** Carefully spoon softened ice cream into chilled crust. Cover; freeze 2 hours or until firm.

**3** Remove pie from freezer 10 to 15 minutes before cutting. Top individual servings with fudge topping; garnish with whole cashews.

**1 Serving:** Calories 520; Total Fat 28g (Saturated Fat 16g; Trans Fat 1.5g); Cholesterol 55mg; Sodium 400mg; Total Carbohydrate 61g (Dietary Fiber 3g); Protein 7g **Exchanges:** 3 Other Carbohydrate, 1 Low-Fat Milk, 4½ Fat **Carbohydrate Choices:** 4

## Sweet Success Tips

Chocolate-covered coffee beans also make a nice garnish for slices of this pie.

Spray the back of a metal spoon with cooking spray and use it to press the crust mixture into the pie plate.

# Buster Sundae Pie

**8 servings** · **PREP TIME:** 20 Minutes · **START TO FINISH:** 5 Hours 5 Minutes

1  Pillsbury refrigerated pie crust, softened as directed on box

1  quart (4 cups) vanilla ice cream, slightly softened

½  cup caramel topping

½  cup hot fudge topping

¾  cup Spanish peanuts

Additional Spanish peanuts, if desired

**1**  Heat oven to 450°F. Bake pie crust as directed on box for One-Crust Baked Shell using 9-inch glass pie plate. Cool completely on cooling rack.

**2**  Spread 2 cups of the ice cream in cooled baked shell. Drizzle with ¼ cup of the caramel topping and ¼ cup of the hot fudge topping. Sprinkle with ¾ cup peanuts. Carefully spread remaining 2 cups ice cream over peanuts. Cover; freeze 4 hours or overnight.

**3**  Remove pie from freezer about 10 minutes before cutting. Drizzle individual servings with remaining caramel and hot fudge toppings. Sprinkle with additional peanuts.

**1 Serving:** Calories 700; Total Fat 38g (Saturated Fat 16g; Trans Fat 0.5g); Cholesterol 70mg; Sodium 470mg; Total Carbohydrate 77g (Dietary Fiber 3g); Protein 11g **Exchanges:** 1½ Starch, 3½ Other Carbohydrate, 1 High-Fat Meat, 6 Fat **Carbohydrate Choices:** 5

## Sweet Success Tip

For an interesting flavor twist, try using a chocolate cookie crumb crust. Either make your own (recipe on page 11) or save time and buy one already made at the grocery store.

# Berry Ice Cream Pie

**8 servings** • **PREP TIME: 25 Minutes** • **START TO FINISH: 2 Hours 50 Minutes**

## FILLING

- 3 cups (1½ pints) vanilla ice cream
- 2 cups (1 pint) raspberry sherbet
- 1 box (10 oz) frozen raspberries in syrup, thawed

## CRUST

- 1¼ cups crushed vanilla wafer cookies
- ½ cup finely chopped pecans
- ¼ cup butter, melted

## SAUCE

- 3 tablespoons sugar
- 1 tablespoon cornstarch
  Reserved raspberry liquid
- 2 tablespoons orange juice
- 1 container (6 oz) fresh raspberries, if desired

**1** Place ice cream and sherbet in refrigerator to soften. Place thawed raspberries in strainer over 2-cup glass measuring cup to drain; reserve liquid for sauce.

**2** Heat oven to 375°F. In medium bowl, mix all crust ingredients. Press mixture in bottom and up side of ungreased 9-inch glass pie plate. Bake 5 to 8 minutes or until edge just begins to brown. Cool completely on cooling rack.

**3** Scoop 1½ cups ice cream into cooled baked crust. In large bowl, fold drained raspberries into sherbet. Spoon evenly over ice cream. Scoop remaining ice cream over top. Freeze at least 2 hours or until firm.

**4** In 1-quart saucepan, mix sugar and cornstarch. Stir in reserved raspberry liquid. Cook over medium heat, stirring constantly, until mixture becomes clear and thickened. Stir in orange juice. Cool at room temperature at least 10 minutes before serving.

**5** Cut pie into slices; serve with sauce. Garnish with fresh raspberries. Cover and store remaining pie in freezer and sauce in refrigerator.

**1 Serving:** Calories 390; Total Fat 20g (Saturated Fat 9g; Trans Fat 1g); Cholesterol 40mg; Sodium 160mg; Total Carbohydrate 49g (Dietary Fiber 4g); Protein 4g **Exchanges:** 1 Starch, 2 Other Carbohydrate, 4 Fat **Carbohydrate Choices:** 3

## Sweet Success Tips

Instead of layering the ice cream and sherbet, for a different look, you can fold and swirl them together.

For easier spreading, stir the ice cream until it is smooth before spreading it on top of the pie.

Ginger–Lemon Curd Petite Pies
(page 162)

# tarts
# &
# mini pies

# Caramel Apple–Marshmallow Tarts

**8 tarts  •  PREP TIME:  20 Minutes  •  START TO FINISH:  1 Hour 15 Minutes**

1  box Pillsbury refrigerated pie
    crusts, softened as directed
    on box
1  cup apple pie filling
    (from 21-oz can)
¾  cup miniature marshmallows
3  tablespoons caramel topping

**1**  Heat oven to 400°F. Unroll pie crusts on work surface. With 4½-inch round cookie cutter, cut 4 rounds from each crust.

**2**  Spoon about 2 tablespoons pie filling onto center of each round. Firmly fold edge of crust over sides of filling, ruffling decoratively. Place on ungreased large cookie sheet.

**3**  Bake 15 to 20 minutes or until crust is golden brown. Sprinkle marshmallows over filling. Bake 3 to 4 minutes longer or until marshmallows are puffed and just beginning to brown. Cool completely, about 30 minutes.

**4**  Just before serving, drizzle about 1 teaspoon caramel topping over each tart.

**1 Tart:** Calories 280; Total Fat 12g (Saturated Fat 5g; Trans Fat 0g); Cholesterol 5mg; Sodium 310mg; Total Carbohydrate 42g (Dietary Fiber 0g); Protein 0g **Exchanges:** 3 Other Carbohydrate, 2½ Fat **Carbohydrate Choices:** 3

## Sweet Success Tip

Let the kids help assemble these tarts, spooning the pie filling on the pastry rounds and adding the marshmallows. Then for dessert or an after-school snack, they can enjoy the fruits of their labor!

# Apple Harvest Turnovers

**8 turnovers · PREP TIME: 25 Minutes · START TO FINISH: 45 Minutes**

1 box Pillsbury refrigerated pie crusts, softened as directed on box
2 cups diced peeled apples
⅓ cup sugar
1 tablespoon all-purpose flour
1½ teaspoons ground cinnamon

**1** Heat oven to 400°F. Unroll pie crusts on work surface. Cut each crust into quarters, making 8 wedges.

**2** In medium bowl, mix apples, sugar, flour and cinnamon. Top half of each crust wedge with ⅓ cup apple mixture. Fold untopped sides of wedges over filling. With fork, press edges to seal. Place on ungreased cookie sheet. Cut several small slits in top of each turnover.

**3** Bake 15 to 20 minutes or until light golden brown. Serve warm or cool.

**1 Turnover:** Calories 260; Total Fat 12g (Saturated Fat 5g; Trans Fat 0g); Cholesterol 5mg; Sodium 280mg; Total Carbohydrate 37g (Dietary Fiber 0g); Protein 0g **Exchanges:** 2½ Other Carbohydrate, 2½ Fat **Carbohydrate Choices:** 2½

## Sweet Success Tip

**Make these turnovers even quicker by substituting 1 can (21 ounces) apple pie filling for the apples, sugar, flour and cinnamon.**

# Apple Spice Jumbo Pie Cupcakes

**12 cupcakes** • **PREP TIME: 25 Minutes** • **START TO FINISH: 1 Hour 45 Minutes**

1 box Pillsbury refrigerated pie crusts, softened as directed on box

1 box spice cake mix with pudding in the mix

Water, vegetable oil and eggs called for on cake mix box

½ cup apple pie filling (from 21-oz can)

1 container cream cheese creamy ready-to-spread frosting

**1** Heat oven to 450°F. Unroll pie crusts on work surface. Cut 6 (4¾-inch) rounds from each crust. Firmly press 1 round in bottom and up side of each of 12 nonstick jumbo muffin cups. Bake 5 minutes.

**2** Reduce oven temperature to 350°F. Make cake mix as directed on box, using water, oil and eggs. Divide apple pie filling evenly among crust-lined muffin cups. Top evenly with cake batter.

**3** Bake 30 to 33 minutes or until toothpick inserted in center of cake comes out clean. Cool 10 minutes; remove from pan to cooling rack. Cool completely. Frost cupcakes with cream cheese frosting.

**1 Cupcake:** Calories 390; Total Fat 21g (Saturated Fat 6g; Trans Fat 2g); Cholesterol 55mg; Sodium 290mg; Total Carbohydrate 47g (Dietary Fiber 0g); Protein 3g **Exchanges:** 1 Starch, 2 Other Carbohydrate, 4 Fat **Carbohydrate Choices:** 3

## Sweet Success Tip

**Try other flavors of pie filling in these creative cupcake treats.**

# Chocolate-Coconut Jumbo Pie Cupcakes

**12 cupcakes · PREP TIME: 25 Minutes · START TO FINISH: 1 Hour 45 Minutes**

1 box Pillsbury refrigerated pie crusts, softened as directed on box

1 box chocolate fudge cake mix with pudding in the mix

Water, vegetable oil and eggs called for on cake mix box

¾ cup semisweet chocolate chips

½ cup shredded coconut

1 container vanilla whipped ready-to-spread frosting

**1** Heat oven to 450°F. Unroll pie crusts on work surface. Cut 6 (4¾-inch) rounds from each crust. Firmly press 1 round in bottom and up side of each of 12 nonstick jumbo muffin cups. Bake 5 minutes.

**2** Reduce oven temperature to 350°F. Make cake mix as directed on box, using water, oil and eggs. Place 1 tablespoon chocolate chips and 1 teaspoon coconut in each crust-lined muffin cup. Top evenly with cake batter.

**3** Bake 30 to 33 minutes or until toothpick inserted in center of cake comes out clean. Cool 10 minutes; remove from pan to cooling rack. Cool completely. Frost cupcakes with vanilla frosting. Top each with 1 teaspoon coconut.

**1 Cupcake:** Calories 550; Total Fat 29g (Saturated Fat 10g; Trans Fat 2g); Cholesterol 55mg; Sodium 540mg; Total Carbohydrate 68g (Dietary Fiber 1g); Protein 4g **Exchanges:** 2 Starch, 2½ Other Carbohydrate, 5½ Fat **Carbohydrate Choices:** 4½

## Sweet Success Tip

Do you love both pie and cupcakes? There's no need to choose between the two with this fantastic dessert!

# Pear Tartlets

**4 tartlets** · **PREP TIME: 10 Minutes** · **START TO FINISH: 40 Minutes**

1 sheet frozen puff pastry (from 17.3-oz package), thawed
1 ripe pear, peeled, quartered
¼ cup peach preserves

**1** Heat oven to 400°F. Unfold pastry sheet on work surface; cut into 4 squares. Place pastry squares on ungreased cookie sheet.

**2** Slice each pear quarter into very thin slices. Arrange slices on pastry squares, leaving ½-inch border.

**3** Bake about 20 minutes or until pastry is puffed and browned. Spread 1 tablespoon preserves over top of each warm tartlet to cover pears. Cool on cookie sheet 10 minutes before serving.

**1 Tartlet:** Calories 430; Total Fat 24g (Saturated Fat 8g; Trans Fat 2.5g); Cholesterol 75mg; Sodium 160mg; Total Carbohydrate 49g (Dietary Fiber 2g); Protein 5g **Exchanges:** 1½ Starch, 1½ Other Carbohydrate, 4½ Fat **Carbohydrate Choices:** 3

## Sweet Success Tips

Thaw the frozen puff pastry on the counter for about 15 minutes. The pastry should be chilled but still pliable when you're ready to work with it. If the pastry gets too warm, the butter layers will flatten and the pastry won't puff as high when it bakes.

Keep puff pastry in the freezer for those occasions when you need a quick dessert like these tartlets.

# Cherry-Filled Heart-Shaped Pies

**6 pies • PREP TIME: 45 Minutes • START TO FINISH: 2 Hours 45 Minutes**

### FILLING

- ⅔ cup granulated sugar
- 2 tablespoons cornstarch
- 1 can (15 oz) pitted dark sweet cherries, drained, 3 tablespoons juice reserved
- 1 teaspoon grated orange peel
- ½ cup orange juice
- 1 tablespoon unsalted butter
- 1 vanilla bean

### CRUST

Two-Crust Pastry (page 8) or 1 box Pillsbury refrigerated pie crusts, softened as directed on box

### TOPPING

- 1 egg
- 1 tablespoon whipping cream
- 2 tablespoons coarse sugar or sanding sugar

**1** In 2-quart saucepan, mix granulated sugar and cornstarch with whisk. Stir in cherries, reserved juice, the orange peel, orange juice and butter. Cut slit down center of vanilla bean; scrape out seeds. Add seeds and bean to cherry mixture. Heat to boiling; boil 1 minute, stirring constantly. Pour into shallow container. Remove and discard vanilla bean. Refrigerate until ready to assemble.

**2** Meanwhile, on lightly floured surface, roll 1 pastry round or pie crust to ⅛-inch thickness. With 5½-inch heart-shaped cookie cutter, cut out 6 hearts. Place on ungreased cookie sheet. Repeat with second pastry or pie crust. With 1½-inch heart-shaped cookie cutter, cut out small heart from center of second batch of hearts. Spread 2 tablespoons filling on each plain heart. Cover with cutout hearts so filling shows. Press edges together with fork. Refrigerate 1 hour or until firm.

**3** Heat oven to 400°F. In small bowl, beat egg and whipping cream. Brush over hearts. Sprinkle with coarse sugar.

**4** Bake 25 to 30 minutes or until lightly golden. Remove from cookie sheet to cooling rack; cool at least 30 minutes before serving.

**1 Pie:** Calories 570; Total Fat 27g (Saturated Fat 8g; Trans Fat 0g); Cholesterol 40mg; Sodium 410mg; Total Carbohydrate 75g (Dietary Fiber 2g); Protein 6g **Exchanges:** 2 Starch, 1 Fruit, 2 Other Carbohydrate, 5 Fat **Carbohydrate Choices:** 5

## Sweet Success Tips

Sprinkle the pies with powdered sugar after baking for a different look.

If a vanilla bean is not available, substitute ½ to 1 teaspoon pure vanilla.

# Mini Wedding Pies

**72 mini pies (24 of each flavor)** • **PREP TIME: 3 Hours** • **START TO FINISH: 5 Hours**

## CRUSTS

- 6 recipes Two-Crust Pastry (page 8) or 6 boxes Pillsbury refrigerated pie crusts, softened as directed on box
- 1 tablespoon whipping cream
- 1 to 2 tablespoons coarse sugar or sanding sugar

## APPLE-CHERRY FILLING AND TOPPING

- 2 lb tart apples, peeled, chopped (about 5½ cups)
- ¾ cup water
- ¾ cup granulated sugar
- 1 teaspoon ground cinnamon
- ½ teaspoon ground ginger
- ¼ teaspoon nutmeg
  Dash salt
- 1 tablespoon finely chopped crystallized ginger
- ¾ cup dried cherries
- 4½ teaspoons cornstarch
- 3 tablespoons cold water
- 1½ cups whipping cream
- ¼ cup granulated sugar or powdered sugar
- ¼ cup caramel topping

## DOUBLE-BERRY FILLING

- 3 cups fresh raspberries
- 3 cups fresh blackberries
- ¾ cup granulated sugar
- ⅓ cup cornstarch
- ¼ cup cold water

## PEACH FILLING AND TOPPING

- 5 medium peaches, peeled, chopped, or 2 bags (16 oz each) frozen sliced peaches, thawed, chopped (3 cups)
- ¼ cup granulated sugar
- 1 teaspoon ground cinnamon
- ½ teaspoon nutmeg
- ¼ cup crème fraîche
- ¾ cup all-purpose flour
- ⅓ cup packed brown sugar
- 1 teaspoon ground cinnamon
- ⅓ cup cold butter
- ⅓ cup slivered almonds, toasted✳, coarsely chopped

**1** Heat oven to 400°F. On lightly floured surface with floured rolling pin, roll 1 pastry round or pie crust at a time to 13-inch round. From each pastry, cut 6 (4-inch) rounds. From scraps, cut a total of 24 (1½-inch) hearts and 24 (1-inch) hearts.

**2** Press pastry rounds in bottoms and up sides of 72 ungreased regular-size muffin cups, leaving top edge slightly ruffled (dough should come slightly over top of cup); set aside until ready to fill. Place hearts on ungreased cookie sheets. Brush with 1 tablespoon whipping cream; sprinkle with coarse sugar. Bake 5 to 7 minutes or until light golden brown. Cool 2 minutes; remove from cookie sheets to cooling racks.

**3** In 12-inch skillet, cook apples, ¾ cup water and ¾ cup granulated sugar over medium heat about 10 minutes, stirring occasionally, until tender. Add 1 teaspoon cinnamon, the ground ginger, ¼ teaspoon nutmeg, the salt, crystallized ginger and dried cherries; mix well. In small bowl, beat 4½ teaspoons cornstarch and 3 tablespoons cold water with whisk. Add to apple mixture; stir until thickened and bubbly. Remove from heat; cool to room temperature.

**4** Meanwhile, in large bowl, place raspberries and blackberries. In 1½-quart saucepan, stir ¾ cup granulated sugar, ⅓ cup cornstarch and ¼ cup cold water with whisk. Cook over medium-high heat, stirring constantly, until mixture just comes to a boil. Pour over berries; mix well. Immediately spoon berry mixture into 24 of the crust-lined muffin cups. Bake 25 to 30 minutes or until crust is golden brown and filling is bubbly. If fruit bubbled up onto pan, run knife around edge of cup. Cool 10 minutes; remove from pans to cooling racks. Cool completely. Just before serving, place 1 large heart and 1 small heart on each Double-Berry Mini Pie.

**5** In medium bowl, stir peaches, sugar, 1 teaspoon cinnamon, ½ teaspoon nutmeg and crème fraîche. Spoon filling into 24 crust-lined muffin cups. In a small bowl, mix flour, brown sugar and 1 teaspoon cinnamon. Cut in butter, using pastry blender or fork, until crumbly. Stir in almonds. Sprinkle topping evenly over filling. Bake 18 to 22 minutes or until topping is golden brown and filling is bubbly. Cool 10 minutes; remove from pans to cooling racks. Cool completely.

**6** Spoon cooled apple-cherry filling into remaining 24 crust-lined muffin cups. Bake 25 to 30 minutes or until crust is golden brown and filling is bubbly. Cool 10 minutes; remove from pans to cooling racks. Cool completely.

**7** Just before serving, in chilled large bowl, beat 1½ cups whipping cream and ¼ cup granulated sugar with electric mixer on high speed until soft peaks form. Spoon about 2 tablespoons whipped cream on top of each Apple-Cherry Mini Pie. Drizzle with caramel topping.

✳To toast almonds, heat oven to 350°F. Spread almonds in ungreased shallow pan. Bake uncovered 6 to 10 minutes, stirring occasionally, until light brown.

**1 Mini Pie:** Calories 270; Total Fat 15g (Saturated Fat 4.5g; Trans Fat 0g); Cholesterol 10mg; Sodium 210mg; Total Carbohydrate 31g (Dietary Fiber 2g); Protein 3g **Exchanges:** 1 Starch, 1 Other Carbohydrate, 3 Fat **Carbohydrate Choices:** 2

# Individual Wedding Pies

9 pies • PREP TIME: 1 Hour 15 Minutes • START TO FINISH: 4 Hours

## CRUST

| | |
|---|---|
| 5 | Pillsbury refrigerated pie crusts, softened as directed on box |
| 9 | (5×1⅝ inch) individual foil tart pans |
| 1 | tablespoon milk |
| 2 | tablespoons coarse sugar or granulated sugar |

## BLUEBERRY-GINGER FILLING

| | |
|---|---|
| ½ | cup granulated sugar |
| ¼ | cup all-purpose flour |
| 3 | cups fresh blueberries |
| 1 | tablespoon finely chopped crystallized ginger |
| 1 | tablespoon lemon juice |
| 1 | tablespoon cold butter, if desired |

## PEACH-CINNAMON FILLING

| | |
|---|---|
| ½ | cup granulated sugar |
| ¼ | cup all-purpose flour |
| ¼ | teaspoon ground cinnamon |
| 3 | cups cut-up (1-inch pieces) fresh peaches (3 to 5 medium) or 3 cups cut-up (1-inch pieces) frozen peaches, partially thawed, drained |
| 1 | tablespoon lemon juice |
| 1 | tablespoon cold butter, if desired |

## CHERRY-ALMOND FILLING

| | |
|---|---|
| ¾ | cup granulated sugar |
| ⅓ | cup all-purpose flour |
| 4 | cups pitted fresh sour cherries or 4 cups unsweetened pitted frozen tart cherries, thawed, drained |
| 1 | teaspoon almond extract |
| 1 | tablespoon cold butter, if desired |

**1** Heat oven to 425°F. On lightly floured work surface, unroll 3 pie crusts. With 6-inch round cutter or bowl, cut 4 rounds from each crust. Reroll scraps as needed; cut 1 additional round to make total of 9 rounds. Fit rounds in bottoms and up sides of tart pans, pressing firmly. Prick bottoms and sides of crusts generously with fork. Place pans on ungreased cookie sheets.

**2** If desired, cut small heart shapes from remaining pie crust scraps; place on cookie sheets with tart pans. Prick hearts with fork; sprinkle lightly with coarse sugar.

**3** Bake tart shells and hearts 6 to 8 minutes or just until shells are dry (only partially baked) and hearts are golden brown. Remove from oven; remove hearts from cookie sheet; place on cooling rack.

**4** Meanwhile, unroll remaining 2 pie crusts. With 6-inch round cutter or bowl, cut 4 rounds from each crust. Reroll scraps as needed; cut 1 additional round to make a total of 9 rounds. Use small letter or heart-shaped cookie cutters to cut 1 shape out of each of the 9 rounds. Set aside.

**5** To make blueberry pies: In large bowl, mix ½ cup granulated sugar and ¼ cup flour. Stir in blueberries, ginger and 1 tablespoon lemon juice. Spoon into 3 pastry-lined tart pans. Cut 1 tablespoon butter into small pieces; sprinkle over blueberries.

**6** To make peach pies: In large bowl, mix ½ cup granulated sugar, ¼ cup flour and the cinnamon. Stir in peaches and 1 tablespoon lemon juice. Spoon into 3 pastry-lined tart pans. Cut 1 tablespoon butter into small pieces; sprinkle over peaches.

**7** To make cherry pies: In large bowl, mix ¾ cup granulated sugar and ⅓ cup flour. Stir in cherries and almond extract. Spoon into 3 pastry-lined tart pans. Cut 1 tablespoon butter into small pieces; sprinkle over cherries.

**8** Cover each of the 9 pies with top crust; seal and flute. Brush top crusts with milk; sprinkle with coarse sugar.

**9** Place pies on ungreased cookie sheets with unbaked cutouts. Bake cutouts 6 to 8 minutes, pies 30 to 35 minutes, or until crust is golden brown and juice begins to bubble through slits in crust. Cover pies with sheet of foil after 15 minutes of baking to prevent overbrowning. Cool pies on cooling rack at least 2 hours. Garnish with pie crust cutouts.

**1 Pie:** Calories 780; Total Fat 27g (Saturated Fat 11g; Trans Fat 0g); Cholesterol 15mg; Sodium 580mg; Total Carbohydrate 126g (Dietary Fiber 3g); Protein 6g **Exchanges:** 2 Starch, 1 Fruit, 5½ Other Carbohydrate, 5 Fat **Carbohydrate Choices:** 8½

## Sweet Success Tip

**If you don't have a 6-inch round cutter, use the top of a 6-inch diameter bowl as a pattern. Place the bowl upside down on the crust, and cut around the bowl using a sharp paring knife.**

# Pie Poppers

**24 poppers** • **PREP TIME: 30 Minutes** • **START TO FINISH: 1 Hour 15 Minutes**

1 box Pillsbury refrigerated pie crusts, softened as directed on box
½ cup canned pie filling or lemon curd
½ cup powdered sugar, if desired
3 to 4 teaspoons milk, if desired

**1** Heat oven to 450°F. Unroll pie crusts on work surface. Cut each crust into 12 squares (some squares will have a rounded edge). Place 1 teaspoon filling on each square.

**2** Bring all sides of square together in center; press to seal. With fingers, pinch dough firmly about ¼ inch below edges, making a pouch with points extending over top. Repeat with remaining crust squares. Place poppers in 24 ungreased mini muffin cups or place mini paper baking cup in each of 24 mini muffin cups, and place popper inside baking cup.

**3** Bake 11 to 14 minutes or light golden brown. Remove from pans to cooling racks; cool 10 minutes.

**4** In small bowl, mix powdered sugar and enough milk until glaze is smooth and thin enough to drizzle. Drizzle glaze over poppers; let stand until set, about 30 minutes.

**1 Popper:** Calories 90; Total Fat 4g (Saturated Fat 1.5g; Trans Fat 0g); Cholesterol 0mg; Sodium 100mg; Total Carbohydrate 13g (Dietary Fiber 0g); Protein 0g **Exchanges:** 1 Other Carbohydrate, 1 Fat **Carbohydrate Choices:** 1

## Sweet Success Tip

These portable single-serving poppers are great for parties, picnics and lunchtime or after-school treats. Make them with two or three kinds of fillings for variety.

# Raspberry–White Chocolate Pie Pops

**8 pie pops** • **PREP TIME:** 20 Minutes • **START TO FINISH:** 45 Minutes

1 box Pillsbury refrigerated pie crusts, softened as directed on box

24 fresh raspberries

8 white candy melts or coating wafers, chopped

8 craft sticks (flat wooden sticks with round ends)

1 egg, beaten

2 tablespoons coarse white sparkling sugar

**1** Heat oven to 450°F. Spray cookie sheet with cooking spray.

**2** Unroll pie crusts on floured work surface. With 3½-inch round cutter, cut 8 rounds from each crust. Place 8 rounds on cookie sheet. Place 3 raspberries in center of each round; sprinkle chopped candy melts evenly over raspberries.

**3** Place 1 craft stick on each round, so tip of stick is in center of round. Top each with 1 remaining round. Press edges together; seal and flute. Cut 4 or 5 small slits in top crust. Brush tops with egg; sprinkle with sugar.

**4** Bake 10 to 13 minutes or until golden brown. Remove from cookie sheet to cooling rack; cool 10 minutes before serving.

**1 Pie Pop:** Calories 150; Total Fat 8g (Saturated Fat 3.5g; Trans Fat 0g); Cholesterol 25mg; Sodium 140mg; Total Carbohydrate 18g (Dietary Fiber 0g); Protein 1g **Exchanges:** ½ Starch, ½ Other Carbohydrate, 1½ Fat **Carbohydrate Choices:** 1

# Strawberry-Rhubarb Pie Pops

**8 pie pops • PREP TIME: 30 Minutes • START TO FINISH: 1 Hour 25 Minutes**

¾   cup frozen strawberries, thawed, chopped, drained and juice reserved

⅓   cup granulated sugar

2   teaspoons cornstarch

1   cup frozen chopped rhubarb, thawed

1   box Pillsbury refrigerated pie crusts, softened as directed on box

8   craft sticks (flat wooden sticks with round ends)

1   egg white, beaten

1   teaspoon granulated sugar

⅓   cup powdered sugar, if desired

2   to 3 teaspoons milk, if desired

**1** Heat oven to 450°F. In medium bowl, place reserved strawberry juice. In small bowl, mix ⅓ cup granulated sugar and the cornstarch. Add to strawberry juice, beating with whisk. Stir in strawberries and rhubarb.

**2** Unroll pie crusts on work surface. Using 3½-inch round cutter, cut 8 rounds from each crust. Place 8 rounds on ungreased cookie sheet. Spoon fruit mixture evenly on each round to within ½ inch of edge. Place 1 craft stick in filling on each round.

**3** Flatten remaining rounds to 4-inch diameter. Brush underside of rounds with egg white; place over fruit. Press edges together; seal with fork. Cut small slit in tops of pies. Brush tops with egg white; sprinkle evenly with 1 teaspoon granulated sugar.

**4** Bake 10 to 13 minutes or until golden brown. Remove from cookie sheet to cooling rack; cool 10 minutes.

**5** In small bowl, mix powdered sugar and enough milk until glaze is smooth and thin enough to drizzle. Drizzle glaze over pie pops; let stand until set, about 30 minutes.

**1 Pie Pop:** Calories 310; Total Fat 12g (Saturated Fat 5g; Trans Fat 0g); Cholesterol 5mg; Sodium 270mg; Total Carbohydrate 49g (Dietary Fiber 1g); Protein 2g **Exchanges:** ½ Starch, 1½ Fruit, 1 Other Carbohydrate, 2½ Fat **Carbohydrate Choices:** 3

## Sweet Success Tip

**Make other flavors of pie pops by substituting 1 cup of your favorite canned pie filling for the strawberry-rhubarb filling.**

# Strawberry-Rhubarb Mini Pies

6 pies • PREP TIME: 30 Minutes • START TO FINISH: 1 Hour 10 Minutes

2 cups frozen strawberries, thawed, drained and juice reserved

1 cup sugar

2 tablespoons cornstarch

3 cups frozen chopped rhubarb, partially thawed

1 box Pillsbury refrigerated pie crusts, softened as directed on box

**1** Heat oven to 450°F. In medium bowl, place reserved strawberry juice. In small bowl, mix ⅓ cup of the sugar and the cornstarch. Add to strawberry juice, beating with whisk. Stir in strawberries and rhubarb.

**2** Unroll pie crusts on work surface. Cut 3 (3½-inch) rounds and 3 (4¾-inch) rounds from each crust. Firmly press 4¾-inch rounds in bottom and up side of 6 ungreased 6-oz custard cups. Divide fruit mixture evenly among crust-lined cups.

**3** Place 3½-inch rounds over filling; crimp edges to seal. Cut slits in tops of pies. Sprinkle evenly with remaining ⅔ cup sugar. Place cups in 15×10×1-inch pan.

**4** Bake 32 to 36 minutes or until golden brown. Serve warm.

**1 Pie:** Calories 670; Total Fat 16g (Saturated Fat 7g; Trans Fat 0g); Cholesterol 10mg; Sodium 350mg; Total Carbohydrate 127g (Dietary Fiber 4g); Protein 3g **Exchanges:** 1 Starch, 1½ Fruit, 6 Other Carbohydrate, 3 Fat **Carbohydrate Choices:** 8½

## Sweet Success Tips

If desired, replace the strawberry-rhubarb filling with a 21-ounce can of pie filling, such as cherry, blueberry or apple.

For variety, add a lattice crust to one or more of the mini pies. For each lattice crust, cut each 3½-inch round into 6 (½-inch wide) strips. Place 3 of the strips over top of pie. Weave remaining 3 strips over and under first strips; crimp edges slightly. Bake as directed.

## Tips for Perfect Pie Pastry

**Keep It Cold:** Use ice water (add an ice cube to the water) when making the pastry.

**Pick the Right Utensil:** Use a pastry blender or fork to mix the shortening and flour.

**Use a Light Touch:** Overworking the pastry dough makes it tough, so handle it as little as possible.

**Chill Out:** Refrigerate pastry for 45 minutes; this helps make it easier to roll out.

**Roll with Ease:** Use a floured pastry cloth or board to roll pastry.

**Go for Even Color:** Place pieces of foil or a pie crust shield ring loosely over areas that are getting brown too fast.

**Get Flaky:** Cool pie on cooling rack so crust won't get soggy.

# Blueberry-Mango Hand Pies

10 pies • PREP TIME: 1 Hour • START TO FINISH: 2 Hours 30 Minutes

## CRUST

Two-Crust Pastry (page 8)
or 1 box Pillsbury refrigerated
pie crusts, softened as directed
on box

## FILLING

2 cups fresh or frozen (thawed)
blueberries

¼ cup granulated sugar

2 tablespoons cornstarch

1 teaspoon grated lemon peel

1 tablespoon lemon juice

¾ teaspoon ground ginger

1 mango, seed removed, peeled
and thinly sliced or 1½ cups
well-drained mango slices
(from 20-oz jar)

1 egg

2 tablespoons whipping cream
or milk

## GLAZE

1 cup powdered sugar

2 to 4 teaspoons water

1 teaspoon almond extract

**1** Heat oven to 375°F. Line large cookie sheet with cooking parchment paper. On well-floured surface, roll 1 pastry round to 15×10-inch rectangle about ⅛ inch thick. Cut into 5 rows by 2 rows. Repeat with second pastry.

**2** In medium bowl, crush ½ cup of the blueberries with fork. Add granulated sugar, cornstarch, lemon peel, lemon juice and ginger; stir to combine. Stir in remaining 1½ cups blueberries.

**3** Cut mango slices in half; evenly arrange slices on 10 of the pastry rectangles. Top each with heaping tablespoon of blueberry mixture, leaving 1-inch border around edges. Place remaining 10 pastry rectangles on fruit-topped rectangles; press edges firmly with fork to seal. Cut slits in top crust. Place pies on cookie sheet. In small bowl, beat egg and whipping cream. Brush over pies.

**4** Bake 25 to 30 minutes or until golden brown. Remove from cookie sheet to cooling rack; cool at least 1 hour before serving.

**5** In small bowl, mix powdered sugar with enough water to make thin glaze. Stir in almond extract. Drizzle glaze over pies.

**1 Pie:** Calories 350; Total Fat 16g (Saturated Fat 4.5g; Trans Fat 0g); Cholesterol 25mg; Sodium 250mg; Total Carbohydrate 48g (Dietary Fiber 2g); Protein 4g **Exchanges:** 1½ Starch, 1 Fruit, ½ Other Carbohydrate, 3 Fat **Carbohydrate Choices:** 3

## Sweet Success Tips

**You can freeze the hand pies before or after baking. If frozen before baking, thaw them first.**

**To cut a mango, peel the fruit and carefully cut with a knife just around the seed. Cut into 2 flat pieces, and slice or dice.**

# Berry-Lemon Cheesecake Squares

**8 servings** • **PREP TIME: 50 Minutes** • **START TO FINISH: 1 Hour 20 Minutes**

## CRUST

- 1 box Pillsbury refrigerated pie crusts, softened as directed on box
- 1 teaspoon milk
- 2 teaspoons sugar

## FILLING

- ½ cup whipping cream
- 1 package (8 oz) cream cheese, softened
- ¼ cup sugar
- 1 to 2 teaspoons grated lemon peel

## TOPPING

- 1 cup fresh blackberries
- ½ cup fresh raspberries
- ½ cup fresh blueberries

**1** Heat oven to 450°F. Unroll pie crusts on lightly floured work surface. With rolling pin, roll each crust into 11½-inch round. Cut 8½-inch square out of center of each round. Cut 4 squares from each large square, making 8 (4¼-inch) squares. Fold up all sides of each square ½ inch and roll inward to form thick crust edge. Brush edges with milk; sprinkle with 2 teaspoons sugar. Place on ungreased large cookie sheet.

**2** Bake 6 to 8 minutes or until light golden brown. Remove from cookie sheet to cooling rack. Cool completely, about 10 minutes.

**3** Using small star-shaped cookie cutters, cut stars out of crust scraps. Place on ungreased cookie sheet. Bake 2 to 3 minutes or until lightly browned. Cool completely, about 5 minutes.

**4** Meanwhile, in small bowl, beat whipping cream with electric mixer on high speed until stiff peaks form. In another small bowl, beat cream cheese, ¼ cup sugar and the lemon peel on medium speed until fluffy. Fold in whipped cream.

**5** Just before serving, spoon rounded 3 tablespoons filling on each pastry square. Arrange berries and stars over filling.

**1 Serving:** Calories 380; Total Fat 25g (Saturated Fat 13g; Trans Fat 0g); Cholesterol 55mg; Sodium 320mg; Total Carbohydrate 34g (Dietary Fiber 1g); Protein 4g **Exchanges:** 1 Starch, ½ Fruit, 1 Other Carbohydrate, 5 Fat **Carbohydrate Choices:** 2

## Sweet Success Tips

Here's a great Fourth of July favorite! Red, white and blue fruit and filling plus pastry stars make this dessert perfect for any patriotic occasion. Vary the cutout shapes for another celebration.

Add a little glaze with a mixture of 2 tablespoons honey and 1 teaspoon lemon juice brushed over the berries, if you like.

# Bourbon-Chocolate-Pecan Mini Pies

12 pies • PREP TIME: 45 Minutes • START TO FINISH: 1 Hour 40 Minutes

## CRUST

1⅓ cups all-purpose flour
¼ cup unsweetened baking cocoa
2 tablespoons granulated sugar
¾ teaspoon salt
½ cup shortening
¼ cup ice-cold water

## FILLING

¾ cup whole pecan halves, toasted ✱
4 oz bittersweet baking chocolate, coarsely chopped
1 egg
¼ cup packed dark brown sugar
2 tablespoons unsalted butter, melted
2 tablespoons light or dark corn syrup
2 tablespoons real maple syrup
1 tablespoon bourbon
½ teaspoon vanilla

## TOPPING

¾ cup whipping cream
2 tablespoons granulated sugar or powdered sugar
2 tablespoons shaved bittersweet chocolate

**1** Heat oven to 375°F. In food processor, place flour, cocoa, 2 tablespoons granulated sugar and the salt. Cover; process, using quick on-and-off motions, until blended. Add shortening. Cover; process, using quick on-and-off motions, until particles are size of small peas. With food processor running, pour water all at once through feed tube just until dough leaves side of bowl. Gather dough into a ball.

**2** Divide dough evenly among 12 ungreased regular-size muffin cups, pressing dough in bottoms and up sides of cups. Sprinkle pecan halves and chopped chocolate into crust-lined cups. In medium bowl, beat egg, brown sugar, melted butter, corn syrup, maple syrup, bourbon and vanilla with whisk. Spoon mixture evenly into muffin cups, about 4 teaspoons per cup.

**3** Bake 20 to 25 minutes or until filling is golden and slightly puffed in center. Cool 30 minutes; remove from pan to cooling rack.

**4** In chilled small bowl, beat whipping cream and 2 tablespoons granulated sugar with electric mixer on high speed until soft peaks form. To serve, spoon about 2 tablespoons whipped cream onto each mini pie. Sprinkle with shaved chocolate.

✱ To toast pecans, heat oven to 350°F. Spread pecans in ungreased shallow pan. Bake uncovered 6 to 10 minutes, stirring occasionally, until light brown.

**1 Pie:** Calories 430; Total Fat 27g (Saturated Fat 11g; Trans Fat 0g); Cholesterol 40mg; Sodium 170mg; Total Carbohydrate 43g (Dietary Fiber 3g); Protein 4g **Exchanges:** 1½ Starch, 1½ Other Carbohydrate, 5 Fat **Carbohydrate Choices:** 3

## Sweet Success Tips

Baked pies can be frozen up to 1 month when well wrapped. Thaw them at room temperature. To serve warm, reheat the pies in the oven.

To make shaved chocolate, let a wrapped large bar of chocolate (any type) stand in a warm place (80°F to 85°F) until slightly softened, about 10 minutes. Scrape a vegetable peeler against the chocolate, using short quick strokes.

# Peanut Butter and Jelly Cookie–Stuffed Pies

**8 pies** • **PREP TIME: 10 Minutes** • **START TO FINISH: 25 Minutes**

1 box Pillsbury refrigerated pie crusts, softened as directed on box

1 roll (16.5 oz) refrigerated peanut butter cookies

8 teaspoons strawberry jelly

1 teaspoon sugar

**1** Heat oven to 450°F. Unroll pie crusts on work surface. Cut 8 (3½-inch) rounds from each crust. Remove wrapper from cookie dough; cut 8 (⅓-inch) slices from cookie dough roll.

**2** Place 1 unbaked cookie slice in center of 8 of the crust rounds; top each with 1 teaspoon jelly. Brush crust edges with water. Top with remaining 8 crust rounds. Press edges together with fork to seal. Brush tops with water; sprinkle with sugar.

**3** Bake 10 to 12 minutes or until golden brown. Serve warm or cool. Slice remaining cookie dough and bake as directed on package; save for another use.

**1 Pie:** Calories 480; Total Fat 24g (Saturated Fat 8g; Trans Fat 2g); Cholesterol 10mg; Sodium 530mg; Total Carbohydrate 61g (Dietary Fiber 0g); Protein 5g **Exchanges:** 2 Starch, 2 Other Carbohydrate, 4½ Fat **Carbohydrate Choices:** 4

# Peanut Butter Cup Cookie–Stuffed Pies

**5 pies** · **PREP TIME: 10 Minutes** · **START TO FINISH: 25 Minutes**

1 box Pillsbury refrigerated pie crusts, softened as directed on box

5 refrigerated ready-to-bake peanut butter cookies with mini peanut butter cups (from 16-oz package)

1 teaspoon sugar

¼ cup semisweet chocolate chips, if desired

½ teaspoon shortening, if desired

**1** Heat oven to 450°F. Unroll pie crusts on work surface. Cut 5 (4-inch) rounds from each crust.

**2** Place 1 unbaked cookie in center of 5 of the crust rounds. Brush crust edges with water. Top with remaining 5 crust rounds; press edges together with fork to seal. Brush tops with water; sprinkle with sugar.

**3** Bake 10 to 12 minutes or until golden brown.

**4** In small microwavable bowl, microwave chocolate chips and shortening uncovered on High 20 to 30 seconds, stirring once, until melted and smooth. Drizzle glaze over pies. Serve warm or cool.

**1 Pie:** Calories 740; Total Fat 38g (Saturated Fat 15g; Trans Fat 3.5g); Cholesterol 10mg; Sodium 780mg; Total Carbohydrate 92g (Dietary Fiber 0g); Protein 7g **Exchanges:** 2½ Starch, 3½ Other Carbohydrate, 7 Fat **Carbohydrate Choices:** 6

## Sweet Success Tip

**Change up these easy-to-make pies by trying different kinds of cookies inside.**

# Chocolate Chip Cookie–Stuffed Pies

**8 pies** • **PREP TIME: 10 Minutes** • **START TO FINISH: 25 Minutes**

1   box Pillsbury refrigerated pie crusts, softened as directed on box

8   refrigerated ready-to-bake chocolate chip cookies (from 16-oz package)

8   milk chocolate candy drops or pieces, unwrapped

1   teaspoon sugar

**1**   Heat oven to 450°F. Unroll pie crusts on work surface. Cut 8 (3½-inch) rounds from each crust.

**2**   Place 1 unbaked cookie in center of 8 of the crust rounds; top each with 1 candy, pointed end into cookie. Brush crust edges with water. Top with remaining 8 crust rounds; press edges together with fork to seal. Brush tops with water; sprinkle with sugar.

**3**   Bake 10 to 12 minutes or until golden brown. Serve warm or cool.

**1 Pie:** Calories 510; Total Fat 27g (Saturated Fat 11g; Trans Fat 3g); Cholesterol 20mg; Sodium 450mg; Total Carbohydrate 63g (Dietary Fiber 0g); Protein 4g **Exchanges:** 1 Starch, 3 Other Carbohydrate, 5½ Fat **Carbohydrate Choices:** 4

# Ginger–Lemon Curd Petite Pies

**16 pies · PREP TIME: 40 Minutes · START TO FINISH: 1 Hour 10 Minutes**

### LEMON CURD

- ½ cup granulated sugar
- 1 tablespoon cornstarch
- 2 teaspoons grated lemon peel
- ½ cup lemon juice
- 2 eggs, slightly beaten
- 1 tablespoon finely chopped crystallized ginger

### CRUST

Two-Crust Pastry (page 8) or 1 box Pillsbury refrigerated pie crusts, softened as directed on box

### GARNISH

Powdered sugar

**1** In 1-quart saucepan, mix granulated sugar and cornstarch. Stir in lemon peel, lemon juice, eggs and ginger with whisk until blended. Cook over medium heat about 2 minutes, stirring constantly, until mixture thickens and boils. Remove from heat; pour into medium bowl. Cover with plastic wrap; refrigerate 30 minutes or until completely cool.

**2** Meanwhile, heat oven to 375°F. Line 2 cookie sheets with cooking parchment paper. On lightly floured surface, roll 1 pastry round or pie crust to ⅛-inch thickness. With 3-inch round cookie cutter, cut out 16 rounds (you may need to reroll scraps to get 16 rounds). Place on cookie sheet. With fork, poke holes all over rounds. Repeat with second pastry or pie crust— except don't poke with fork. With 1½-inch flower- or heart-shaped cookie cutter, cut out flower or heart from center of second batch of rounds. Place on cookie sheet.

**3** Bake 8 to 10 minutes or until golden brown. Remove from cookie sheets to cooling racks; cool completely.

**4** To serve, place 1 plain pastry round in each of 16 jumbo paper baking cups. Top each with about 1 tablespoon lemon curd. Sprinkle powdered sugar over rounds with flower or heart cutouts; place 1 round over lemon curd in each cup.

**1 Pie:** Calories 180; Total Fat 9g (Saturated Fat 2.5g; Trans Fat 0g); Cholesterol 25mg; Sodium 160mg; Total Carbohydrate 21g (Dietary Fiber 0g); Protein 2g **Exchanges:** 1 Starch, ½ Other Carbohydrate, 1½ Fat **Carbohydrate Choices:** 1½

## Sweet Success Tip

**For a more decorative look, use fluted cookie cutters to cut the crust rounds.**

# Lemon Curd Jumbo Pie Cupcakes

**12 cupcakes • PREP TIME: 25 Minutes • START TO FINISH: 1 Hour 45 Minutes**

1 box Pillsbury refrigerated pie crusts, softened as directed on box

1 box lemon cake mix with pudding in the mix

Water, vegetable oil and eggs called for on cake mix box

½ cup lemon curd

1 container vanilla whipped ready-to-spread frosting

**1** Heat oven to 450°F. Unroll pie crusts on work surface. Cut 6 (4¾-inch) rounds from each crust. Firmly press 1 round in bottom and up side of each of 12 nonstick jumbo muffin cups. Bake 5 minutes.

**2** Reduce oven temperature to 350°F. Make cake mix as directed on box, using water, oil and eggs. Divide lemon curd evenly among crust-lined muffin cups. Top evenly with cake batter.

**3** Bake 30 to 33 minutes or until toothpick inserted in center of cake comes out clean. Cool 10 minutes; remove from pan to cooling rack. Cool completely. Frost cupcakes with vanilla frosting.

**1 Cupcake:** Calories 530; Total Fat 26g (Saturated Fat 8g; Trans Fat 2g); Cholesterol 65mg; Sodium 490mg; Total Carbohydrate 71g (Dietary Fiber 0g); Protein 3g **Exchanges:** 1 Starch, 3½ Other Carbohydrate, 5 Fat **Carbohydrate Choices:** 5

## Sweet Success Tip

**Look for lemon curd in jars in the baking aisle, or with jams and jellies, at the grocery store.**

# Mini S'mores Hand Pies

**10 pies** • **PREP TIME: 35 Minutes** • **START TO FINISH: 50 Minutes**

## CRUST

1 box Pillsbury refrigerated pie crusts, softened as directed on box

½ cup graham cracker crumbs

¼ cup sugar

3 tablespoons butter, melted

## FILLING

½ cup marshmallow creme

2 tablespoons cream cheese, softened

2 tablespoons sugar

½ cup semisweet or milk chocolate chips

**1** Heat oven to 425°F. Line cookie sheet with cooking parchment paper.

**2** Unroll pie crusts on work surface. With 3-inch round cutter, cut 10 rounds from each crust. In shallow bowl, mix cracker crumbs and ¼ cup sugar. Brush both sides of pie crust rounds with butter; dip into crumb mixture to coat.

**3** In small bowl, stir together all filling ingredients. Spoon about 1 heaping tablespoon filling in center of 10 coated rounds. Top with remaining 10 rounds; pinch edges to seal. Place on cookie sheet.

**4** Bake 9 to 12 minutes or until golden brown. Serve warm or cool. Store in refrigerator.

**1 Pie:** Calories 320; Total Fat 17g (Saturated Fat 8g; Trans Fat 0g); Cholesterol 20mg; Sodium 280mg; Total Carbohydrate 39g (Dietary Fiber 0g); Protein 2g **Exchanges:** 1½ Starch, 1 Other Carbohydrate, 3 Fat **Carbohydrate Choices:** 2½

## Sweet Success Tip

For the cream cheese, use 1 ounce of a 3-ounce package, or scoop out 2 tablespoons from an 8-ounce container of cream cheese spread.

# Choco-Coco-Nut Mini Ice Cream Pies

**12 pies • PREP TIME: 15 Minutes • START TO FINISH: 3 Hours 50 Minutes**

1 roll (16.5 oz) refrigerated
   chocolate chip cookies
⅓ cup hot fudge topping
⅓ cup roasted chopped almonds
1 cup coconut ice cream

**1** Heat oven to 350°F. Grease 12 regular-size muffin cups with shortening or cooking spray. Cut cookie dough into 12 slices. Firmly press 1 slice in bottom and up side of each muffin cup.

**2** Bake 9 to 11 minutes or until golden brown. Cool 5 minutes; remove from pan to cooling rack. Cool completely, about 15 minutes.

**3** Spoon 1 teaspoon hot fudge topping into each cookie cup; top each with 1 teaspoon chopped almonds. Divide ice cream evenly among cups. Freeze uncovered until firm, about 3 hours.

**4** Remove pies from freezer 5 minutes before serving. Garnish with remaining hot fudge topping and almonds.

**1 Pie:** Calories 220; Total Fat 12g (Saturated Fat 4.5g; Trans Fat 0g); Cholesterol 10mg; Sodium 220mg; Total Carbohydrate 24g (Dietary Fiber 0g); Protein 2g **Exchanges:** ½ Starch, 1 Other Carbohydrate, 2½ Fat **Carbohydrate Choices:** 1½

## Sweet Success Tip

**These versatile little pies can be made with practically any kind of refrigerated cookies, topping, nuts and ice cream. Experiment to make your own delicious creation!**

# Lime Cooler Mini Ice Cream Pies

**12 pies • PREP TIME: 15 Minutes • START TO FINISH: 3 Hours 45 Minutes**

1 box Pillsbury refrigerated pie crusts, softened as directed on box

1 cup lime sherbet

1 cup vanilla ice cream

½ cup frozen whipped topping, thawed

Grated lime peel, if desired

**1** Heat oven to 450°F. Unroll pie crusts on work surface. Cut 6 (4-inch) rounds from each crust. Firmly press each round in bottom and up side of each of 12 ungreased regular-size muffin cups. Prick crusts with fork.

**2** Bake 8 to 10 minutes or until lightly browned. Cool 5 minutes; remove from pan to cooling rack. Cool completely, about 15 minutes.

**3** In medium bowl, gently mix sherbet and ice cream. Divide mixture evenly among pie crust cups. Freeze uncovered until firm, about 3 hours.

**4** Remove pies from freezer 5 minutes before serving. Garnish with whipped topping and lime peel.

**1 Pie:** Calories 190; Total Fat 10g (Saturated Fat 5g; Trans Fat 0g); Cholesterol 10mg; Sodium 190mg; Total Carbohydrate 23g (Dietary Fiber 0g); Protein 1g **Exchanges:** ½ Starch, 1 Other Carbohydrate, 2 Fat **Carbohydrate Choices:** 1½

# Orange Dream Mini Ice Cream Pies

**12 pies • PREP TIME: 15 Minutes • START TO FINISH: 3 Hours 45 Minutes**

1 box Pillsbury refrigerated pie crusts, softened as directed on box

1 cup orange sherbet

1 cup vanilla ice cream

½ cup frozen whipped topping, thawed

Orange peel twists, if desired

**1** Heat oven to 450°F. Unroll pie crusts on work surface. Cut 6 (4-inch) rounds from each crust. Firmly press each round in bottom and up side of each of 12 ungreased regular-size muffin cups. Prick crusts with fork.

**2** Bake 8 to 10 minutes or until lightly browned. Cool 5 minutes; remove from pan to cooling rack. Cool completely, about 15 minutes.

**3** In medium bowl, gently mix sherbet and ice cream. Divide mixture evenly among pie crust cups. Freeze uncovered until firm, about 3 hours.

**4** Remove pies from freezer 5 minutes before serving. Garnish with whipped topping and orange peel.

**1 Pie:** Calories 190; Total Fat 10g (Saturated Fat 5g; Trans Fat 0g); Cholesterol 10mg; Sodium 190mg; Total Carbohydrate 23g (Dietary Fiber 0g); Protein 1g **Exchanges:** ½ Starch, 1 Other Carbohydrate, 2 Fat **Carbohydrate Choices:** 1½

## Sweet Success Tip

To make an orange peel twist for the garnish, use a vegetable peeler to peel an orange in a circular motion, being careful to cut only the orange peel and not the white part or pith. A tool called a zester also can be helpful to make long, thin strips of citrus peel.

# Impossibly Easy Mini Pumpkin Pies

**12 pies • PREP TIME: 10 Minutes • START TO FINISH: 1 Hour**

½ cup Original Bisquick® mix
½ cup sugar
1½ teaspoons pumpkin pie spice
1 cup canned pumpkin
(not pumpkin pie mix)
¾ cup evaporated milk
1 teaspoon vanilla
2 eggs
1 cup frozen whipped topping,
thawed, if desired

**1** Heat oven to 375°F. Spray 12 regular-size muffin cups with cooking spray.

**2** In medium bowl, stir all ingredients except whipped topping until blended. Spoon ¼ cup of mixture into each muffin cup.

**3** Bake about 30 minutes or until tops are golden brown and edges are starting to pull away from sides of pan. Cool 10 minutes. With thin knife, loosen sides of pies from pan; remove from pan and place top side up on cooling rack. Cool 10 minutes longer. Garnish with whipped topping.

**1 Pie:** Calories 90; Total Fat 2g (Saturated Fat 1g; Trans Fat 0g); Cholesterol 35mg; Sodium 90mg; Total Carbohydrate 15g (Dietary Fiber 0g); Protein 2g **Exchanges:** ½ Starch, ½ Other Carbohydrate, ½ Fat **Carbohydrate Choices:** 1

## Sweet Success Tip

To make your own pumpkin pie spice, combine these ground spices: 4 teaspoons cinnamon, 1 teaspoon ginger, ½ teaspoon allspice, ½ teaspoon nutmeg and ½ teaspoon cloves. Use what you need for this recipe and store the remainder in a tightly covered container.

# Easy Apple Tart

**8 servings** • PREP TIME: **30 Minutes** • START TO FINISH: **2 Hours 5 Minutes**

One-Crust Pastry (page 7)
or Easy Buttermilk Pastry
(page 11)
⅔ cup packed brown sugar
⅓ cup all-purpose flour
4 cups thinly sliced peeled tart
apples (4 medium)
1 tablespoon cold butter
Granulated sugar, if desired

**1** Heat oven to 425°F. Make pastry as directed—except roll into 13-inch round. Place on ungreased large cookie sheet. Cover with plastic wrap while making filling.

**2** In large bowl, mix brown sugar and flour. Stir in apples. Remove plastic wrap from pastry. Mound apple mixture in center of pastry to within 3 inches of edge. Cut butter into small pieces; sprinkle over apples. Fold edge of pastry over apples, making pleats so it lays flat on apples (pastry will not cover apples in center). Sprinkle pastry with sugar.

**3** Bake 30 to 35 minutes or until crust is light golden brown. Cover center of pie with 5-inch square of foil during last 10 to 15 minutes of baking to prevent excessive browning. Cool on cookie sheet on cooling rack 1 hour, or serve warm if desired.

**1 Serving:** Calories 290; Total Fat 12g (Saturated Fat 3.5g; Trans Fat 2g); Cholesterol 0mg; Sodium 160mg; Total Carbohydrate 43g (Dietary Fiber 2g); Protein 2g **Exchanges:** 1 Starch, 1 Fruit, 1 Other Carbohydrate, 2 Fat **Carbohydrate Choices:** 3

## Sweet Success Tip

**There's no pie plate required for this simple recipe—place the pastry on a cookie sheet, top with the apple filling, fold up the edges and bake!**

# Maple-Apple Walnut Tart

**8 servings** • **PREP TIME: 40 Minutes** • **START TO FINISH: 3 Hours 30 Minutes**

### CRUST
1   box Pillsbury refrigerated pie crusts, softened as directed on box

### FILLING
2   eggs
½   cup packed brown sugar
¾   cup real maple syrup
¼   cup butter, melted
2   tablespoons all-purpose flour
    Dash salt
2   cups sliced peeled apples (2 medium)
¾   cup chopped walnuts
    Milk, if desired

### GARNISH, IF DESIRED
    Additional real maple syrup
1½   cups Sweetened Whipped Cream (page 80)

**1**   Heat oven to 375°F. Unroll 1 pie crust in 10-inch tart pan with removable bottom; trim crust even with top of pan.

**2**   In large bowl, beat eggs, brown sugar, ¾ cup syrup, the butter, flour and salt with whisk. Stir in apples and walnuts. Pour into crust-lined pan.

**3**   Cut second crust into 1-inch-wide strips. Place half of the strips about ½ inch apart across filling. Weave remaining strips over and under first strips. Trim ends of strips; seal edges. Brush top with milk.

**4**   Bake 45 to 50 minutes or until crust is golden brown and filling is bubbly. Cool on cooling rack at least 2 hours before serving. Remove tart from side of pan. Drizzle tart with additional syrup. Serve with whipped cream. Store in refrigerator.

**1 Serving:** Calories 510; Total Fat 26g (Saturated Fat 10g; Trans Fat 0g); Cholesterol 70mg; Sodium 350mg; Total Carbohydrate 64g (Dietary Fiber 1g); Protein 5g **Exchanges:** 1½ Starch, 3 Other Carbohydrate, 5 Fat **Carbohydrate Choices:** 4

## Sweet Success Tip
To make an easy lattice top, after placing the first pastry strips across the filling, simply place the remaining strips crosswise over the first strips instead of weaving them.

# Fresh Pear Crostata

**8 servings** • **PREP TIME: 25 Minutes** • **START TO FINISH: 1 Hour**

½ cup sugar

3 tablespoons all-purpose flour

4 cups chopped peeled ripe pears
(8 to 9 medium)

1 Pillsbury refrigerated pie crust,
softened as directed on box

1 teaspoon sugar

2 tablespoons sliced almonds

**1** Heat oven to 450°F. In medium bowl, mix ½ cup sugar and the flour. Gently stir in pears to coat. Unroll pie crust into 15×10×1-inch pan.

**2** Spoon pear mixture onto center of crust to within 2 inches of edge. Carefully fold 2-inch edge of crust up and over pear mixture, pleating crust slightly as necessary. Sprinkle 1 teaspoon sugar over crust edge.

**3** Bake 14 to 20 minutes, sprinkling almonds over filling during last 5 minutes of baking, until pears are tender and crust is golden brown. Cool 15 minutes. Cut into wedges; serve warm. Store in refrigerator.

**1 Serving:** Calories 240; Total Fat 8g (Saturated Fat 2.5g; Trans Fat 0g); Cholesterol 0mg; Sodium 110mg; Total Carbohydrate 41g (Dietary Fiber 3g); Protein 0g **Exchanges:** ½ Fruit, 2 Other Carbohydrate, 2 Fat **Carbohydrate Choices:** 3

## Sweet Success Tips

**Turn this into an apple crostata by using 4 cups chopped peeled apples instead of the pears.**

**Cinnamon ice cream makes a delicious topping for this crostata.**

# Fresh Strawberry Tarts

**6 tarts** · **PREP TIME: 30 Minutes** · **START TO FINISH: 1 Hour 15 Minutes**

1 Pillsbury refrigerated pie crust, softened as directed on box

¾ teaspoon sugar

2½ cups sliced fresh strawberries

½ cup strawberry glaze

6 tablespoons hot fudge topping, heated

⅓ cup frozen whipped topping, thawed

**1** Heat oven to 450°F. Unroll pie crust on work surface. Sprinkle sugar over crust; press in lightly. Cut 6 rounds from crust with 4-inch round cutter, or trace 6 rounds with top of large plastic glass and cut out with sharp knife (piece scraps slightly for 6th round).

**2** Spray back of muffin pan with cooking spray. Fit rounds, sugared side up, alternately over backs of muffin cups. Pinch 5 equally spaced pleats around side of each cup. Prick pastry generously with fork.

**3** Bake 5 to 7 minutes or until lightly browned. Cool 5 minutes; carefully remove from muffin cups to cooling rack. Cool completely, about 30 minutes.

**4** Meanwhile, in large bowl, gently mix strawberries and glaze. Refrigerate until thoroughly chilled, about 30 minutes.

**5** Just before serving, spoon 1 tablespoon fudge topping into each cooled baked shell. Spoon about ⅓ cup berry mixture into each shell. Garnish with whipped topping.

**1 Tart:** Calories 360; Total Fat 16g (Saturated Fat 9g; Trans Fat 0g); Cholesterol 0mg; Sodium 240mg; Total Carbohydrate 52g (Dietary Fiber 2g); Protein 2g **Exchanges:** ½ Starch, ½ Fruit, 2½ Other Carbohydrate, 3 Fat **Carbohydrate Choices:** 3½

## Sweet Success Tips

Look for containers of strawberry glaze in the produce section at the supermarket.

If you have mint growing in your garden, it makes a pretty garnish for these berry tarts—and it has an amazing aroma too!

# Blueberry-Lemon Tart

**16 servings · PREP TIME: 20 Minutes · START TO FINISH: 1 Hour 15 Minutes**

1   box Pillsbury refrigerated pie crusts, softened as directed on box

2   containers (6 oz each) lemon fat-free yogurt

1   package (8 oz) cream cheese, softened

1   can (21 oz) blueberry pie filling

1   cup fresh blueberries

**1**   Heat oven to 375°F. Unroll 1 pie crust on center of ungreased large cookie sheet. Unroll second pie crust and place over first crust, matching edges and pressing to seal. With rolling pin, roll into 14-inch round.

**2**   Fold ½ inch of crust edge under, forming border; press to seal seam (if desired, flute edge). Prick crust generously with fork.

**3**   Bake 20 to 25 minutes or until golden brown. Cool completely on cooling rack.

**4**   In medium bowl, beat yogurt and cream cheese with electric mixer on medium speed until blended. Spread evenly over cooled baked crust. Spread pie filling evenly over yogurt mixture. Top with blueberries. Cut into wedges to serve. Store in refrigerator.

**1 Serving:** Calories 230; Total Fat 12g (Saturated Fat 6g; Trans Fat 0g); Cholesterol 20mg; Sodium 160mg; Total Carbohydrate 29g (Dietary Fiber 0g); Protein 2g **Exchanges:** ½ Starch, 1½ Other Carbohydrate, 2½ Fat **Carbohydrate Choices:** 2

## Sweet Success Tip

**Get a head start on this recipe by baking the crust a day before you plan to assemble and serve the tart.**

# Nectarine-Plum Crostata

**8 servings** • **PREP TIME: 40 Minutes** • **START TO FINISH: 2 Hours 50 Minutes**

## CRUST

| | |
|---|---|
| 1½ | cups all-purpose flour |
| 1 | teaspoon sugar |
| ¼ | teaspoon salt |
| ½ | cup cold butter |
| 1 | egg yolk |
| 4 | to 5 tablespoons cold water |

## FILLING

| | |
|---|---|
| ½ | cup sugar |
| 3 | tablespoons all-purpose flour |
| ¼ | teaspoon ground cinnamon |
| 3 | cups sliced nectarines |
| 2 | cups sliced plums |
| 1 | tablespoon lemon juice |
| 2 | tablespoons cold butter |
| 1 | tablespoon sugar |

**1** In medium bowl, mix 1½ cups flour, 1 teaspoon sugar and the salt. Cut in ½ cup butter, using pastry blender or fork, until crumbly. Stir in egg yolk with fork. Sprinkle with water, 1 tablespoon at a time, tossing until ball of dough forms. Flatten ball to ½-inch thickness. Wrap in plastic wrap; refrigerate 30 minutes.

**2** Heat oven to 425°F. On lightly floured surface, roll pastry into 13-inch round, about ⅛ inch thick. Place on ungreased large cookie sheet.

**3** In large bowl, mix ½ cup sugar, 3 tablespoons flour and the cinnamon. Stir in nectarines and plums until coated. Sprinkle with lemon juice; mix. Spoon fruit mixture onto center of pastry, spreading to within 3 inches of edge. Cut 2 tablespoons butter into small pieces; sprinkle over filing. Fold edge of pastry up and over fruit mixture, pleating crust slightly as necessary. Brush edge of pastry with small amount of water; sprinkle with 1 tablespoon sugar.

**4** Bake 30 to 40 minutes or until crust is golden brown and fruit is tender. Cool on cooling rack at least 1 hour before serving.

**1 Serving:** Calories 340; Total Fat 15g (Saturated Fat 9g; Trans Fat 0.5g); Cholesterol 65mg; Sodium 180mg; Total Carbohydrate 45g (Dietary Fiber 2g); Protein 4g **Exchanges:** 1 Starch, 1 Fruit, 1 Other Carbohydrate, 3 Fat **Carbohydrate Choices:** 3

## Sweet Success Tips

You can keep a fruit crostata at room temperature for 2 days; after that, store it loosely covered in the refrigerator up to 2 days longer.

Serve the crostata with ice cream or whipped cream (page 80), if desired.

# Mixed Berry Crumble Tart

**8 servings • PREP TIME: 40 Minutes • START TO FINISH: 1 Hour 25 Minutes**

One-Crust Pastry (page 7)
or 1 Pillsbury refrigerated pie
crust, softened as directed
on box

1½ cups sliced fresh strawberries

1½ cups fresh blueberries

1 cup fresh raspberries

⅔ cup sugar

2 tablespoons cornstarch

¾ cup all-purpose flour

½ cup sugar

1 teaspoon grated orange peel

⅓ cup butter, melted

**1** Heat oven to 425°F. Roll pastry round or pie crust into 13-inch round. Fold into fourths and place in 10- or 11-inch tart pan with removable bottom; unfold and press against bottom and side of pan. Trim overhanging edge of pastry even with top of pan.

**2** In large bowl, gently toss berries with ⅔ cup sugar and the cornstarch. Spoon into pastry-lined pan.

**3** In small bowl, stir flour, ½ cup sugar, the orange peel and melted butter with fork until crumbly. Sprinkle evenly over berries.

**4** Bake 35 to 45 minutes or until fruit bubbles in center. Remove tart from side of pan. Serve warm.

**1 Serving:** Calories 420; Total Fat 18g (Saturated Fat 6g; Trans Fat 2g); Cholesterol 20mg; Sodium 200mg; Total Carbohydrate 60g (Dietary Fiber 3g); Protein 3g **Exchanges:** 1 Starch, 3 Fruit, 3½ Fat **Carbohydrate Choices:** 4

# Mixed Pluot Tart

**8 servings** • **PREP TIME: 30 Minutes** • **START TO FINISH: 3 Hours 5 Minutes**

6   fresh pluots (mixed variety), thinly sliced
¾   cup sugar
2   tablespoons quick-cooking tapioca
½   teaspoon ground cinnamon
¼   teaspoon ground nutmeg
1   box Pillsbury refrigerated pie crusts, softened as directed on box
1   egg white, beaten
2   tablespoons sugar

**1**   Heat oven to 450°F. In large bowl, mix pluots, ¾ cup sugar, the tapioca, cinnamon and nutmeg. Let stand 15 minutes.

**2**   Meanwhile, make pie crusts as directed on box for Two-Crust Pie using 9-inch tart pan with removable bottom. Brush egg white over crust. Pour fruit mixture into crust-lined pan. Top with second crust; seal and flute. Cut slits in several places in top crust. Brush crust with egg white; sprinkle with 2 tablespoons sugar.

**3**   Bake 25 to 35 minutes or until golden brown. Cover with sheet of foil during last 10 minutes of baking to prevent excessive browning. Cool on cooling rack at least 2 hours before serving. Remove tart from side of pan.

Lorraine Demeter of West Allis, Wisconsin, won the Pillsbury Refrigerated Pie Crust Pie Baking Championship at the 2009 Wisconsin State Fair with this recipe.

**1 Serving:** Calories 330; Total Fat 12g (Saturated Fat 5g; Trans Fat 0g); Cholesterol 5mg; Sodium 290mg; Total Carbohydrate 54g (Dietary Fiber 0g); Protein 0g **Exchanges:** 1 Starch, ½ Fruit, 2 Other Carbohydrate, 2 Fat **Carbohydrate Choices:** 3½

## Sweet Success Tips

Pluots are a hybrid of the plum and apricot. They have a smooth skin, plum-like shape and sweet flavor.

To add a special serving touch, warm apricot jam in the microwave and drizzle it on dessert plates before adding slices of the pluot tart.

# Strawberries and Cream Tart

10 servings • PREP TIME: 25 Minutes • START TO FINISH: 1 Hour 40 Minutes

### CRUST

1   box Pillsbury refrigerated pie crusts, softened as directed on box

### FILLING

1   package (8 oz) cream cheese, softened

⅓   cup sugar

¼   teaspoon almond extract

1   cup whipping cream, whipped

### TOPPING

4   cups fresh strawberries, hulled, halved

½   cup semisweet chocolate chips

1   tablespoon shortening

**1**   Heat oven to 450°F. Bake pie crust as directed on box for One-Crust Baked Shell using 10-inch tart pan with removable bottom or 9-inch glass pie plate. Cool completely on cooling rack.

**2**   In large bowl, beat cream cheese with electric mixer on medium speed until fluffy. Gradually add sugar and almond extract; beat well. Fold in whipped cream. Spread filling into cooled baked shell. Arrange strawberry halves over filling. Refrigerate while making chocolate drizzle.

**3**   In 1-quart saucepan, melt chocolate chips and shortening over low heat, stirring constantly, until smooth. Drizzle over strawberries and filling. Refrigerate until set, about 30 minutes. Remove tart from side of pan. Store in refrigerator.

**1 Serving:** Calories 340; Total Fat 24g (Saturated Fat 13g; Trans Fat 0.5g); Cholesterol 55mg; Sodium 190mg; Total Carbohydrate 28g (Dietary Fiber 1g); Protein 3g **Exchanges:** 1 Fruit, 1 Other Carbohydrate, ½ High-Fat Meat, 4 Fat **Carbohydrate Choices:** 2

## Sweet Success Tips

For a different look, leave the strawberries whole and dip the pointed end of each berry into melted chocolate so it's half covered. Place the dipped berries, stem ends down, on a waxed paper–lined tray. Refrigerate until set. Arrange berries on top of the tart.

If you enjoy a more pronounced almond flavor, use another ¼ teaspoon almond extract in the filling.

# Raspberry-Lemon Meringue Tart

**8 servings** • **PREP TIME: 1 Hour** • **START TO FINISH: 4 Hours**

### CRUST

1 box Pillsbury refrigerated pie crusts, softened as directed on box

### RASPBERRY FILLING

¼ cup sugar

2 tablespoons cornstarch

1 bag (12 oz) frozen raspberries, thawed, drained and juice reserved

### LEMON FILLING

1 cup sugar

2 tablespoons cornstarch

2 tablespoons all-purpose flour

¼ teaspoon salt

1½ cups water

3 egg yolks, beaten

1 tablespoon grated lemon peel

⅓ cup lemon juice

1 tablespoon butter

### MERINGUE

⅓ cup sugar

1 tablespoon cornstarch

⅓ cup water

3 egg whites

⅛ teaspoon salt

**1** Heat oven to 450°F. Bake pie crust as directed on box for One-Crust Baked Shell using 9-inch tart pan with removable bottom or 9-inch glass pie plate. Cool completely on cooling rack.

**2** In 2-quart saucepan, mix ¼ cup sugar and 2 tablespoons cornstarch. If necessary, add water to reserved raspberry juice to measure ½ cup; gradually add raspberry liquid to sugar mixture. Cook and stir over medium heat until thickened. Gently fold in raspberries. Cool 10 minutes. Spread in cooled baked shell.

**3** In another 2-quart saucepan, mix 1 cup sugar, 2 tablespoons cornstarch, the flour and ¼ teaspoon salt. Gradually stir in 1½ cups water, stirring until smooth. Heat to boiling over medium heat; cook and stir 1 minute longer. Remove from heat. Quickly stir about ½ cup hot mixture into beaten egg yolks; mix well. Gradually stir egg mixture back into hot mixture. Stir in lemon peel and juice. Cook over medium heat about 5 minutes, stirring constantly. Remove from heat. Add butter; stir until melted. Let stand 10 minutes.

**4** Meanwhile, heat oven to 350°F. In 1-quart saucepan, mix ⅓ cup sugar and 1 tablespoon cornstarch. Stir in ⅓ cup water; cook and stir over medium heat until thickened. Cool completely by placing in freezer about 15 minutes. In small bowl, beat egg whites and ⅛ teaspoon salt with electric mixer on high speed until soft peaks form. Add cooled cornstarch mixture, beating on medium speed until stiff peaks form. Carefully pour hot lemon filling over raspberry filling. Gently spread meringue over lemon filling carefully sealing meringue to edge of crust to prevent shrinking or weeping.

**5** Bake 20 to 25 minutes or until meringue reaches 160°F. Cool on cooling rack 2 hours; refrigerate until serving time. Remove tart from side of pan. Store in refrigerator.

**1 Serving:** Calories 360; Total Fat 9g (Saturated Fat 4g; Trans Fat 0g); Cholesterol 85mg; Sodium 280mg; Total Carbohydrate 64g (Dietary Fiber 3g); Protein 4g **Exchanges:** 1 Starch, ½ Fruit, 3 Other Carbohydrate, 1½ Fat **Carbohydrate Choices:** 4

## Sweet Success Tip

**Egg whites will really fluff up during beating if you let them stand at room temperature for about 30 minutes first.**

# White and Dark Chocolate Raspberry Tart

**10 servings • PREP TIME: 1 Hour • START TO FINISH: 5 Hours 15 Minutes**

1 Pillsbury refrigerated pie crust, softened as directed on box

2 tablespoons orange juice

1 teaspoon unflavored gelatin

1½ cups whipping cream

1 package (6 oz) white chocolate baking bars, chopped

1 bag (12 oz) frozen raspberries, thawed, drained and juice reserved

1 tablespoon cornstarch

1 tablespoon sugar

1 cup fresh raspberries, if desired

2 oz semisweet baking chocolate, cut into pieces

2 tablespoons butter

**1** Heat oven to 450°F. Place pie crust in 10-inch tart pan with removable bottom or 10-inch springform pan, pressing 1 inch up side of pan. Bake as directed on box for One-Crust Baked Shell. Cool completely on cooling rack.

**2** Pour orange juice into 2-quart saucepan. Sprinkle gelatin over juice; let stand 5 minutes to soften. Stir in ¾ cup of the whipping cream; heat over low heat, stirring frequently, until gelatin is dissolved. Stir in white chocolate until melted and smooth. Transfer to medium bowl; refrigerate about 30 minutes, stirring occasionally, until cool but not set.

**3** In blender or food processor, place thawed raspberries and any juice. Cover; blend until pureed. Set strainer over 2-cup measuring cup. Press puree with back of spoon through strainer to remove seeds. If necessary, add water to raspberry puree to measure ½ cup. In 1-quart saucepan, mix cornstarch and sugar. Gradually add raspberry puree. Cook and stir over low heat until thickened. Fold in fresh raspberries; spread over crust. Refrigerate 15 minutes.

**4** Meanwhile, in chilled small bowl, beat remaining ¾ cup whipping cream with electric mixer on high speed until stiff peaks form. Fold whipped cream into white chocolate mixture. Spoon and spread over raspberry layer. Refrigerate 1 hour or until filling is set.

**5** In 1-quart saucepan, melt semisweet chocolate and butter over low heat, stirring frequently; carefully pour and spread over white chocolate layer. Refrigerate at least 2 hours or until set. Remove from refrigerator about 30 minutes before serving to soften chocolate layers. Remove tart from side of pan. Store in refrigerator.

**1 Serving:** Calories 390; Total Fat 27g (Saturated Fat 16g; Trans Fat 0g); Cholesterol 50mg; Sodium 135mg; Total Carbohydrate 33g (Dietary Fiber 2g); Protein 3g **Exchanges:** 1 Starch, 1 Other Carbohydrate, 5½ Fat **Carbohydrate Choices:** 2

## Sweet Success Tips

This elegant tart can be a year-round favorite—just leave out the fresh raspberries when unavailable.

Garnish slices of tart with white chocolate curls and additional fresh raspberries, if desired.

# Creamy Three-Berry Tart

10 servings • PREP TIME: 30 Minutes • START TO FINISH: 3 Hours

## CINNAMON CRUST

1½ cups finely crushed graham crackers (24 squares)

⅓ cup butter, melted

3 tablespoons sugar

1 teaspoon ground cinnamon

## FILLING

1 package (8 oz) cream cheese, room temperature

½ cup sugar

2 tablespoons lemon juice

1 cup whipping cream

1 cup fresh blueberries

1 cup fresh blackberries

1 cup fresh raspberries

¼ cup strawberry jam

1 tablespoon orange juice

**1** Heat oven to 350°F. In medium bowl, mix all crust ingredients. Press mixture firmly and evenly against bottom and up side of 9-inch tart pan with removable bottom. Bake 8 to 12 minutes or until golden brown. Cool completely on cooling rack.

**2** In large bowl, beat cream cheese, ½ cup sugar and the lemon juice with an electric mixer on low speed until blended. Add whipping cream; beat on high speed 3 to 5 minutes or until light and fluffy. Spread filling in cooled baked tart shell. Refrigerate at least 2 hours.

**3** If necessary, use a thin-bladed knife to loosen side of pan from any places where it sticks to the crust. Remove tart from side of pan. Arrange berries on filling.

**4** In small microwavable bowl, microwave jam uncovered on High about 20 seconds or until warm. Stir in orange juice with fork; mix well. Gently brush glaze over berries.

**1 Serving:** Calories 380; Total Fat 23g (Saturated Fat 14g; Trans Fat 1g); Cholesterol 70mg; Sodium 220mg; Total Carbohydrate 39g (Dietary Fiber 2g); Protein 3g **Exchanges:** 1 Starch, ½ Fruit, 1 Other Carbohydrate, 4½ Fat **Carbohydrate Choices:** 2½

## Sweet Success Tips

Instead of using mixed berries, you can use 3 cups of just blueberries, blackberries or raspberries.

To remove the tart from the pan, place pan on a wide, short can and pull down the side of the pan. If you don't have a can available, hold the tart in both hands and push the bottom up, letting the side of the pan slip onto your arm.

# Ultimate Fresh Fruit Tart

8 servings · PREP TIME: 30 Minutes · START TO FINISH: 5 Hours

1 Pillsbury refrigerated pie crust, softened as directed on box

2 oz unsweetened baking chocolate

1¼ cups whipping cream

4 egg yolks

6 tablespoons butter

⅓ cup sugar

1 tablespoon cornstarch

3 teaspoons vanilla

1½ cups fresh fruit (such as raspberries, blackberries, sliced nectarines, sliced kiwifruit)

½ cup apricot jam

1 tablespoon water

1  Heat oven to 450°F. Press pie crust in 10-inch tart pan with removable bottom; prick bottom and side with fork. Bake 10 minutes; reduce oven temperature to 350°F. Bake about 10 minutes longer or until golden brown.

2  In 1-quart saucepan, heat chocolate and ¼ cup of the whipping cream over low heat until chocolate is melted; stir until smooth. Spread mixture in bottom of baked crust. Refrigerate.

3  In small bowl, beat egg yolks; set aside. In heavy 2-quart saucepan, cook butter, sugar and cornstarch over medium-high heat, stirring constantly, until mixture thickens and boils; boil 1 minute. Stir small amount of hot sugar mixture into egg yolks. Slowly add egg mixture to remaining sugar mixture in saucepan, stirring rapidly to avoid lumps. Cook 1 minute over low heat. Remove from heat; stir in vanilla. Transfer to medium bowl. Cover; refrigerate 3 hours.

4  In chilled medium bowl, beat remaining 1 cup whipping cream with electric mixer on high speed until stiff peaks form. Fold cold egg mixture into whipped cream with whisk. Spread filling over chocolate layer in crust. Arrange fruit on filling.

5  In small microwavable bowl, microwave jam and water uncovered on High 1 minute. Brush glaze over fruit. Refrigerate 1 hour 30 minutes before serving. Remove tart from side of pan. Store in refrigerator.

**Marjorie Weiner from Brooklyn, Connecticut, entered this winning recipe at the 2010 Connecticut State Fair Pie Contest.**

**1 Serving:** Calories 480; Total Fat 32g (Saturated Fat 18g; Trans Fat 1g); Cholesterol 170mg; Sodium 220mg; Total Carbohydrate 42g (Dietary Fiber 3g); Protein 4g **Exchanges:** 2 Starch, 1 Other Carbohydrate, 6 Fat **Carbohydrate Choices:** 3

## Sweet Success Tip

**Did you know? Unsweetened baking chocolate is chocolate in its rawest form, containing 50 to 58 percent cocoa butter.**

# Cranberry-Chocolate Tart

10 servings • PREP TIME. 50 Minutes • START TO FINISH· 2 Hours 25 Minutes

## PASTRY

- 1¼ cups all-purpose flour
- ⅓ cup shortening
- 1 teaspoon vinegar
- 2 to 4 tablespoons cold water
- ½ cup semisweet chocolate chips
- ¼ cup half-and-half

## TOPPING

- 2 cups fresh or frozen cranberries
- 1 cup sugar
- ½ cup water

## FILLING

- ¾ cup milk
- 1 box (4-serving size) vanilla instant pudding and pie filling mix
- 1 cup sour cream
- 1 tablespoon grated orange peel or 2 tablespoons orange-flavored liqueur

**1** Heat oven to 450°F. In medium bowl, place flour. Cut in shortening, using pastry blender or fork, until mixture looks like coarse crumbs. Sprinkle with vinegar. Add water, 1 tablespoon at a time, mixing lightly with fork, until dough is just moist enough to hold together.

**2** Shape dough into a ball. With floured fingers, press dough evenly in bottom and up side of 10-inch tart pan with removable bottom or 9-inch glass pie plate. Flute edge, if desired. Prick bottom and side of pastry generously with fork. Bake 8 to 12 minutes or until lightly browned.

**3** In 1-quart saucepan, melt chocolate chips and half-and-half, stirring until smooth. Spread in baked shell. Cool slightly; refrigerate until chocolate is firm, about 15 minutes.

**4** Meanwhile, in another 1-quart saucepan, heat all topping ingredients to boiling, stirring until sugar is dissolved. Boil gently 3 to 4 minutes or until most of cranberries pop. Cool at least 30 minutes.

**5** In small bowl, beat milk and pudding mix with electric mixer on low speed about 1 minute or until blended; stir in sour cream and orange peel. Let stand 5 minutes. Pour over chocolate layer, spreading to cover evenly. Spoon cooled cranberry topping over filling, covering completely. Refrigerate at least 1 hour. Remove from refrigerator 10 minutes before serving. Remove tart from side of pan. Store in refrigerator.

**1 Serving:** Calories 350; Total Fat 15g (Saturated Fat 7g; Trans Fat 1.5g); Cholesterol 20mg; Sodium 160mg; Total Carbohydrate 51g (Dietary Fiber 2g); Protein 3g **Exchanges:** ½ Starch, 3 Other Carbohydrate, 3 Fat **Carbohydrate Choices:** 3½

## Sweet Success Tip

Use a small cookie or canapé cutter to cut leaf shapes out of crust scraps. Bake the cutouts on an ungreased cookie sheet 6 to 8 minutes or until golden brown. Use the cutouts to garnish the tart.

# Merry Cherry-Plum-Berry Tart

**8 servings** • **PREP TIME: 30 Minutes** • **START TO FINISH: 2 Hours 40 minutes**

## CRUST AND TOPPING

- 1 box Pillsbury refrigerated pie crusts
- ¼ cup chopped almonds
- 3 tablespoons turbinado sugar (raw sugar)

## FILLING

- ½ cup dried cranberries
- ½ cup dried cherries
- ¾ cup amaretto
- 1¼ cups fresh blueberries
- 2 plums, cut into pieces
- 4½ teaspoons cornstarch

## WHITE AMARETTO TRUFFLE SAUCE

- ⅓ cup white vanilla baking chips
- ½ cup whipping cream
- 2 tablespoons amaretto

**1** Heat oven to 425°F. Let 1 of the pie crusts stand at room temperature 15 minutes to soften (keep remaining crust cold). Unroll softened crust in 9-inch tart pan with removable bottom; lightly press crust into fluted edge of pan. Run rolling pin across top of pan to cut off excess crust. Prick side and bottom of crust with fork. Bake 10 minutes.

**2** Chop cold pie crust into small pieces, adding almonds and sugar while chopping, to make crumbly topping. Set aside.

**3** In 2-quart saucepan, heat cranberries, cherries and ¾ cup amaretto over medium heat 5 minutes. Add blueberries and plums. Cook 15 minutes longer. Stir in cornstarch. Pour filling into partially baked crust. Sprinkle crumbly topping over filling.

**4** Bake 30 to 35 minutes or until top is golden brown and filling is bubbly. Cool on cooling rack at least 15 minutes before serving.

**5** Meanwhile, place white chips in small heatproof bowl. In 1-quart saucepan, heat cream over low heat. As soon as bubbles form around edge of pan, remove from heat and pour warm cream over chips; stir until melted and smooth. Stir in 2 tablespoons amaretto. Refrigerate 1 hour, stirring every 15 minutes.

**6** Remove tart from side of pan. Cut into slices. Stir sauce well. Drizzle each slice of tart with about 2 tablespoons sauce. Store tart and sauce in refrigerator.

**1 Serving:** Calories 500; Total Fat 22g (Saturated Fat 9g; Trans Fat 0g); Cholesterol 25mg; Sodium 240mg; Total Carbohydrate 64g (Dietary Fiber 2g); Protein 2g **Exchanges:** 1 Starch, 1 Fruit, 2½ Other Carbohydrate, 4½ Fat **Carbohydrate Choices:** 4

# Amaretto Peach Tart

**10 servings** • **PREP TIME: 25 Minutes** • **START TO FINISH: 2 Hours 25 Minutes**

### CRUST

1   Pillsbury refrigerated pie crust, softened as directed on box

### FILLING

1   package (8 oz) cream cheese, softened

⅓   cup sugar

2   tablespoons amaretto or ¼ teaspoon almond extract

2   eggs

### TOPPING

2   tablespoons peach preserves

1   tablespoon amaretto or ⅛ teaspoon almond extract

2   cups thinly sliced peeled peaches (2 to 3 medium)

**1**   Heat oven to 450°F. Place pie crust in 10-inch tart pan with removable bottom as directed on box for One-Crust Filled Pie. Press in bottom and up side of pan. Trim edge if necessary. DO NOT PRICK CRUST. Bake 10 minutes. If crust puffs in center, flatten gently with back of wooden spoon. Cool on cooling rack 15 minutes. Reduce oven temperature to 375°F.

**2**   In medium bowl, beat cream cheese and sugar with electric mixer on medium speed until light and fluffy. Beat in 2 tablespoons amaretto and the eggs until well blended. Pour into partially baked crust.

**3**   Bake 18 to 22 minutes or until filling is set. Cool 10 minutes. Refrigerate 1 hour or until completely cooled and set.

**4**   Just before serving, in medium microwavable bowl, microwave preserves on High 20 seconds. Stir in 1 tablespoon amaretto. Add peaches; stir to coat. Arrange peach slices over top of tart. Remove tart from side of pan. Cover and refrigerate any remaining tart.

**1 Serving:** Calories 250; Total Fat 15g (Saturated Fat 7g; Trans Fat 0g); Cholesterol 70mg; Sodium 170mg; Total Carbohydrate 25g (Dietary Fiber 0g); Protein 3g **Exchanges:** 1 Starch, ½ Other Carbohydrate, 3 Fat **Carbohydrate Choices:** 1½

## Sweet Success Tip

**One bag (16 ounces) frozen sliced peaches without syrup, thawed and well drained, can be substituted for the fresh peaches.**

# Rhubarb Custard Tart

**12 servings** • **PREP TIME: 20 Minutes** • **START TO FINISH: 1 Hour 40 Minutes**

### CRUST

1 Pillsbury refrigerated pie crust, softened as directed on box

### TOPPING

½ cup all-purpose flour

½ cup packed brown sugar

¼ cup quick-cooking oats

¼ cup cold butter

### FILLING

¾ cup granulated sugar

3 tablespoons all-purpose flour

½ cup whipping cream

2 tablespoons apricot preserves

1 egg yolk

3 cups sliced fresh or frozen rhubarb, thawed, drained

**1** Heat oven to 375°F. Place cookie sheet on middle oven rack while oven heats. Place pie crust in 9-inch tart pan with removable bottom or 9-inch glass pie plate as directed on box for One-Crust Filled Pie. Press in bottom and up side of pan. Trim edge if necessary.

**2** In small bowl, mix ½ cup flour, the brown sugar and oats. Cut in butter, using pastry blender or fork, until mixture is crumbly; set aside.

**3** In large bowl, mix granulated sugar and 3 tablespoons flour. Stir in whipping cream, preserves and egg yolk until well blended. Stir in rhubarb. Pour into crust-lined pan. Sprinkle topping evenly over filling.

**4** Place tart on heated cookie sheet. Bake 40 to 50 minutes or until filling bubbles around edge and topping is deep golden brown. Cool on cooling rack 30 minutes before serving. Remove tart from side of pan. Cover and refrigerate any remaining tart.

**1 Serving:** Calories 280; Total Fat 12g (Saturated Fat 6g; Trans Fat 0g); Cholesterol 40mg; Sodium 110mg; Total Carbohydrate 40g (Dietary Fiber 0g); Protein 2g **Exchanges:** 1 Starch, 1½ Other Carbohydrate, 2½ Fat **Carbohydrate Choices:** 2½

## Sweet Success Tips

**Rhubarb is highly perishable and should be stored tightly wrapped in the refrigerator; use within 3 days of purchase.**

**Top slices of this warm tart with a spoonful of whipped cream or scoop of ice cream.**

# Country Rhubarb Crostata

**8 servings • PREP TIME: 20 Minutes • START TO FINISH: 4 Hours 20 Minutes**

## CRUST

1   box Pillsbury refrigerated pie crusts, softened as directed on box

## FILLING

1   cup sugar
3   tablespoons all-purpose flour
½   teaspoon grated orange peel
3   eggs, slightly beaten
½   cup sour cream
3½   cups sliced fresh or frozen rhubarb

## TOPPING

¼   cup sugar
¼   cup all-purpose flour
2   tablespoons butter, softened

**1**   Heat oven to 375°F. Place pie crust in 9-inch glass pie plate as directed on box for One-Crust Filled Pie (do not trim or flute crust).

**2**   In medium bowl, mix 1 cup sugar, 3 tablespoons flour and the orange peel. Stir in eggs and sour cream. Add rhubarb; toss gently. Spoon filling into crust-lined plate. Fold edges of crust over filling, ruffling decoratively.

**3**   In small bowl, mix all topping ingredients until crumbly. Sprinkle evenly over filling.

**4**   Bake 50 to 60 minutes or until crust is light golden brown. Cool on cooling rack 3 hours before serving. Store in refrigerator.

**1 Serving:** Calories 350; Total Fat 14g (Saturated Fat 7g; Trans Fat 0g); Cholesterol 100mg; Sodium 190mg; Total Carbohydrate 52g (Dietary Fiber 1g); Protein 4g **Exchanges:** ½ Starch, 1 Fruit, 2 Other Carbohydrate, 3 Fat **Carbohydrate Choices:** 3½

## Sweet Success Tips

If you're using frozen rhubarb in this tart, there's no need to thaw it first.

The grated orange peel adds zip to the filling, but feel free to leave it out if you don't care for it.

# Piña Colada Tart

**12 servings** • **PREP TIME:** 20 Minutes • **START TO FINISH:** 1 Hour 50 Minutes

1    Pillsbury refrigerated pie crust, softened as directed on box

¼    cup sugar

¼    cup cornstarch

1    cup canned cream of coconut (not coconut milk)

1    cup whole milk

2    egg yolks

1    tablespoon butter

2    tablespoons dark rum or 1½ teaspoons rum extract

1    can (20 oz) sliced pineapple, drained, slices cut in half

¼    cup apricot jam

1    tablespoon dark rum or orange juice

2    tablespoons flaked coconut, toasted✱

**1**    Heat oven to 425°F. Bake pie crust as directed on box for One-Crust Baked Shell using 10-inch tart pan with removable bottom. Cool completely on cooling rack.

**2**    Meanwhile, in 2-quart saucepan, mix sugar and cornstarch. In small bowl, mix cream of coconut, milk and egg yolks; gradually stir into sugar mixture. Cook and stir over medium heat until mixture thickens and boils. Boil 1 minute, stirring constantly; remove from heat. Beat in butter and 2 tablespoons rum with whisk. Cool at room temperature 1 hour.

**3**    Pour cooled filling into cooled baked shell. Arrange pineapple slices in decorative pattern over filling.

**4**    In small microwavable bowl, microwave jam uncovered on High 20 seconds. Add 1 tablespoon rum; mix well with fork. Brush glaze over pineapple. Sprinkle with toasted coconut. Remove tart from side of pan. Store tart covered in refrigerator.

✱ To toast coconut, heat the oven to 350°F. Spread the coconut in an ungreased shallow pan. Bake uncovered 5 to 7 minutes, stirring occasionally, until golden brown.

**1 Serving:** Calories 230; Total Fat 14g (Saturated Fat 10g; Trans Fat 0g); Cholesterol 40mg; Sodium 105mg; Total Carbohydrate 24g (Dietary Fiber 1g); Protein 2g **Exchanges:** 1 Starch, ½ Other Carbohydrate, 2½ Fat **Carbohydrate Choices:** 1½

## Sweet Success Tips

**Cream of coconut is a canned mixture of coconut paste, water and sugar. It's available in supermarkets, usually near the soft drinks, and in liquor stores.**

# Fruit Pizza

**12 servings • PREP TIME: 20 Minutes • START TO FINISH: 2 Hours 10 Minutes**

1 roll (16.5 oz) refrigerated sugar cookies

1 package (8 oz) cream cheese, softened

⅓ cup sugar

½ teaspoon vanilla

2 kiwifruit, peeled, halved lengthwise and sliced

1 cup halved or quartered fresh strawberries

1 cup fresh blueberries

½ cup apple jelly

**1** Heat oven to 350°F. Spray 12-inch pizza pan with cooking spray. In pan, break up cookie dough; press dough evenly in pan to form crust.

**2** Bake 16 to 20 minutes or until golden brown. Cool completely on cooling rack, about 30 minutes.

**3** In small bowl, beat cream cheese, sugar and vanilla with electric mixer on medium speed until fluffy. Spread mixture over cooled baked crust. Arrange fruit over cream cheese layer. Stir jelly until smooth; spoon or brush over fruit. Refrigerate until chilled, at least 1 hour.

**4** Cut into wedges or squares to serve. Store any remaining fruit pizza covered in refrigerator.

**1 Serving:** Calories 320; Total Fat 15g (Saturated Fat 6g; Trans Fat 2g); Cholesterol 35mg; Sodium 170mg; Total Carbohydrate 43g (Dietary Fiber 1g); Protein 3g **Exchanges:** 1 Starch, 2 Other Carbohydrate, 3 Fat **Carbohydrate Choices:** 3

## Sweet Success Tips

For best results, keep the cookie dough very cold until you're ready to use it.

If fresh blueberries aren't available, frozen berries can be used. Be sure to thaw and drain them. Raspberries, halved green grapes and sliced almonds would also be great toppings for this fruit pizza.

Jeweled Cranberry-Apricot Tart (page 242)

# holiday pies

# Apple-Ginger Tart with Cider-Bourbon Sauce

8 servings • PREP TIME: 25 Minutes • START TO FINISH: 1 Hour 45 Minutes

## CRUST

- 1 Pillsbury refrigerated pie crust, softened as directed on box

## FILLING

- ½ cup packed brown sugar
- 2 tablespoons cornstarch
- 2 tablespoons finely chopped crystallized ginger
- 1 teaspoon ground cinnamon
- 4 cups thinly sliced peeled cooking apples (4 medium)

## SAUCE

- 1¼ cups apple cider
- 2 tablespoons butter
- 2 tablespoons packed brown sugar
- 1 tablespoon cornstarch
- 2 tablespoons bourbon

**1** Heat oven to 450°F. Place cookie sheet in oven while oven heats. Place pie crust in 9-inch tart pan with removable bottom as directed on box for One-Crust Filled Pie. Bake on preheated cookie sheet 7 minutes.

**2** Meanwhile, in large bowl, mix ½ cup brown sugar, 2 tablespoons cornstarch, the ginger and cinnamon until blended. Add apples; toss until evenly coated. Arrange apples in concentric circles in partially baked crust, overlapping slices and beginning at outside edge and working toward center.

**3** Cover top of tart with foil; place on preheated cookie sheet. Bake 40 minutes. Remove foil; bake 8 to 10 minutes longer or until apples are tender and crust is golden brown. Cool on cooling rack 30 minutes while making sauce.

**4** In 1-quart saucepan, heat cider to boiling over high heat. Boil 4 to 6 minutes, stirring occasionally, until reduced to 1 cup. Stir in butter and 2 tablespoons brown sugar; continue boiling 2 minutes, stirring occasionally. In small bowl, stir 1 tablespoon cornstarch into bourbon until dissolved. Stir bourbon mixture into sauce; boil 1 minute, stirring constantly.

**5** To serve, remove tart from side of pan. Cut tart into wedges; serve with warm sauce.

**1 Serving:** Calories 280; Total Fat 10g (Saturated Fat 4.5g; Trans Fat 0g); Cholesterol 10mg; Sodium 140mg; Total Carbohydrate 46g (Dietary Fiber 1g); Protein 0g **Exchanges:** 3 Other Carbohydrate, 2 Fat **Carbohydrate Choices:** 3

## Sweet Success Tip

Try not to stretch the pie crust when you fit it into the tart pan—just press gently. The crust may shrink during baking if it's stretched.

# Sour Cream–Apple Pie

**8 servings** • **PREP TIME: 30 Minutes** • **START TO FINISH: 3 Hours 40 Minutes**

## CRUST

1 Pillsbury refrigerated pie crust, softened as directed on box

## FILLING

1¼ cups sour cream
¾ cup granulated sugar
¼ cup all-purpose flour
¼ teaspoon salt
2 teaspoons vanilla
1 egg
6 cups thinly sliced peeled baking apples (6 medium)

## TOPPING

½ cup all-purpose flour
½ cup chopped walnuts
¼ cup granulated sugar
¼ cup packed light brown sugar
½ teaspoon ground cinnamon
Dash salt
3 tablespoons cold butter

**1** Heat oven to 400°F. Place pie crust in 9-inch glass pie plate as directed on box for One-Crust Filled Pie.

**2** In large bowl, beat all filling ingredients except apples with whisk until well blended. Stir in apples. Spoon filling into crust-lined plate. Cover crust edge with pie shield ring or strips of foil to prevent excessive browning.

**3** Bake 15 minutes. Reduce oven temperature to 350°F; bake 30 minutes longer.

**4** Meanwhile, in medium bowl, mix all topping ingredients except butter. Cut in butter, using pastry blender or fork, until mixture looks like coarse crumbs; refrigerate until ready to use.

**5** Sprinkle topping over pie. Bake 20 to 25 minutes or until topping is golden brown. Cool on cooling rack at least 2 hours before serving. Store covered in refrigerator.

**1 Serving:** Calories 500; Total Fat 24g (Saturated Fat 10g; Trans Fat 0g); Cholesterol 65mg; Sodium 260mg; Total Carbohydrate 67g (Dietary Fiber 2g); Protein 4g **Exchanges:** 1 Starch, 3½ Other Carbohydrate, 4½ Fat **Carbohydrate Choices:** 4½

## Sweet Success Tip

**The best baking apples are slightly tart. Top choices are Granny Smith, Braeburn, Cortland, Northern Spy and Rome Beauty.**

# Caramel-Apple-Ginger Crostata

**6 servings • PREP TIME: 20 Minutes • START TO FINISH: 1 Hour 25 Minutes**

1   Pillsbury refrigerated pie crust, softened as directed on box

6   cups thinly sliced peeled baking apples (6 medium)

½   cup packed brown sugar

3   tablespoons all-purpose flour

2   tablespoons finely chopped crystallized ginger

1   teaspoon ground cinnamon

1   tablespoon cold butter

1   tablespoon granulated sugar

⅓   cup caramel topping

**1**   Heat oven to 450°F. Line 15×10×1-inch pan with cooking parchment paper. Unroll pie crust in pan.

**2**   In large bowl, toss apples, brown sugar, flour, ginger and cinnamon. Mound apple mixture in center of crust, leaving 2-inch border. Cut butter into small pieces; sprinkle over apples. Fold edge of crust over apples, pleating to fit. Brush crust edge with water; sprinkle with granulated sugar.

**3**   Loosely cover top and sides of crostata with foil; bake 20 minutes. Remove foil; bake 9 to 13 minutes longer or until crust is golden brown and apples are tender. Immediately run spatula or pancake turner under crust to loosen. Cool 30 minutes.

**4**   To serve, cut crostata into wedges; drizzle with caramel topping.

**1 Serving:** Calories 380; Total Fat 10g (Saturated Fat 4.5g; Trans Fat 0g); Cholesterol 10mg; Sodium 260mg; Total Carbohydrate 70g (Dietary Fiber 2g); Protein 2g **Exchanges:** 1 Starch, ½ Fruit, 3 Other Carbohydrate, 2 Fat **Carbohydrate Choices:** 4½

## Sweet Success Tip

**Shop for crystallized ginger, usually packed in plastic containers, in the spice section or produce department at the grocery store.**

# Caramel Apple Pie

**8 servings • PREP TIME: 40 Minutes • START TO FINISH: 3 Hours 50 Minutes**

1   box Pillsbury refrigerated pie crusts, softened as directed on box
1   cup granulated sugar
1¼ cups all-purpose flour
1   teaspoon ground cinnamon
5   cups thinly sliced peeled apples (5 medium)
½   cup caramel apple dip
2   tablespoons milk
½   cup packed brown sugar
½   cup cold butter
    Ice cream, if desired

**1** Heat oven to 375°F. Place 1 pie crust in 9-inch glass pie plate as directed on box for One-Crust Filled Pie.

**2** In large bowl, mix granulated sugar, ¼ cup of the flour and the cinnamon. Add apples; toss to coat. Spoon mixture into crust-lined plate. In small bowl, mix 2 tablespoons of the caramel apple dip and the milk; drizzle over apples.

**3** In medium bowl, mix remaining 1 cup flour and the brown sugar. Cut in butter, using pastry blender or fork, until mixture looks like coarse crumbs. Sprinkle over filling.

**4** Cut second crust into ½-inch-wide strips. Place half of the strips across filling in pie plate. Weave remaining strips with first strips to form lattice. Trim ends of strips even with edge of bottom crust. Fold trimmed edge of bottom crust over ends of strips, forming a high stand-up rim; seal and flute.

**5** Bake 50 to 60 minutes or until golden brown. Cool 10 minutes. Drizzle remaining 6 tablespoons caramel apple dip over pie. Cool on cooling rack at least 2 hours before serving. Serve with ice cream.

**Judith Waldron of Rossville, Indiana, won the Pillsbury Refrigerated Pie Crust Pie Baking Championship at the 2009 Indiana State Fair with this recipe.**

**1 Serving:** Calories 630; Total Fat 24g (Saturated Fat 12g; Trans Fat 0g); Cholesterol 40mg; Sodium 420mg; Total Carbohydrate 100g (Dietary Fiber 2g); Protein 4g **Exchanges:** 2 Starch, ½ Fruit, 4 Other Carbohydrate, 4½ Fat **Carbohydrate Choices:** 6½

# Steps to Great Crust

**Using Pillsbury refrigerated pie crust makes pie making a snap! It's the secret shortcut to fresh, homemade pies in no time, because it's ready to fill in seconds and is the perfect base for any pie.**

## GET TO GREAT CRUST IN 5 EASY STEPS

### 1 Warm Them Up

Refrigerated crusts need to warm up a bit in order move and shape them. Let crusts stand at room temperature 15 minutes, or microwave 1 pouch on Defrost for 10 to 20 seconds before unrolling. Remove frozen crusts from the box and let stand 1 hour to 1 hour 30 minutes at room temperature before unrolling.

### 2 Fix the Cracks

Repairing any cracks before baking will reduce the chance of cracks reappearing while baking. Wet your fingers slightly with cold water and press edges together. For wide cracks, patch with extra dough and seal with wet fingers.

### 3 Pick the Perfect Pan

Made for 8- or 9-inch pie plates or 10-inch tart pans, Pillsbury refrigerated pie crusts can also be rolled and cut into other shapes, as long as you don't stretch the dough (or it may shrink while baking). For best results, follow the guidelines in Choosing Pie Plates, page 6.

### 4 Keep the Crust in Its Place

Keep the crust anchored to the pan by pressing it firmly (without stretching) against the side and bottom of the pan. Keep the crust flat, if baking an unfilled pie crust, by generously pricking the side and bottom of the crust with a fork before baking.

### 5 Watch the Browning

Keep the edge of the pastry on pies from getting too brown while baking by carefully covering with a pie shield ring or strips of foil after the first 15 minutes of baking (or as directed in the recipe).

# Pear Cream Pie

**8 servings** • **PREP TIME: 1 Hour** • **START TO FINISH: 5 Hours 20 Minutes**

## CRUST

1 box Pillsbury refrigerated pie crusts, softened as directed on box

## FRUIT FILLING

5 cups sliced peeled pears
¾ teaspoon lemon juice
¾ cup sugar
1¼ cups water

## CREAM FILLING

3 egg yolks
1 cup sugar
3 tablespoons cornstarch
¼ teaspoon salt
1¼ cups milk
¾ cup evaporated milk (from 12-oz can)
1½ teaspoons vanilla
¼ cup butter, cut into small pieces

## TOPPING

1 cup whipping cream
¼ cup sugar
½ teaspoon vanilla

**1** Heat oven to 450°F. Place 1 pie crust in 9-inch glass pie plate as directed on box for One-Crust Baked Shell. Bake 9 to 11 minutes or until light brown.

**2** Cut second crust into ½-inch-wide strips. Line large cookie sheet with cooking parchment paper. On cookie sheet, weave strips together to make lattice design; trim to fit top of pie. Bake 7 to 8 minutes or until golden brown.

**3** Meanwhile, place pears in large saucepan; sprinkle with lemon juice. Add ¾ cup sugar and the water. Cook over medium heat until pears are tender and almost all liquid has evaporated. Cool slightly while cooking cream filling.

**4** In medium saucepan, beat egg yolks with whisk or fork. Stir in 1 cup sugar. Add cornstarch and salt; mix well. Stir in 1¼ cups milk, the evaporated milk and 1½ teaspoons vanilla until blended. Stir in butter. Cook and stir over medium heat until thick and bubbly.

**5** Spread fruit filling in cooled baked shell. Spread cream filling over top. Carefully slide lattice top onto pie. Cool; refrigerate 4 hours or until filling is set.

**6** In chilled medium bowl, beat all topping ingredients with electric mixer on high speed until stiff peaks form (do not overbeat). Pipe whipped cream around edge of pie, or garnish as desired. Store covered in refrigerator.

**Bill Blake of Star City, Arkansas, won the Pillsbury Refrigerated Pie Crust Pie Baking Championship at the 2009 Arkansas State Fair with this recipe.**

**1 Serving:** Calories 690; Total Fat 32g (Saturated Fat 17g; Trans Fat 0.5g); Cholesterol 145mg; Sodium 420mg; Total Carbohydrate 95g (Dietary Fiber 3g); Protein 5g **Exchanges:** 2 Starch, ½ Fruit, 4 Other Carbohydrate, 6 Fat **Carbohydrate Choices:** 6

## Sweet Success Tip

Use a pastry cutter (also called a pastry wheel) to cut the lattice strips for a special touch.

# Almond-Pear Pie

8 servings • PREP TIME: 20 Minutes • START TO FINISH: 2 Hours 25 Minutes

1 box Pillsbury refrigerated pie crusts, softened as directed on box
1 can (8 oz) or tube (7 oz) almond paste
5 cups ½-inch slices ripe but firm peeled pears (about 4 medium)
2 tablespoons sugar
2 tablespoons all-purpose flour
1¼ teaspoons apple pie spice
1 tablespoon lemon juice
1 egg, beaten
¼ cup sliced almonds
1 teaspoon sugar

**1** Heat oven to 375°F. Make pie crusts as directed on box for Two-Crust Pie using 9-inch glass pie plate. Shape almond paste into a disk. On lightly floured surface, roll or pat disk into 8-inch round. Place in crust-lined plate.

**2** In large bowl, mix pears, 2 tablespoons sugar, the flour, apple pie spice and lemon juice. Spoon mixture over almond paste. Top with second crust; seal and flute. Cut slits in several places in top crust. Brush crust with egg. Sprinkle with almonds and 1 teaspoon sugar.

**3** Bake 55 to 65 minutes or until pears are tender and crust is deep golden brown. Cool on cooling rack at least 1 hour before serving.

**1 Serving:** Calories 360; Total Fat 16g (Saturated Fat 3.5g; Trans Fat 0g); Cholesterol 30mg; Sodium 120mg; Total Carbohydrate 49g (Dietary Fiber 5g); Protein 5g **Exchanges:** ½ Starch, ½ Fruit, 2 Other Carbohydrate, ½ High-Fat Meat, 2½ Fat **Carbohydrate Choices:** 3

## Sweet Success Tips

Pears are best picked when hard and green (underripe) and they will continue ripening after picking. If your pears are still too firm, plan on ripening them at home for a few days before you use them.

Anjou pears are a great fall and winter pear. They're juicy when ripe but hold their shape well.

# Pumpkin Pie

**8 servings** • **PREP TIME: 20 Minutes** • **START TO FINISH: 3 Hours 35 Minutes**

One-Crust Pastry (page 7) or 1 Pillsbury refrigerated pie crust, softened as directed on box

2 eggs

½ cup sugar

1 teaspoon ground cinnamon

½ teaspoon salt

½ teaspoon ground ginger

⅛ teaspoon ground cloves

1 can (15 oz) pumpkin (not pumpkin pie mix)

1 can (12 oz) evaporated milk

Sweetened Whipped Cream (page 80), if desired

**1** Heat oven to 425°F. Place pastry round or pie crust in 9-inch glass pie plate. Bake as directed for Partially Baked One-Crust Pie (page 9).

**2** In medium bowl, beat eggs slightly with whisk. Beat in remaining ingredients except whipped cream. Pour filling into partially baked crust (to prevent spilling, place pie plate on oven rack before adding filling). Cover crust edge with pie crust shield ring or strips of foil to prevent excessive browning.

**3** Bake 15 minutes. Reduce oven temperature to 350°F. Bake about 45 minutes longer or until knife inserted in center comes out clean, removing shield or foil during last 15 minutes of baking. Cool on cooling rack 1 hour; refrigerate uncovered until completely chilled, at least 1 hour.

**4** Serve pie with whipped cream. Store any remaining pie loosely covered in refrigerator.

**1 Serving:** Calories 300; Total Fat 15g (Saturated Fat 5g; Trans Fat 2g); Cholesterol 65mg; Sodium 360mg; Total Carbohydrate 33g (Dietary Fiber 2g); Protein 7g **Exchanges:** 1 Starch, 1 Fruit, 3 Fat **Carbohydrate Choices:** 2

**Praline Pumpkin Pie** Make pie as directed—except decrease second bake time to 35 minutes. Mix ⅓ cup packed brown sugar, ⅓ cup chopped pecans and 1 tablespoon butter, softened. Sprinkle over pie. Bake about 10 minutes longer or until knife inserted in center comes out clean.

## Sweet Success Tip
Be sure to use canned pumpkin, not pumpkin pie mix, in this recipe. The mix has sugar and spices already in it, so if you have purchased the pumpkin pie mix, follow the directions on that label.

# Pumpkin Cheese Tart

10 servings · PREP TIME: 40 Minutes · START TO FINISH: 1 Hour 30 Minutes

## CRUST

- ⅓ cup quick-cooking oats
- 1 cup gingersnap cookie crumbs (about 20 cookies)
- 3 tablespoons butter, melted
- ¼ teaspoon ground cinnamon

## CREAM CHEESE FILLING

- 2 containers (8 oz each) reduced-fat cream cheese
- ⅓ cup granulated sugar
- 2 tablespoons fat-free (skim) milk
- 1 tablespoon all-purpose flour
- ½ teaspoon vanilla
- 1 egg

## PUMPKIN FILLING

- 1 cup canned pumpkin (not pumpkin pie mix)
- ⅓ cup packed brown sugar
- ½ teaspoon pumpkin pie spice

## CARAMEL SAUCE

- ½ cup packed brown sugar
- ¼ cup fat-free (skim) milk
- ¼ cup corn syrup
- 2 tablespoons water
- 1 tablespoon butter
- ¼ teaspoon vanilla

**1** Heat oven to 375°F. Spray 10-inch tart pan with removable bottom with cooking spray. In small bowl, mix all crust ingredients. Press in bottom and up side of pan. Bake 6 to 8 minutes or until set. Cool on cooling rack.

**2** In large bowl, beat all cream cheese filling ingredients with electric mixer on medium speed until smooth and creamy. Reserve ⅔ cup cream cheese filling; set aside.

**3** In small bowl, mix all pumpkin filling ingredients. Add to remaining cream cheese filling; mix well. Spoon into partially baked crust. Spoon dollops of reserved cream cheese filling randomly over pumpkin filling. Swirl with knife to marble mixtures.

**4** Bake 25 to 30 minutes or until set. Cool 10 minutes. Remove tart from side of pan. Serve warm, or cool 1 hour and refrigerate until serving time.

**5** Just before serving, in 1-quart saucepan, heat all caramel sauce ingredients to boiling over medium heat, stirring constantly. Boil 1 minute. Remove from heat. Serve warm over tart. Store in refrigerator.

**1 Serving:** Calories 370; Total Fat 17g (Saturated Fat 10g; Trans Fat 1g); Cholesterol 70mg; Sodium 310mg; Total Carbohydrate 47g (Dietary Fiber 1g); Protein 7g **Exchanges:** 1 Starch, 2 Other Carbohydrate, ½ High-Fat Meat, 2½ Fat **Carbohydrate Choices:** 3

## Sweet Success Tip

**Instead of making the caramel sauce from scratch, use purchased caramel topping. For an extra-special presentation, use the caramel sauce or topping to create a design on each guest's plate before serving.**

# Pumpkin Meringue Pie

**8 servings** • **PREP TIME: 25 Minutes** • **START TO FINISH: 5 Hours 50 Minutes**

1    Pillsbury refrigerated pie crust, softened as directed on box

3    whole eggs

¾    cup packed brown sugar

1    can (15 oz) pumpkin (not pumpkin pie mix)

1    cup half-and-half

1    teaspoon ground cinnamon

¾    teaspoon ground ginger

¼    teaspoon salt

¼    teaspoon ground cloves

1    teaspoon vanilla

6    egg whites

½    teaspoon cream of tartar

1    cup granulated sugar

**1**    Heat oven to 425°F. Place pie crust in 9-inch glass pie plate as directed on box for One-Crust Filled Pie. Prick bottom and side of crust thoroughly with fork. Bake 12 to 15 minutes or until light golden brown. Cool on cooling rack 15 minutes. Reduce oven temperature to 350°F.

**2**    In medium bowl, beat whole eggs with whisk. Stir in brown sugar and pumpkin until well blended. Stir in half-and-half, cinnamon, ginger, salt, cloves and vanilla until blended. Pour filling into partially baked crust. Bake 45 to 50 minutes or until golden brown and center is almost set.

**3**    In large bowl, beat egg whites and cream of tartar with electric mixer on medium speed until soft peaks form. Gradually add granulated sugar, 2 tablespoons at a time, beating on high speed until stiff glossy peaks form. Gently spread meringue over hot filling carefully sealing meringue to edge of crust to prevent shrinking or weeping.

**4**    Bake 15 to 17 minutes or until meringue is light brown. Cool on cooling rack away from drafts 4 hours. Store in refrigerator.

**1 Serving:** Calories 390; Total Fat 12g (Saturated Fat 5g; Trans Fat 0g); Cholesterol 85mg; Sodium 290mg; Total Carbohydrate 64g (Dietary Fiber 2g); Protein 7g **Exchanges:** 4½ Other Carbohydrate, ½ Very Lean Meat, ½ Lean Meat, 2 Fat **Carbohydrate Choices:** 4

## Sweet Success Tip

Investing in good-quality cooling racks is worth it. The metal tines should be heavy-duty so they can support the weight of fruit-filled or custard pies without sagging in the center. The clearance between the rack and countertop allows for proper air circulation, which results in even cooling.

# Pumpkin–Butterscotch Cream Tart

**10 servings** • **PREP TIME: 30 Minutes** • **START TO FINISH: 3 Hours 10 Minutes**

## CRUST

1 Pillsbury refrigerated pie crust, softened as directed on box

## FILLING

1 can (15 oz) pumpkin (not pumpkin pie mix)
2 eggs
½ cup granulated sugar
½ cup packed light brown sugar
1 tablespoon ground cinnamon
1 teaspoon ground ginger
½ teaspoon ground mace
½ teaspoon ground cloves
1 cup heavy whipping cream

## BUTTERSCOTCH CREAM

1 package (3 oz) cream cheese, softened
2½ cups frozen reduced-fat whipped topping, thawed
¼ cup butterscotch instant pudding and pie filling mix

## GARNISH

½ cup whipping cream
1 tablespoon white chocolate instant pudding and pie filling mix
1 teaspoon vanilla
Pecan halves, if desired

**1** Heat oven to 450°F. Place pie crust in 10-inch tart pan with removable bottom as directed on box for One-Crust Filled Pie. Press in bottom and up side of pan. Trim edge if necessary. DO NOT PRICK CRUST.

**2** In large bowl, beat all filling ingredients with whisk until thoroughly combined. Pour filling into crust-lined pan.

**3** Bake 20 minutes. Reduce oven temperature to 400°F. Bake 15 to 20 minutes longer or until knife inserted in center comes out clean. If necessary, cover crust edge with pie shield ring or strips of foil to prevent excessive browning. Cool on cooling rack 1 hour. Refrigerate at least 1 hour or until cold.

**4** In medium bowl, beat cream cheese with electric mixer on medium speed until creamy. Add whipped topping and dry butterscotch pudding mix; beat until smooth and creamy. Spread over filling.

**5** Remove tart from side of pan. In chilled small bowl, beat ½ cup whipping cream, the white chocolate pudding mix and vanilla with electric mixer on high speed until stiff peaks form. Spoon cream mixture into decorating bag; pipe cream around edge and center of tart. Garnish with pecan halves. Store covered in refrigerator.

**Susan Brown from Minneapolis, Minnesota, won a blue ribbon at the 2010 Minnesota State Fair Pie Contest.**

**1 Serving:** Calories 420; Total Fat 25g (Saturated Fat 14g; Trans Fat 0.5g); Cholesterol 105mg; Sodium 250mg; Total Carbohydrate 45g (Dietary Fiber 2g); Protein 4g **Exchanges:** 1 Starch, 2 Other Carbohydrate, 5 Fat **Carbohydrate Choices:** 3

## Sweet Success Tip
If you prefer to cook your own pumpkin, choose smaller pumpkins—the pumpkin flesh will be more tender and juicy. You'll need 1½ cups cooked pumpkin to substitute for the 15-oz can.

# Roasted Sweet Potato Pie

**8 servings** • **PREP TIME: 15 Minutes** • **START TO FINISH: 6 Hours 30 Minutes**

1½  lb dark-orange sweet potatoes
(about 2 medium-large)

1  Pillsbury refrigerated pie crust,
softened as directed on box

½  cup packed brown sugar

½  cup granulated sugar

½  teaspoon ground cinnamon

½  teaspoon ground nutmeg

¼  teaspoon salt

½  cup butter, softened

½  cup whipping cream

2  tablespoons bourbon
or 1 teaspoon vanilla

2  eggs

**1**  Heat oven to 400°F. Line cookie sheet with foil. Place sweet potatoes on cookie sheet. Roast 1 hour or until tender. Cut potatoes in half. Scoop out pulp into medium bowl; discard skins. Reduce oven temperature to 350°F.

**2**  Place pie crust in 9½-inch glass deep-dish pie plate as directed on box for One-Crust Filled Pie. Beat sweet potato pulp with electric mixer on medium speed until creamy. Add remaining ingredients; beat 1 minute or until well blended. Pour filling into crust-lined plate.

**3**  Bake 1 hour 15 minutes or until knife inserted near center comes out clean. Cool completely on cooling rack, about 4 hours. Store in refrigerator.

**1 Serving:** Calories 440; Total Fat 24g (Saturated Fat 14g; Trans Fat 0.5g); Cholesterol 100mg; Sodium 360mg; Total Carbohydrate 51g (Dietary Fiber 2g); Protein 3g **Exchanges:** 3 Other Carbohydrate, 1 Vegetable, 5 Fat **Carbohydrate Choices:** 3½

## Sweet Success Tip

For a special topping on top of each slice of pie, fold flaked or shredded coconut into some sweetened whipped cream.

# Pecan-Pumpkin Pie

8 servings  •  PREP TIME: 25 Minutes  •  START TO FINISH: 3 Hours 15 Minutes

## CRUST

1 Pillsbury refrigerated pie crust, softened as directed on box

1 teaspoon all-purpose flour

## PUMPKIN FILLING

1 cup canned pumpkin (not pumpkin pie mix)

1 egg, beaten

½ cup half-and-half

½ cup granulated sugar

1½ teaspoons pumpkin pie spice

## PECAN FILLING

¼ cup light or dark corn syrup

2 eggs, beaten

2 tablespoons butter, melted

¼ cup packed brown sugar

½ teaspoon vanilla

1½ cups pecan halves

**1** Heat oven to 450°F. Unroll pie crust. Sprinkle each side of crust with ½ teaspoon flour; smooth flour over crust. Place crust in 9-inch glass pie plate. Carefully line pastry with double thickness of foil, gently pressing foil to bottom and side of pastry. Let foil extend over edge to prevent excessive browning.

**2** Bake 10 minutes. Carefully remove foil; bake 3 to 4 minutes longer or until pastry begins to brown and has set. Reduce oven temperature to 350°F.

**3** In medium bowl, beat all pumpkin filling ingredients with whisk until blended. Pour filling into partially baked crust. In another medium bowl, beat all pecan filling ingredients except pecans with whisk until blended. Stir in pecans. Carefully spoon mixture over pumpkin layer.

**4** Bake 30 to 35 minutes or until knife inserted 1 inch from edge comes out clean. Cool completely on cooling rack, about 2 hours. Store covered in refrigerator.

**1 Serving:** Calories 440; Total Fat 26g (Saturated Fat 7g; Trans Fat 0g); Cholesterol 95mg; Sodium 190mg; Total Carbohydrate 46g (Dietary Fiber 2g); Protein 5g **Exchanges:** 1½ Starch, 1½ Other Carbohydrate, 5 Fat **Carbohydrate Choices:** 3

## Sweet Success Tip

Sprinkling flour on the pie crust ensures that the crust will be well baked and helps keep the filling from seeping into the crust, making it soggy.

# Streusel-Topped Sweet Potato Pie Squares

**15 servings** • **PREP TIME: 25 Minutes** • **START TO FINISH: 3 Hours 35 Minutes**

## CRUST

- 1 Pillsbury refrigerated pie crust, softened as directed on box

## FILLING

- 3 cans (15 oz each) sweet potatoes in syrup, drained, mashed
- 1 can (14 oz) sweetened condensed milk (not evaporated)
- 3 eggs, beaten
- ¾ cup half-and-half
- 2 teaspoons pumpkin pie spice
- ½ teaspoon salt

## TOPPING

- ½ cup packed brown sugar
- ½ cup quick-cooking oats
- ¼ cup all-purpose flour
- ½ teaspoon ground cinnamon
- ¼ cup cold butter

## GARNISH

- 1 cup whipping cream
- 2 tablespoons powdered sugar

**1** Heat oven to 400°F. Unroll pie crust in 13×9-inch pan. Press crust in bottom and ¼ inch up sides of pan, cutting to fit; press seams firmly to seal. DO NOT PRICK CRUST. Bake 10 minutes. Immediately press bubbles down with back of wooden spoon.

**2** Reduce oven temperature to 350°F. In large bowl, beat all filling ingredients with whisk until blended. Pour over partially baked crust.

**3** Bake 40 minutes. Meanwhile, in medium bowl, mix brown sugar, oats, flour and cinnamon. Cut in butter, using pastry blender or fork, until mixture looks like coarse crumbs. Sprinkle over filling.

**4** Bake 15 to 20 minutes longer or until knife inserted in center comes out clean (surface may be puffy in spots). Cool completely on cooling rack. Refrigerate at least 2 hours before serving.

**5** In chilled medium bowl, beat whipping cream and powdered sugar with electric mixer on high speed until soft peaks form. Cut dessert into squares; serve with whipped cream. Store in refrigerator.

**1 Serving:** Calories 400; Total Fat 17g (Saturated Fat 10g; Trans Fat 0g); Cholesterol 90mg; Sodium 270mg; Total Carbohydrate 55g (Dietary Fiber 3g), Protein 6g **Exchanges:** 3 Other Carbohydrate, ½ Milk, ½ Vegetable, 2½ Fat **Carbohydrate Choices:** 3½

## Sweet Success Tips

You can substitute fresh cooked dark-orange sweet potatoes for the canned version. Two pounds sweet potatoes will yield about 3 cups mashed.

Use a food processor to easily mash the sweet potatoes.

# Pecan Pie

**8 servings** • **PREP TIME: 20 Minutes** • **START TO FINISH: 1 Hour 10 Minutes**

One-Crust Pastry (page 7),
Easy Buttermilk Pastry
(page 11) or Press-in-the-Pan
Pastry (page 11)

⅔ cup sugar

⅓ cup butter, melted

1 cup light or dark corn syrup

3 eggs

1 cup pecan halves or broken
pecans

**1** Heat oven to 375°F. Place pastry in 9-inch glass pie plate.

**2** In medium bowl, beat sugar, butter, corn syrup and eggs with whisk until well blended. Stir in pecans. Pour into pastry-lined plate.

**3** Bake 40 to 50 minutes or until center is set. Serve warm or chilled.

**1 Serving:** Calories 530; Total Fat 29g (Saturated Fat 8g; Trans Fat 2g); Cholesterol 100mg; Sodium 420mg; Total Carbohydrate 62g (Dietary Fiber 2g); Protein 5g **Exchanges:** 2 Starch, 2 Other Carbohydrate, 6 Fat **Carbohydrate Choices:** 4

**Kentucky Pecan Pie** Add 2 tablespoons bourbon or 1 teaspoon brandy extract with the corn syrup. Stir in 1 cup semisweet chocolate chips (6 ounces) with the pecans.

## Sweet Success Tip

Instead of granulated sugar, use a combination of ⅓ cup granulated sugar and ⅓ cup packed light or dark brown sugar, if you like. The flavor will be just a bit more caramel-like.

# Browned Butter Pecan Pie

**8 servings** • **PREP TIME: 30 Minutes** • **START TO FINISH: 5 Hours 25 Minutes**

½ cup butter (do not use margarine)

1 cup sugar

1 cup light corn syrup

1 teaspoon vanilla bean paste or vanilla

¼ teaspoon salt

4 eggs, beaten

1 Pillsbury refrigerated pie crust, softened as directed on box

1¼ cups pecan halves

**1** In 2-quart saucepan, melt butter over medium heat, stirring frequently. Cook 2 to 5 minutes, stirring often, until butter stops foaming and browned bits form at bottom of pan. Stir in sugar and corn syrup. Cook over low heat 15 to 18 minutes, stirring frequently, until sugar is dissolved. Cool 1 hour. Add vanilla bean paste, salt and eggs; beat with whisk until well blended.

**2** Heat oven to 325°F. Place pie crust in 9-inch glass pie plate as directed on box for One-Crust Filled Pie. Pour filling into crust-lined plate. Arrange pecan halves in concentric circles on top of filling. With fork, gently press pecans into filling to glaze, keeping pecans in circular pattern.

**3** Bake 50 to 55 minutes or until filling is set and crust is golden brown. Cover crust edge with strips of foil after 40 minutes to prevent excessive browning. Cool completely on cooling rack, 3 to 4 hours, before slicing.

**1 Serving:** Calories 590; Total Fat 31g (Saturated Fat 12g; Trans Fat 0g); Cholesterol 125mg; Sodium 360mg; Total Carbohydrate 72g (Dietary Fiber 1g); Protein 5g **Exchanges:** ½ Starch, 4½ Other Carbohydrate, ½ Medium-Fat Meat, 5½ Fat **Carbohydrate Choices:** 5

# Spiced Chocolate Chip–Pecan Pie

**8 servings** · **PREP TIME: 20 Minutes** · **START TO FINISH: 1 Hour 30 Minutes**

## CRUST

1 Pillsbury refrigerated pie crust, softened as directed on box

## FILLING

¾ cup light corn syrup
½ cup sugar
3 tablespoons butter, melted
1 teaspoon ground cinnamon
¼ teaspoon ground nutmeg
1 teaspoon vanilla
3 eggs
1 cup coarsely chopped pecans
¾ cup semisweet chocolate chips

## TOPPING

¼ cup semisweet chocolate chips
1 teaspoon shortening
1½ cups Sweetened Whipped Cream (page 80), if desired

**1** Heat oven to 325°F. Place pie crust in 9-inch glass pie plate as directed on box for One-Crust Filled Pie.

**2** In large bowl, beat corn syrup, sugar, butter, cinnamon, nutmeg, vanilla and eggs with whisk. Stir in pecans and ¾ cup chocolate chips. Spread evenly in crust-lined plate. Cover crust edge with pie shield ring or strips of foil to prevent excessive browning.

**3** Bake 30 minutes. Remove pie shield ring or foil; bake 15 to 25 minutes longer or until pie is deep golden brown and filling is set. Cool 15 minutes.

**4** In small microwavable bowl, microwave ¼ cup chocolate chips and the shortening uncovered on High 1 minute; stir until smooth. Drizzle chocolate over top of pie. Serve warm or cool. Garnish with whipped cream. Store in refrigerator.

**1 Serving:** Calories 550; Total Fat 30g (Saturated Fat 11g; Trans Fat 0g); Cholesterol 95mg; Sodium 190mg; Total Carbohydrate 66g (Dietary Fiber 2g); Protein 4g **Exchanges:** 1 Starch, 3½ Other Carbohydrate, 6 Fat **Carbohydrate Choices:** 4½

## Sweet Success Tips

Flavor the whipped cream with a little brown sugar and a dash of cinnamon.

If you like dark chocolate, substitute dark chocolate chips for the semisweet chips.

# Golden Pecan Pie

**8 servings** • **PREP TIME: 15 Minutes** • **START TO FINISH: 3 Hours 5 Minutes**

1   Pillsbury refrigerated pie crust, softened as directed on box
⅓   cup packed brown sugar
1½   teaspoons all-purpose flour
1¼   cups light corn syrup
1¼   teaspoons vanilla
3   eggs
1½   cups pecan halves or pieces
2   tablespoons butter, melted

**1**   Heat oven to 375°F. Place pie crust in 9-inch glass pie plate as directed on box for One-Crust Filled Pie.

**2**   In large bowl, mix brown sugar, flour, corn syrup, vanilla and eggs until well blended. Stir in pecans and butter. Pour filling into crust-lined plate.

**3**   Bake 40 to 50 minutes or until filling is puffed and pie is golden brown. Cool completely on cooling rack, about 2 hours, before serving. Store in refrigerator.

**1 Serving:** Calories 500; Total Fat 24g (Saturated Fat 6g; Trans Fat 0g); Cholesterol 80mg; Sodium 210mg; Total Carbohydrate 65g (Dietary Fiber 2g); Protein 5g **Exchanges:** 1½ Starch, 3 Other Carbohydrate, 4½ Fat **Carbohydrate Choices:** 4

**Orange Pecan Pie** Add ½ teaspoon grated orange peel to the filling. If desired, garnish with candied orange peel.

# Bittersweet Chocolate Pecan Pie

**8 servings** • **PREP TIME: 15 Minutes** • **START TO FINISH: 3 Hours 5 Minutes**

1 Pillsbury refrigerated pie crust, softened as directed on box
½ cup sugar
1 cup dark corn syrup
2 tablespoons all-purpose flour
3 tablespoons bourbon, if desired
1 tablespoon butter, melted
1 teaspoon vanilla
2 eggs
1¼ cups pecan halves
1 cup bittersweet chocolate chips, melted, cooled

**1** Heat oven to 350°F. Place pie crust in 9-inch glass pie plate as directed on box for One-Crust Filled Pie.

**2** In large bowl, beat sugar, corn syrup, flour, bourbon, butter, vanilla and eggs with whisk. Stir in pecans and melted chocolate. Pour filling into crust-lined plate.

**3** Bake 48 to 50 minutes or until set. Cool completely on cooling rack, about 2 hours, before serving.

**1 Serving:** Calories 560; Total Fat 26g (Saturated Fat 9g; Trans Fat 0g); Cholesterol 55mg; Sodium 190mg; Total Carbohydrate 74g (Dietary Fiber 3g); Protein 5g **Exchanges:** 1½ Starch, 3½ Other Carbohydrate, 5 Fat **Carbohydrate Choices:** 5

## Sweet Success Tip

Serve slices of pie with sweetened whipped cream (page 80). For an extra kick, add bourbon to the whipped cream (1 tablespoon bourbon to 1 cup whipped cream).

# Fudgy Brownie Pie with Caramel Sauce

**16 servings** • **PREP TIME:** 20 Minutes • **START TO FINISH:** 2 Hours 10 Minutes

### CRUST

1 Pillsbury refrigerated pie crust, softened as directed on box

### FILLING

1 cup butter

2 cups sugar

2 teaspoons vanilla

4 eggs, slightly beaten

1½ cups all-purpose flour

¾ cup unsweetened baking cocoa

¼ teaspoon salt

1 cup semisweet chocolate chunks

1 cup chopped pecans

### SAUCE

1 bag (14 oz) caramels, unwrapped

⅔ cup half-and-half

**1** Heat oven to 350°F. Place pie crust in 9-inch glass pie plate as directed on box for One-Crust Filled Pie.

**2** In 2-quart saucepan, melt butter over low heat; remove from heat. Stir in sugar, vanilla and eggs until well blended. Stir in flour, cocoa and salt until smooth. Stir in chocolate chunks and pecans. Spread filling evenly in crust-lined plate.

**3** Bake 45 to 50 minutes or until set. Cool on cooling rack 1 hour.

**4** In 2-quart saucepan, heat sauce ingredients over low heat, stirring constantly, until caramels are melted and mixture is smooth. Serve hot caramel sauce over slices of pie.

**1 Serving:** Calories 560; Total Fat 28g (Saturated Fat 13g; Trans Fat 0.5g); Cholesterol 85mg; Sodium 290mg; Total Carbohydrate 70g (Dietary Fiber 3g); Protein 6g **Exchanges:** 2 Starch, 2½ Other Carbohydrate, 5½ Fat **Carbohydrate Choices:** 4½

# Turtle Cheesecake Tartlets

**24 tartlets • PREP TIME: 35 Minutes • START TO FINISH: 3 Hours**

1   box Pillsbury refrigerated pie crusts, softened as directed on box

½   cup milk chocolate chips

4   oz (half of 8-oz package) cream cheese, softened

¼   cup packed brown sugar

2   tablespoons caramel topping

1   egg

½   teaspoon vegetable oil

2   tablespoons finely chopped pecans

**1** Heat oven to 450°F. Unroll 1 pie crust on work surface; roll lightly with rolling pin. With 2½- to 2¾-inch cookie cutter, cut 12 rounds from crust. Press rounds in bottoms and up sides of 12 miniature muffin cups, with edges extending above cups about ⅛ inch. Repeat with second pie crust.

**2** Place about 5 of the chocolate chips in each crust. Bake 6 minutes. Leave crusts in pan. Reduce oven temperature to 375°F.

**3** In medium bowl, beat cream cheese, brown sugar, caramel topping and egg with electric mixer on medium speed until creamy. Spoon evenly over chocolate chips, about 1½ teaspoons for each tartlet.

**4** Bake 10 to 12 minutes or until cheesecake is set. Cool 10 minutes; remove from pans to cooling racks.

**5** In small microwavable bowl, microwave remaining chocolate chips and the oil uncovered on High 30 seconds; stir. Microwave about 30 seconds longer or until melted; stir. Drizzle chocolate over each tartlet; immediately sprinkle with pecans. Refrigerate at least 2 hours before serving. Store in refrigerator.

**1 Tartlet:** Calories 130; Total Fat 7g (Saturated Fat 3.5g; Trans Fat 0g); Cholesterol 15mg; Sodium 115mg; Total Carbohydrate 14g (Dietary Fiber 0g); Protein 1g **Exchanges:** ½ Starch, ½ Other Carbohydrate, 1½ Fat **Carbohydrate Choices:** 1

## Sweet Success Tip

**If you prefer your chocolate less sweet, use semisweet chocolate chips instead of the milk chocolate chips.**

# The Scoop on Refrigerated Pie Crust

**They're convenient, easy to use and make any pie taste great. So here's everything you'll want to know about using Pillsbury refrigerated pie crusts.**

**Q** How long can I store an unopened box of pie crusts?

**A** The recommendation for best quality is to use refrigerated pie crusts before the "use-by" date on the package.

**Q** Can I freeze unbaked pie crusts?

**A** Absolutely! Pie crusts may be frozen for up to 2 months if placed in the freezer before the "use-by" date.

**Q** Can I thaw frozen, unbaked crusts in the microwave?

**A** No because the uneven heat of a microwave may melt some parts of the crust.

**Q** Can I soften refrigerated crusts in the microwave?

**A** Yes, this works well. See Warm Them Up (page 211), for directions.

**Q** How can I keep the bottom crust from getting soggy?

**A** Most recipes will provide directions for baking the pie the best way. But if you ever have a problem with a soggy bottom crust using refrigerated pie crust, here are some tips that might help.

- See Choosing Pie Plates (page 6).
- For a two-crust pie, brush the bottom crust with egg white before filling.
- For a one-crust filled pie, such as pumpkin or custard, bake the crust for 3 to 5 minutes before filling.
- Bake the pie on the lowest oven rack.
- Bake the pie on a preheated cookie sheet.
- Use a cooling rack to cool the pie.

**Q** Can I freeze pies that are assembled, but not baked?

**A** Some pies, like pumpkin or pecan, have to be baked before freezing. But you can freeze fruit pies before baking. Follow these tips when assembling and freezing an unbaked fruit pie:

- Brush the bottom crust with egg white before filling to help prevent sogginess.
- Cover the pie with an inverted paper plate, wrap it thoroughly, and freeze it for up to 3 months.
- See Freezing Filled Pies (page 6).

**Q** Can I freeze pies that are already baked?

**A** See Freezing Filled Pies (page 6).

**Q** How long should a pie cool before serving?

**A** See Cooling Pies and Tarts (page 6).

**Q** What's the easiest way to cut a pie?

**A** See Cutting/Serving Pies and Tarts (page 6).

**Q** How should I store baked pies?

**A** See Storing Baked Pies and Tarts (page 6).

# Salted Cashew–Bittersweet Chocolate Tart

**16 servings** • **PREP TIME: 20 Minutes** • **START TO FINISH: 2 Hours 35 Minutes**

One-Crust Pastry (page 7) or 1 Pillsbury refrigerated pie crust, softened as directed on box

1¼   cups whipping cream

12   oz bittersweet baking chocolate, chopped

½   cup cashew halves and pieces, coarsely chopped

1   can (13.4 oz) dulce de leche (caramelized sweetened condensed milk)

2   tablespoons cashew halves and pieces

¼   teaspoon coarse (kosher or sea) salt

**1**  Heat oven to 450°F. Place pastry or pie crust in 9-inch tart pan with removable bottom. DO NOT PRICK CRUST. Bake 10 to 12 minutes or until light golden brown. (Check crust after 5 minutes; if crust puffs in center, flatten gently with back of wooden spoon.) Cool completely, about 20 minutes.

**2**  Meanwhile, in 2-quart saucepan, heat whipping cream over medium-high heat just to boiling. Remove from heat; stir in chocolate with whisk until smooth. Stir in ½ cup chopped cashews. Pour into cooled baked shell. Refrigerate 2 hours or until firm.

**3**  Spread dulce de leche over chocolate layer. Sprinkle 2 tablespoons cashews and the salt evenly over top. Remove tart from side of pan. Store in refrigerator.

**1 Serving:** Calories 370; Total Fat 26g (Saturated Fat 14g; Trans Fat 0g); Cholesterol 30mg; Sodium 150mg; Total Carbohydrate 28g (Dietary Fiber 4g); Protein 6g **Exchanges:** 1 Starch, 1 Other Carbohydrate, ½ Medium-Fat Meat, 4½ Fat **Carbohydrate Choices:** 2

## Sweet Success Tips

**Semisweet chocolate can be substituted for the bittersweet chocolate.**

**For easier cutting, use a thin, sharp knife, wiping it clean with paper towels and running it under hot water between cutting each slice.**

# Chocolate-Cashew-Cranberry Tart

**16 servings** · **PREP TIME:** 40 Minutes · **START TO FINISH:** 4 Hours 20 Minutes

1 Pillsbury refrigerated pie crust, softened as directed on box
1¼ cups dark chocolate chips
½ cup granulated sugar
½ cup packed light brown sugar
¼ cup light corn syrup
1 cup whipping cream
1 teaspoon vanilla
1 bag (6 oz) sweetened dried cranberries (1⅓ cups)
1 container (9.25 oz) roasted cashew halves and pieces
1 teaspoon vegetable oil

**1** Heat oven to 425°F. Place pie crust in 10-inch tart pan with removable bottom as directed on box for One-Crust Filled Pie. Press in bottom and up side of pan; trim edge. Bake 9 to 11 minutes or until lightly browned and dry in appearance. If crust puffs in center, flatten gently with back of wooden spoon.

**2** Sprinkle 1 cup of the chocolate chips over hot crust. Let stand 5 minutes to soften. Gently spread chocolate over crust. Refrigerate to set chocolate. Reduce oven temperature to 375°F.

**3** In 2-quart saucepan, heat granulated sugar, brown sugar, corn syrup and whipping cream to full rolling boil over medium-high heat, stirring constantly with whisk, until sugar is dissolved. Reduce heat to medium-low to just maintain a full boil. Cook 8 to 10 minutes, stirring frequently, until mixture thickens and starts to turn a slightly darker caramel color. Remove from heat; stir in vanilla and cranberries. Let stand 15 minutes. Stir in cashews. Spoon mixture evenly over chocolate layer.

**4** Bake 20 to 25 minutes or until filling is bubbly and cashews are golden brown.

**5** In small microwavable bowl, microwave remaining ¼ cup chocolate chips and the oil uncovered on High 1 minute, stirring twice, until smooth. Drizzle over tart. Cool completely on cooling rack, about 2 hours. Refrigerate about 1 hour or until chocolate is set. Remove tart from side of pan. Store in refrigerator.

**1 Serving:** Calories 390; Total Fat 21g (Saturated Fat 9g; Trans Fat 0g); Cholesterol 25mg; Sodium 130mg; Total Carbohydrate 45g (Dietary Fiber 2g); Protein 4g **Exchanges:** 1½ Starch, 1½ Other Carbohydrate, 4 Fat **Carbohydrate Choices:** 3

## Sweet Success Tip

This decadent tart is delicious on its own, but for a little added flair, serve each slice topped with a small scoop of ice cream—either vanilla or chocolate!

# Chocolate-Macadamia Tart

**8 servings** · **PREP TIME: 10 Minutes** · **START TO FINISH: 2 Hours**

1   Pillsbury refrigerated pie crust, softened as directed on box

1   egg

½   cup packed brown sugar

2   tablespoons unsalted butter, melted

¼   cup light corn syrup

1   tablespoon dark rum or rum extract

1   cup macadamia nuts, coarsely chopped

½   cup miniature semisweet chocolate chips

2   oz bittersweet baking chocolate, melted

**1**   Heat oven to 450°F. Place pie crust in 9-inch tart pan with removable bottom as directed on box for One-Crust Filled Pie. Press in bottom and up side of pan; trim edge if necessary. DO NOT PRICK CRUST.

**2**   Bake 10 to 12 minutes or until golden brown. If crust puffs in center, flatten gently with back of wooden spoon. Cool crust 10 minutes. Reduce oven temperature to 375°F.

**3**   In medium bowl, beat egg and brown sugar with electric mixer on medium speed until well blended. Beat in butter, corn syrup and rum. Stir in macadamia nuts and chocolate chips. Pour filling into partially baked crust.

**4**   Bake 25 minutes or until deep golden brown and center is almost set. Cool completely on cooling rack. Remove tart from side of pan; cut tart into 8 wedges. Drizzle each wedge with melted chocolate.

**1 Serving:** Calories 440; Total Fat 27g (Saturated Fat 10g; Trans Fat 0g); Cholesterol 35mg; Sodium 150mg; Total Carbohydrate 44g (Dietary Fiber 3g); Protein 4g **Exchanges:** 1 Starch, 2 Other Carbohydrate, 5½ Fat **Carbohydrate Choices:** 3

## Sweet Success Tip

When placing the crust into the tart pan, ease it in rather than stretching it to fit. If the crust is stretched, it will spring back into shape or shrink during the initial bake.

# Cranberry-Raisin Maple Nut Pie

**8 servings** • **PREP TIME:** 25 Minutes • **START TO FINISH:** 3 Hours 5 Minutes

- 1 box Pillsbury refrigerated pie crusts, softened as directed on box
- ⅓ cup packed brown sugar
- 1 cup chopped walnuts
- ¾ cup packed brown sugar
- ½ cup white vanilla baking chips
- ½ cup real maple syrup
- ¾ cup half-and-half
- 3 eggs, slightly beaten
- ¾ cup sweetened dried cranberries
- ½ cup golden raisins

**1** Heat oven to 425°F. Place 1 pie crust in 9-inch glass pie plate as directed on box for One-Crust Filled Pie.

**2** Unroll second crust on work surface. With floured 2½- to 3-inch and 1- to 1½-inch leaf-shaped cookie cutters, cut 3 leaf shapes of each size from crust; set aside. Cut remaining crust with scissors to look like crumb topping. In small bowl, mix ⅓ cup brown sugar and ¼ cup of the walnuts; stir in cut-up crust.

**3** In 3-quart saucepan, cook ¾ cup brown sugar, the white chips and syrup over medium heat, stirring constantly, just until chips are melted and mixture is smooth. Stir in half-and-half and eggs until well blended. Stir in cranberries, remaining ¾ cup walnuts and the raisins. Pour filling into crust-lined plate. Sprinkle with cut-up crust mixture; top with leaf cutouts.

**4** Cover crust edge with pie shield ring or strips of foil to prevent excessive browning; bake 20 minutes. Remove foil; reduce oven temperature to 350°F. Bake 20 minutes longer. Cool on cooling rack at least 2 hours before serving.

**Donna Buckland of Billerica, Massachusetts, won the Pillsbury Refrigerated Pie Crust Pie Baking Championship at the 2009 Topsfield Fair with this recipe.**

**1 Serving:** Calories 700; Total Fat 32g (Saturated Fat 11g, Trans Fat 0g); Cholesterol 100mg; Sodium 320mg; Total Carbohydrate 96g (Dietary Fiber 2g); Protein 8g **Exchanges:** 2 Starch, ½ Fruit, 4 Other Carbohydrate, 6 Fat **Carbohydrate Choices:** 6½

# Jeweled Cranberry-Apricot Tart

**12 servings • PREP TIME: 25 Minutes • START TO FINISH: 2 Hours 55 Minutes**

## CRUST

- 1 Pillsbury refrigerated pie crust, softened as directed on box

## FILLING

- 1 package (8 oz) cream cheese, softened
- ⅓ cup sugar
- 2 tablespoons orange-flavored liqueur or orange juice
- 2 eggs

## TOPPING

- ½ cup sweetened dried cranberries
- ½ cup chopped dried apricots
- 1 cup cranberry juice cocktail
- ¼ cup seedless raspberry jam
- 1 tablespoon cold water
- 4 teaspoons cornstarch
- ½ teaspoon grated orange peel

**1** Heat oven to 450°F. Place pie crust in 10-inch tart pan with removable bottom as directed on box for One-Crust Filled Pie. Press in bottom and up side of pan; trim edge if necessary. DO NOT PRICK CRUST. Line crust with heavy-duty foil.

**2** Bake 11 minutes. Remove foil; bake 3 to 4 minutes longer or until light golden brown in center and dry in appearance. If crust puffs in center, flatten gently with back of wooden spoon. Cool crust 10 minutes. Reduce oven temperature to 375°F.

**3** In medium bowl, beat cream cheese and sugar with electric mixer on medium speed until light and fluffy. Beat in liqueur and eggs until well blended. Spoon filling into partially baked crust. Bake 15 to 18 minutes or until filling is set. Cool 30 minutes on cooling rack.

**4** Meanwhile, in 1-quart saucepan, heat cranberries, apricots and cranberry juice to boiling over high heat, stirring occasionally. Reduce heat to medium-low; simmer 5 minutes, stirring occasionally. Stir in jam; cook 2 minutes. In small bowl, mix water and cornstarch; stir into fruit mixture. Increase heat to medium. Heat to boiling; boil 1 minute, stirring constantly. Remove from heat; stir in orange peel. Cool to room temperature, about 30 minutes.

**5** Remove tart from side of pan. Spread topping over filling. Refrigerate at least 1 hour before serving. Cover and refrigerate any remaining tart.

**1 Serving:** Calories 240; Total Fat 11g (Saturated Fat 6g; Trans Fat 0g); Cholesterol 60mg; Sodium 160mg; Total Carbohydrate 30g (Dietary Fiber 0g); Protein 3g **Exchanges:** 1½ Other Carbohydrate, ½ Milk, 1½ Fat **Carbohydrate Choices:** 2

## Sweet Success Tip

**Any dried fruit that you like can be substituted for the cranberries and apricots. Chop the fruit into smaller pieces, if necessary. To reduce stickiness while chopping the apricots, wet the knife with water.**

# White Chocolate–Raspberry Pie

**8 servings** • **PREP TIME: 35 Minutes** • **START TO FINISH: 3 Hours 5 Minutes**

1   Pillsbury refrigerated pie crust, softened as directed on box

5   oz white chocolate baking squares

3   tablespoons milk

5   oz cream cheese, softened

½   cup powdered sugar

½   to 1 teaspoon grated orange peel

1   cup whipping cream, whipped

3   cups fresh raspberries

**1**   Heat oven to 450°F. Make pie crust as directed on box for One-Crust Baked Shell using 9-inch glass pie plate. Cool completely on cooling rack.

**2**   In small microwavable bowl, microwave 4 squares of the white chocolate and the milk uncovered on Medium (50%) about 2 minutes or until softened and chocolate can be stirred smooth. Cool to room temperature.

**3**   In small bowl, beat cream cheese, powdered sugar and orange peel with electric mixer on low speed until smooth. Beat in white chocolate mixture. Fold in whipped cream. Spread filling in cooled baked shell. Arrange raspberries on filling.

**4**   Melt remaining 1 square white chocolate; drizzle over pie. Refrigerate about 2 hours or until set. Store in refrigerator.

**1 Serving:** Calories 430; Total Fat 29g (Saturated Fat 16g; Trans Fat 0.5g); Cholesterol 70mg; Sodium 220mg; Total Carbohydrate 37g (Dietary Fiber 3g); Protein 4g **Exchanges:** 1½ Starch, ½ Fruit, ½ Other Carbohydrate, 5½ Fat **Carbohydrate Choices:** 2½

## Sweet Success Tip

**When purchasing white chocolate, check to see if the label states it contains cocoa butter; if not, it's not white chocolate. White chocolate is made of a mixture of sugar, cocoa butter, milk solids, lecithin and vanilla.**

# Cranberry Mousse Mini Tarts

**24 tarts** • **PREP TIME: 45 Minutes** • **START TO FINISH: 2 Hours 5 Minutes**

## FILLING

- 1 envelope unflavored gelatin
- ⅔ cup water
- ½ cup granulated sugar
- 1 cup whole cranberries, chopped
- ½ teaspoon grated orange peel

## CRUST

- 1 box Pillsbury refrigerated pie crusts, softened as directed on box
- 2 tablespoons coarse sugar, if desired

## TOPPING

- ¼ cup whipping cream
- 3 teaspoons powdered sugar

**1** In small bowl, sprinkle gelatin on water to soften; let soak about 15 minutes. In 1½-quart saucepan, heat ½ cup granulated sugar and the cranberries just to boiling over medium heat, stirring occasionally. Remove from heat; stir in gelatin mixture and orange peel. Refrigerate 30 to 40 minutes or until mixture just starts to thicken.

**2** Heat oven to 425°F. Spray 24 miniature muffin cups with cooking spray.

**3** Unroll pie crusts on work surface. With 2½-inch scalloped round cutter, cut 15 rounds from 1 crust and 9 from second crust. Fit rounds into muffin cups, pressing in gently. Generously prick crusts with fork. With 1-inch star-shaped cookie cutter, cut 24 stars from remaining crust; place on ungreased cookie sheet. Sprinkle with coarse sugar.

**4** Bake crusts 6 to 9 minutes or until light golden brown. Cool completely on cooling rack, about 15 minutes; remove from muffin cups; place on cooling rack. Meanwhile, bake star shapes 3 to 4 minutes or until light golden brown.

**5** In small bowl, beat whipping cream until soft peaks form. Add 2 teaspoons of the powdered sugar; beat until stiff peaks form. Fold in cranberry mixture; refrigerate about 10 minutes or until thickened. Spoon about 1 tablespoon filling into each tart shell; top each with 1 star. Store in refrigerator. Just before serving, sprinkle with remaining 1 teaspoon powdered sugar.

**1 Tart:** Calories 80; Total Fat 3.5g (Saturated Fat 1.5g; Trans Fat 0g); Cholesterol 0mg; Sodium 45mg; Total Carbohydrate 10g (Dietary Fiber 0g); Protein 0g **Exchanges:** ½ Other Carbohydrate, 1 Fat **Carbohydrate Choices:** ½

## Sweet Success Tip

**These mini tarts are the perfect dessert for a holiday party. Both the tarts and the stars can be made a day ahead of time. Store the tarts in the refrigerator and the stars at room temperature. Just before serving, top each tart with a star and a sprinkle of powdered sugar.**

# Pomegranate Tartlets

**36 tartlets • PREP TIME: 45 Minutes • START TO FINISH: 2 Hour 5 Minutes**

## CRUST

3  Pillsbury refrigerated pie crusts, softened as directed on box

## FILLING

1  pomegranate

1  box (4-serving size) vanilla pudding and pie filling mix (not instant)

1¾  cups whipping cream

2  tablespoons dark rum or ½ teaspoon rum extract

## TOPPING

1  teaspoon powdered sugar

**1**  Heat oven to 450°F. Unroll pie crusts on work surface. With 2½-inch plain or scalloped round cutter, cut 12 rounds from each crust. Fit rounds into ungreased miniature muffin cups, pressing in gently. Generously prick crusts with fork.

**2**  Bake 7 to 9 minutes or until light golden brown. Remove tartlet shells from muffin cups; place on cooling racks. Cool 10 minutes.

**3**  Meanwhile, cut pomegranate in half; remove seeds. Set aside.

**4**  In 2-quart saucepan, stir pudding mix and whipping cream with whisk until blended. Cook over medium heat about 5 minutes or until mixture comes to a boil, stirring constantly. Remove from heat; stir in rum.

**5**  Immediately spoon about 2 rounded teaspoons filling into each tartlet shell. Top each with about 1 teaspoon pomegranate seeds. Cover loosely; refrigerate at least 1 hour or until serving time. Sprinkle with powdered sugar just before serving.

**1 Tartlet:** Calories 90; Total Fat 6g (Saturated Fat 3g; Trans Fat 0g); Cholesterol 15mg; Sodium 60mg; Total Carbohydrate 8g (Dietary Fiber 0g); Protein 0g **Exchanges:** ½ Other Carbohydrate, 1½ Fat **Carbohydrate Choices:** ½

## Sweet Success Tip

To remove the seeds from a pomegranate, you'll need a sharp knife and bowl of cold water. Score the pomegranate skin from top to bottom about 5 times, evenly spaced. Hold the pomegranate under water in the bowl, and pull it apart into sections. Remove the seeds with your fingers or a small spoon while holding it under water. The seeds will sink to the bottom, and the skin and membrane will float to the top. Remove the membrane with your fingers, and drain the seeds in a strainer.

# Peppermint Candy Tarts

**32 tarts • PREP TIME: 1 Hour • START TO FINISH: 1 Hour 30 Minutes**

### TART SHELLS

½  cup granulated sugar
½  cup butter, softened
½  teaspoon peppermint extract
1  egg
1½  cups all-purpose flour
¼  teaspoon baking soda
¼  teaspoon salt

### FILLING AND GARNISH

2  cups powdered sugar
3  tablespoons butter, softened
2  to 3 drops red food color
2  to 3 tablespoons milk
½  cup crushed hard peppermint candies

**1**  Heat oven to 350°F. Grease bottoms only of 32 mini muffin cups with shortening.

**2**  In large bowl, beat granulated sugar and ½ cup butter with electric mixer on medium speed until fluffy. Beat in peppermint extract and egg until blended. On low speed, beat in flour, baking soda and salt. Shape dough into 1½-inch balls. Press each ball in bottom and up side of muffin cup.

**3**  Bake 9 to 12 minutes or until set and edges are light golden brown. Cool 1 minute; remove from muffin cups to cooling racks. Cool completely, about 15 minutes.

**4**  In small bowl, beat powdered sugar, 3 tablespoons butter, food color and enough milk with electric mixer on medium speed until smooth and creamy. Stir in ¼ cup of the candies. Spoon 1 rounded measuring teaspoon filling into each tart shell. Sprinkle with remaining ¼ cup candies.

**1 Tart:** Calories 110; Total Fat 4g (Saturated Fat 2.5g; Trans Fat 0g); Cholesterol 15mg; Sodium 65mg; Total Carbohydrate 18g (Dietary Fiber 0g); Protein 1g **Exchanges:** 1 Other Carbohydrate, 1 Fat **Carbohydrate Choices:** 1

# Peppermint Cookie Ice Cream Pie

**8 servings • PREP TIME: 10 Minutes • START TO FINISH: 4 Hours 25 Minutes**

½ gallon peppermint ice cream, softened

1 cup chopped creme-filled chocolate sandwich cookies (8 to 10 cookies)

1 creme-filled chocolate sandwich cookie crumb crust (6 oz)

¾ cup chocolate topping that forms hard shell

¼ cup crushed red and green peppermint candies (about 10 candies)

**1** In large bowl, stir ice cream and chopped cookies until blended. Spoon ice cream mixture evenly into crumb crust.

**2** Drizzle chocolate topping over pie; sprinkle with candies. Cover; freeze 4 hours or until firm. Remove from freezer 10 to 15 minutes before serving.

**1 Serving:** Calories 630; Total Fat 34g (Saturated Fat 17g; Trans Fat 0.5g); Cholesterol 60mg; Sodium 300mg; Total Carbohydrate 73g (Dietary Fiber 3g); Protein 7g **Exchanges:** 2½ Starch, 2½ Other Carbohydrate, 6½ Fat **Carbohydrate Choices:** 5

## Sweet Success Tip

One color of peppermint candies will be just as pretty as two—just choose your favorite: red or green.

Muffin Tin Taco Pies (page 284)

# savory pies

# Individual Chicken Pot Pies

**8 pot pies** • **PREP TIME: 35 Minutes** • **START TO FINISH: 1 Hour 15 Minutes**

1 package (17.3 oz) frozen puff pastry sheets, thawed

1 tablespoon olive oil

1 cup diced unpeeled red potatoes

1 medium carrot, thinly sliced (½ cup)

1 medium stalk celery, thinly sliced (½ cup)

1 medium onion, chopped (½ cup)

2 cloves garlic, finely chopped

2 cans (10¾ oz each) condensed 98% fat-free cream of chicken soup with 45% less sodium

1 cup fat-free or regular half-and-half

½ cup dry sherry, nonalcoholic wine or chicken broth

¾ cup water

1½ teaspoons parsley flakes

1 teaspoon poultry seasoning

2 cups cubed cooked chicken breast

1 cup frozen sweet peas, thawed

**1** Heat oven to 400°F. Lightly spray 8 (8-oz) individual baking dishes (ramekins) with cooking spray. Place on large cookie sheet with sides.

**2** Unfold puff pastry on lightly floured surface; cut each sheet into 4 (8-inch) squares. Set aside.

**3** In 3-quart saucepan, heat oil over medium heat. Add potatoes, carrot, celery, onion and garlic; cook about 10 minutes, stirring occasionally, until vegetables are tender. Stir in soup, half-and-half, sherry, water, 1 teaspoon of the parsley flakes, the poultry seasoning, chicken and peas; heat to boiling. Remove from heat.

**4** Divide chicken mixture evenly among baking dishes; top each with puff pastry square. Sprinkle with remaining ½ teaspoon parsley flakes.

**5** Bake 30 to 35 minutes or until pastry is puffed and golden brown. Let stand 5 minutes before serving.

**1 Pot Pie:** Calories 540; Total Fat 29g (Saturated Fat 7g; Trans Fat 6g); Cholesterol 35mg; Sodium 530mg; Total Carbohydrate 48g (Dietary Fiber 2g); Protein 18g **Exchanges:** 3 Starch, ½ Vegetable, 1 Very Lean Meat, 5½ Fat **Carbohydrate Choices:** 3

## Savory Success Tip

**This twist on pot pie is easy to make and easy to serve—and the puff pastry provides a flaky holder for the delicious savory filling.**

# Chicken Pot Pie with Flaky Crust

**4 servings** • **PREP TIME:** 40 Minutes • **START TO FINISH:** 1 Hour 35 Minutes

1 sheet frozen puff pastry (from 17.3-oz package), thawed

1 tablespoon olive or vegetable oil

¾ lb boneless skinless chicken breasts, cut into ½-inch pieces

1 large onion, coarsely chopped (1 cup)

1 cup quartered ready-to-eat baby-cut carrots (5 to 6 oz)

¾ cup frozen sweet peas, thawed

1 jar (12 oz) chicken gravy

½ cup sour cream

2 tablespoons cornstarch

¼ teaspoon dried thyme leaves

¼ teaspoon pepper

1 egg, beaten, if desired

**1** Heat oven to 375°F. Unfold puff pastry on lightly floured surface. With rolling pin, roll pastry into 11-inch square. Cut off corners to make 11-inch round. Cut slits or small designs in several places in pastry; set aside.

**2** In 10-inch skillet, heat oil over medium-high heat. Cook chicken in oil about 5 minutes, stirring occasionally, until no longer pink in center. Add onion and carrots; cook 5 minutes, stirring frequently, until crisp-tender. Remove from heat; stir in peas.

**3** In medium bowl, beat remaining ingredients except egg with whisk until well blended. Stir into chicken mixture in skillet. Spoon into 9½-inch glass deep-dish pie plate. Place pastry over filling, allowing pastry to hang over edge.

**4** Bake 20 minutes. Brush crust with beaten egg. Cover crust edge with strips of foil to prevent excessive browning. Bake 20 to 25 minutes longer or until crust is golden brown. Let stand 10 minutes before serving.

**1 Serving:** Calories 610; Total Fat 37g (Saturated Fat 13g; Trans Fat 2.5g); Cholesterol 135mg; Sodium 720mg; Total Carbohydrate 44g (Dietary Fiber 3g); Protein 27g **Exchanges:** 1 Starch, 1½ Other Carbohydrate, 1 Vegetable, 3 Very Lean Meat, 7 Fat **Carbohydrate Choices:** 3

## Savory Success Tips

You can use 2¾ cups frozen mixed vegetables instead of the onion, carrots and frozen peas. Just stir them into the cooked chicken before adding the gravy mixture.

Use a miniature cookie or canapé cutter to make steam holes in the pastry. Save the pastry cutouts and place on top of the pastry after brushing it with egg. Bake as directed in the recipe.

# Herbed Chicken Lattice Pot Pie

**6 servings** • **PREP TIME: 35 Minutes** • **START TO FINISH: 1 Hour**

1 cup uncooked instant white rice
1 cup water
2 tablespoons olive oil
1¼ lb boneless skinless chicken breasts, cut into ¾-inch pieces
1 large red bell pepper, chopped (about 1½ cups)
1 large onion, chopped (1 cup)
1 medium zucchini, chopped (about 1 cup)
2 tablespoons savory herb with garlic soup mix (from package in 2.4-oz box)
¾ cup milk
1 can (8 oz) refrigerated seamless dough sheet

**1** Heat oven to 375°F. Spray 9-inch glass pie plate with cooking spray. Cook rice in water as directed on package. Pat cooked rice evenly in bottom of pie plate.

**2** In 12-inch nonstick skillet, heat 1 tablespoon of the oil over medium-high heat. Cook chicken in oil about 5 minutes, stirring occasionally, until no longer pink in center. Remove chicken; set aside.

**3** In same skillet, heat remaining 1 tablespoon oil over medium-high heat. Cook bell pepper, onion and zucchini in oil, stirring frequently, until crisp-tender. In small bowl, mix soup mix and milk; stir into vegetables. Heat to boiling over high heat. Remove from heat; stir in chicken (discard chicken juices). Spoon over rice in pie plate.

**4** Unroll dough on work surface; cut lengthwise into 8 strips. Arrange 4 strips evenly in same direction over filling. Top with remaining strips in opposite direction. Fold overhanging ends of strips at an angle around edge of pie plate to form rim.

**5** Bake about 20 minutes or until crust is golden brown. Let stand 5 minutes before serving.

**1 Serving:** Calories 390; Total Fat 15g (Saturated Fat 4.5g; Trans Fat 0g); Cholesterol 60mg; Sodium 570mg; Total Carbohydrate 38g (Dietary Fiber 2g); Protein 26g **Exchanges:** 2 Starch, ½ Other Carbohydrate, 3 Lean Meat, 1 Fat **Carbohydrate Choices:** 2½

## Savory Success Tip

You can substitute 1 can (8 ounces) refrigerated crescent dinner rolls for the seamless dough sheet, but be sure to press the seams together to seal before cutting the dough into strips.

# Moroccan Chicken Pie

**6 servings** • **PREP TIME: 30 Minutes** • **START TO FINISH: 1 Hour 20 Minutes**

2 tablespoons butter

1 large onion, chopped (1 cup)

½ teaspoon ground cinnamon

½ teaspoon ground turmeric

2 tablespoons all-purpose flour

1 cup reduced-sodium chicken broth

⅓ cup raisins

3 cups shredded deli rotisserie chicken (from 2-lb chicken)

¼ cup chopped fresh cilantro

¼ teaspoon salt

¼ teaspoon pepper

16 sheets frozen phyllo (filo) pastry (14×9 inch), thawed

Cooking spray

½ cup slivered almonds, finely ground

**1** Heat oven to 350°F. Lightly spray 9-inch glass pie plate with cooking spray.

**2** In 10-inch nonstick skillet, melt butter over medium heat. Cook onion in butter 5 to 6 minutes, stirring occasionally, until softened and lightly browned. Stir in cinnamon and turmeric. Stir in flour; cook 1 minute, stirring constantly. Slowly stir in broth. Add raisins. Heat to boiling; boil gently 1 minute, stirring occasionally. In large bowl, stir together onion mixture, chicken, cilantro, salt and pepper.

**3** Place phyllo sheets on work surface; cover with clean damp towel. Place 1 phyllo sheet in bottom and up side of pie plate, allowing excess phyllo to extend over edge. Lightly spray with cooking spray; sprinkle with 1½ teaspoons of the ground almonds. Repeat layers, using 7 more phyllo sheets and alternating position of sheets to cover bottom and side of pie plate.

**4** Spoon chicken mixture into pastry-lined plate. Using kitchen scissors, cut excess phyllo from edges. Layer with remaining 8 phyllo sheets, spraying each with cooking spray and sprinkling with almonds. Fold excess phyllo under to form rustic crust edge.

**5** Bake 30 to 40 minutes or until crust is golden brown. Let stand 10 minutes before serving.

**1 Serving:** Calories 440; Total Fat 15g (Saturated Fat 4.5g; Trans Fat 0g); Cholesterol 70mg; Sodium 760mg; Total Carbohydrate 49g (Dietary Fiber 3g); Protein 27g **Exchanges:** 3 Starch, ½ Other Carbohydrate, 2½ Lean Meat, 1 Fat **Carbohydrate Choices:** 3

## Savory Success Tips

**The key to working with phyllo pastry is to work quickly and always keep it covered with a damp towel. Phyllo that is not covered will quickly turn dry and brittle. Don't worry if your phyllo splits or creases when you place it in the pan—you will never notice it once the pie is baked.**

**Turmeric adds bright yellow color to food; in fact, it's what gives American ballpark mustard its distinctive color. In this dish, turmeric adds not only color but also a rich earthy flavor.**

# Chicken Souvlaki Pot Pie

**6 servings** • **PREP TIME: 25 Minutes** • **START TO FINISH: 1 Hour**

2 tablespoons olive or vegetable oil

1¼ lb boneless skinless chicken breasts, cut into bite-size strips

1 medium red onion, chopped (about 1¼ cups)

2 small zucchini, cut in half lengthwise, then cut crosswise into slices (about 2⅓ cups)

2 cloves garlic, finely chopped

2 teaspoons chili powder

1½ teaspoons dried oregano leaves

½ teaspoon salt

1 can (14.5 oz) diced tomatoes, undrained

½ cup plain yogurt

2 tablespoons all-purpose flour

1 Pillsbury refrigerated pie crust, softened as directed on box

**1** Heat oven to 400°F. In 12-inch nonstick skillet, heat 1 tablespoon of the oil over medium-high heat. Cook chicken in oil about 8 minutes, stirring occasionally, until no longer pink in center. Remove chicken from skillet.

**2** In same skillet, heat remaining 1 tablespoon oil over medium-high heat. Cook onion and zucchini in oil about 6 minutes, stirring frequently, until zucchini is crisp-tender. Return chicken to skillet (discard chicken juices). Stir in garlic, chili powder, oregano and salt. Cook 2 minutes, stirring constantly. Stir in tomatoes; cook until thoroughly heated. Remove from heat.

**3** In small bowl, beat yogurt and flour with whisk until blended; stir into chicken mixture. Spoon into ungreased 9-inch glass pie plate.

**4** Unroll pie crust over hot chicken mixture. Fold excess crust under and press to form thick crust edge; flute. Cut slits in several places in crust. Place pie plate on cookie sheet with sides.

**5** Bake 25 to 30 minutes or until crust is golden brown (sauce may bubble slightly over crust). Let stand 5 minutes before serving.

**1 Serving:** Calories 490; Total Fat 24g (Saturated Fat 8g; Trans Fat 0g); Cholesterol 70mg; Sodium 720mg; Total Carbohydrate 42g (Dietary Fiber 2g); Protein 26g **Exchanges:** 2 Starch, ½ Other Carbohydrate, 1½ Vegetable, 2½ Lean Meat, 3 Fat **Carbohydrate Choices:** 3

## Savory Success Tip

Blending flour into the yogurt before the mixture is added to the chicken filling allows the sauce to thicken when heated without separating.

# Mediterranean Chicken Bake

**6 servings (1¼ cups each)** • **PREP TIME: 25 Minutes** • **START TO FINISH: 55 Minutes**

1 lb boneless skinless chicken breasts, cut into 1-inch cubes

1 medium onion, chopped (½ cup)

2 medium zucchini, cut into ⅛-inch slices

½ cup uncooked rosamarina or orzo pasta (3 oz)

½ cup water

2 medium plum (Roma) tomatoes, chopped

1 jar (26 oz) roasted tomato and garlic pasta sauce

2 cups shredded mozzarella cheese (8 oz)

1 teaspoon Italian seasoning

6 sheets frozen phyllo (filo) pastry (14×9 inch), thawed

3 tablespoons butter, melted

**1** Heat oven to 400°F. Spray 3-quart casserole with cooking spray.

**2** In 12-inch nonstick skillet, cook chicken over medium heat 8 to 10 minutes, stirring occasionally, until no longer pink in center. Stir in onion, zucchini, pasta and water. Cook 5 to 6 minutes, stirring occasionally, until vegetables are crisp-tender. Stir in tomatoes, pasta sauce, cheese and Italian seasoning.

**3** Spoon mixture into casserole. Brush top of each phyllo sheet with melted butter. Crumple each phyllo sheet and place on top of chicken mixture.

**4** Bake uncovered 20 to 30 minutes or until phyllo is golden brown.

**1 Serving:** Calories 490; Total Fat 21g (Saturated Fat 10g; Trans Fat 0g); Cholesterol 80mg; Sodium 930mg; Total Carbohydrate 45g (Dietary Fiber 4g); Protein 32g **Exchanges:** 1½ Starch, 1 Other Carbohydrate, 1 Vegetable, 3½ Very Lean Meat, 3½ Fat **Carbohydrate Choices:** 3

## Savory Success Tips

To keep phyllo dough from drying out, cover with a damp towel or damp paper towels until you are ready to use it.

Rosamarina is a tiny rice-shaped pasta. It's ideal for casseroles and soups and makes a great substitute for rice.

# Skillet Chicken Pot Pie

**6 servings** • **PREP TIME:** 35 Minutes • **START TO FINISH:** 45 Minutes

1 tablespoon vegetable oil

1¼ lb boneless skinless chicken breasts, cut into 1-inch pieces

1 teaspoon salt

1½ teaspoons dried thyme leaves

⅛ teaspoon pepper

2 cups sliced fresh carrots (4 medium)

2 cups frozen shredded or diced hash brown potatoes (from 30- to 32-oz bag)

1 jar (12 oz) chicken gravy

1 cup frozen sweet peas, thawed

1 can (12 oz) refrigerated flaky biscuits

½ teaspoon garlic powder

**1** In 12-inch nonstick skillet, heat oil over medium-high heat. Add chicken; sprinkle with salt, ½ teaspoon of the thyme and the pepper. Cook 5 minutes, stirring frequently, until chicken is browned.

**2** Move chicken to one side of skillet. Add carrots and potatoes; cook 5 minutes, stirring frequently. Stir gravy into chicken and vegetables. Heat to boiling; reduce heat to low. Cover; simmer 20 to 25 minutes, stirring occasionally and adding peas during last 5 minutes of cooking, until chicken is no longer pink in center and vegetables are tender.

**3** During last 15 minutes of cooking, heat oven to 400°F. Separate dough into 10 biscuits. Cut each biscuit into quarters; place in large bowl. Sprinkle garlic powder and remaining 1 teaspoon thyme over dough; toss to coat. Place on ungreased cookie sheet.

**4** Bake 8 to 10 minutes or until biscuit pieces are golden brown. Scatter biscuit pieces over top of cooked chicken mixture before serving.

**1 Serving:** Calories 450; Total Fat 16g (Saturated Fat 3.5g; Trans Fat 2.5g); Cholesterol 60mg; Sodium 1430mg; Total Carbohydrate 47g (Dietary Fiber 3g); Protein 28g **Exchanges:** 2½ Starch, ½ Other Carbohydrate, 1 Vegetable, 2½ Lean Meat, 1½ Fat **Carbohydrate Choices:** 3

## Savory Success Tips

Shredded hash brown potatoes are called "country-style," and diced potatoes are called "southern-style." Either type can be used in this recipe.

If you have a bag of frozen mixed vegetables in the freezer, use 3 cups mixed vegetables, thawed, instead of the carrots and peas. After cooking the potatoes, add the mixed veggies with the chicken.

# Chicken Pot Pie Bubble Bake

**6 servings (1½ cups each)** • **PREP TIME: 20 Minutes** • **START TO FINISH: 1 Hour 10 Minutes**

1   can (10¾ oz) condensed cream of chicken soup

1⅓   cups milk

1   teaspoon Italian seasoning

2   cups refrigerated cooked new potato wedges (from 20-oz bag), each cut in half crosswise

3   cups cubed deli rotisserie chicken (without skin)

1   bag (1 lb) frozen mixed vegetables, thawed

1   can (12 oz) refrigerated flaky biscuits

½   cup shredded Cheddar cheese (2 oz)

**1**   Heat oven to 375°F. Spray 13×9-inch (3-quart) glass baking dish with cooking spray.

**2**   In large bowl, mix soup, milk and Italian seasoning. Stir in potatoes, chicken and vegetables.

**3**   Separate dough into 10 biscuits. Cut each biscuit into quarters; add to potato mixture. Stir gently to mix well; spoon into baking dish.

**4**   Bake uncovered 35 to 40 minutes or until top is deep golden brown and biscuits are no longer doughy inside. Sprinkle with cheese. Bake 4 to 6 minutes longer or until cheese is melted.

**1 Serving:** Calories 510; Total Fat 22g (Saturated Fat 7g; Trans Fat 3.5g); Cholesterol 75mg; Sodium 1100mg; Total Carbohydrate 48g (Dietary Fiber 5g); Protein 30g **Exchanges:** 2 Starch, 1 Other Carbohydrate, 1 Vegetable, 3 Lean Meat, 2½ Fat **Carbohydrate Choices:** 3

## Savory Success Tips

If you purchase a 2-pound rotisserie chicken, you'll have enough cubed chicken for this recipe with about 1 cup left over.

To quickly thaw the frozen vegetables, place them in a colander or strainer, then rinse with warm water until they're thawed. Be sure to drain them well.

# Mini Bacon Chicken Pot Pies

**5 pot pies** • PREP TIME: 20 Minutes • START TO FINISH: 45 Minutes

1 can (10.2 oz) large refrigerated flaky biscuits
1 jar (12 oz) homestyle chicken gravy
1 tablespoon cornstarch
¾ cup milk
½ teaspoon dried thyme leaves
¼ teaspoon pepper
2 cups cubed cooked chicken
1 bag (12 oz) frozen mixed vegetables, thawed
1 cup refrigerated cooked diced potatoes with onions (from 20-oz bag)
½ cup shredded Cheddar cheese (2 oz)
5 slices bacon, crisply cooked, crumbled

**1** Heat oven to 350°F. Spray 5 (10-oz) individual baking dishes (ramekins) with cooking spray. Place on large cookie sheet with sides.

**2** Separate dough into 5 biscuits; cut each biscuit into quarters. Set aside.

**3** In 3-quart saucepan, stir gravy and cornstarch with whisk. Stir in milk, thyme, pepper, chicken, vegetables and potatoes. Heat to boiling over medium-high heat, stirring occasionally. Immediately divide hot chicken mixture among baking dishes; top each with 4 biscuit pieces.

**4** Bake 18 to 20 minutes or until biscuits are golden brown. Carefully remove from oven. Sprinkle cheese evenly over tops of biscuits. Bake about 4 minutes longer or until cheese is melted. Sprinkle with bacon.

**1 Pot Pie:** Calories 570; Total Fat 28g (Saturated Fat 9g; Trans Fat 3g); Cholesterol 75mg; Sodium 1700mg; Total Carbohydrate 50g (Dietary Fiber 4g); Protein 30g **Exchanges:** 2½ Starch, ½ Other Carbohydrate, 1 Vegetable, 3 Lean Meat, 3½ Fat **Carbohydrate Choices:** 3

## Savory Success Tip

**The chicken mixture must be piping hot when spooned into the baking dishes in order to bake the biscuits properly.**

# Mini Chicken Pot Pies

**4 pot pies** • **PREP TIME: 15 Minutes** • **START TO FINISH: 30 Minutes**

1½ cups frozen peas and carrots, thawed

1 cup cubed cooked chicken

1 cup refrigerated cooked diced potatoes with onions (from 20-oz bag)

¼ cup milk

½ teaspoon dried thyme leaves

1 can (10¾ oz) condensed cream of chicken soup

1 can (4 oz) refrigerated crescent dinner rolls

1 egg

1 tablespoon water

⅛ teaspoon dried thyme leaves

**1** Heat oven to 400°F. Place 4 (10-oz) individual baking dishes (ramekins) on cookie sheet with sides.

**2** In 2-quart saucepan, mix peas and carrots, chicken, potatoes, milk, ½ teaspoon thyme and the soup. Heat to boiling over medium-high heat, stirring occasionally. Remove from heat. Divide chicken mixture evenly among baking dishes.

**3** Separate dough into 4 triangles; place 1 triangle over each baking dish. In small bowl, beat egg and water. Brush over dough. Sprinkle with ⅛ teaspoon thyme.

**4** Bake 11 to 13 minutes or until crusts are golden brown.

**1 Pot Pie:** Calories 330; Total Fat 15g (Saturated Fat 5g; Trans Fat 1.5g); Cholesterol 90mg; Sodium 920mg; Total Carbohydrate 31g (Dietary Fiber 2g); Protein 18g **Exchanges:** 2 Starch, 1½ Lean Meat, 2 Fat **Carbohydrate Choices:** 2

## Savory Success Tip

**Vary the ingredients of these pot pies to suit your taste, using your favorite frozen veggies, turkey instead of chicken or a different soup, such as cream of celery or cream of mushroom.**

# Impossibly Easy Mini Thai Chicken Pies

**6 servings (2 mini pies each)** • **PREP TIME: 20 Minutes** • **START TO FINISH: 1 Hour 15 Minutes**

### THAI CHICKEN MIXTURE

| | |
|---|---|
| 1 | tablespoon vegetable oil |
| 1 | lb boneless skinless chicken breasts, cut into bite-size pieces |
| 1 | medium onion, chopped (½ cup) |
| ¼ | cup sliced green onions (4 medium) |
| ¼ | cup chopped fresh cilantro |
| ½ | teaspoon Thai red curry paste |
| 1 | tablespoon fresh lime juice |
| 1 | cup shredded mozzarella cheese (4 oz) |

### BAKING MIXTURE

| | |
|---|---|
| ½ | cup Original Bisquick mix |
| ½ | cup milk |
| 2 | eggs |

### GARNISHES

| | |
|---|---|
| ½ | cup salted cocktail peanuts |
| ¼ | cup sliced green onions (4 medium), if desired |

**1** Heat oven to 375°F. Spray 12 regular-size muffin cups with cooking spray.

**2** In 10-inch nonstick skillet, heat oil over medium-high heat. Cook chicken in oil 5 to 7 minutes, stirring occasionally, until no longer pink in center. Add onion; cook 2 to 3 minutes. Add green onions, cilantro, red curry paste and lime juice; cook, stirring occasionally, until thoroughly heated. Cool 5 minutes; stir in cheese.

**3** In medium bowl, stir all baking mixture ingredients with whisk or fork until blended. Spoon slightly less than 1 tablespoon baking mixture into each muffin cup. Top each with about ¼ cup chicken mixture and 1 tablespoon baking mixture.

**4** Bake 10 minutes. Sprinkle peanuts evenly over tops of pies. Bake 20 to 25 minutes longer or until toothpick inserted in center comes out clean and tops of pies are golden brown. Cool 5 minutes. With thin knife, loosen sides of pies from pan; remove from pan and place top side up on cooling rack. Cool 10 minutes longer. Garnish with green onions.

**1 Serving:** Calories 330; Total Fat 18g (Saturated Fat 5g; Trans Fat 0.5g); Cholesterol 120mg; Sodium 430mg; Total Carbohydrate 13g (Dietary Fiber 1g); Protein 28g **Exchanges:** 1 Starch, 3 Very Lean Meat, ½ Medium-Fat Meat, 2½ Fat **Carbohydrate Choices:** 1

# French Onion–Chicken Pot Pies

**8 pot pies** • **PREP TIME: 35 Minutes** • **START TO FINISH: 1 Hour**

¼ cup butter

2½ lb boneless skinless chicken thighs, cut into ½-inch pieces

2 large onions, halved, thinly sliced (about 1½ cups)

2 packages (8 oz each) sliced fresh mushrooms (about 6 cups)

¼ cup all-purpose flour

4 cups water

¼ cup dry sherry or additional water

1 box (2 oz) onion soup mix (2 packages)

¼ teaspoon pepper

1 can (16.3 oz) large refrigerated flaky biscuits

6 oz Gruyère cheese, shredded (1½ cups)

**1** Heat oven to 350°F. Spray 8 (10-oz) individual baking dishes (ramekins) with cooking spray. Place on large cookie sheet with sides.

**2** In 12-inch nonstick skillet, melt 2 tablespoons of the butter over medium-high heat. Cook chicken in butter 5 to 7 minutes, stirring occasionally, until no longer pink in center. Remove chicken from skillet; discard chicken juices.

**3** In same skillet, melt remaining 2 tablespoons butter. Cook onions and mushrooms in butter about 8 minutes, stirring occasionally, until golden brown. Sprinkle with flour; cook 1 minute, stirring constantly. Stir in water, sherry and soup mix; heat to boiling. Boil about 3 minutes, stirring occasionally, until slightly thickened.

**4** Spoon about ½ cup chicken into each baking dish; top each with about ⅔ cup onion mixture. Sprinkle with pepper. Separate dough into 8 biscuits; place 1 biscuit on onion mixture in each baking dish.

**5** Bake about 20 minutes or until biscuits are golden. Carefully remove from oven. Sprinkle 3 tablespoons cheese over each biscuit. Bake 4 to 5 minutes longer or until cheese is melted.

**1 Pot Pie:** Calories 630; Total Fat 33g (Saturated Fat 13g; Trans Fat 4g); Cholesterol 125mg; Sodium 1360mg; Total Carbohydrate 38g (Dietary Fiber 2g); Protein 42g **Exchanges:** 2 Starch, 1 Vegetable, 5 Medium-Fat Meat, 1½ Fat **Carbohydrate Choices:** 2½

## Savory Success Tips

A large cookie sheet measuring 17½ × 13½ inches is large enough to hold all of the ramekins.

Shredded Swiss cheese can be substituted for the Gruyère.

# Harvest Turkey Pot Pie

**5 servings** • **PREP TIME: 25 Minutes** • **START TO FINISH: 50 Minutes**

| | |
|---|---|
| 1 | cup uncooked instant brown rice |
| 1¼ | cups water |
| 1 | tablespoon olive or vegetable oil |
| 2 | medium stalks celery, sliced (about 1 cup) |
| 1 | large onion, chopped (1 cup) |
| 1 | large apple, chopped (about 1½ cups) |
| 3 | cups cut-up cooked turkey |
| 1 | jar (12 oz) turkey gravy |
| ½ | teaspoon salt |
| ½ | teaspoon dried sage leaves |
| 1 | Pillsbury refrigerated pie crust, softened as directed on box |
| 1 | can (14 oz) whole berry cranberry sauce |

**1** Heat oven to 400°F. Spray 2-quart round casserole with cooking spray. Cook rice in water as directed on package. Spread rice in bottom and 1 inch up side of casserole.

**2** In 12-inch nonstick skillet, heat oil over medium-high heat. Cook celery and onion in oil 5 minutes, stirring frequently. Add apple; cook 3 minutes, stirring frequently. Stir in turkey, gravy, salt and sage. Cook about 3 minutes, stirring occasionally, until thoroughly heated. Spoon turkey mixture over rice in casserole.

**3** Unroll pie crust over hot turkey mixture. Fold excess crust under and press to form thick crust edge; flute. Cut slits in several places in crust.

**4** Bake about 25 minutes or until crust is golden and filling is bubbly. Serve with cranberry sauce.

**1 Serving:** Calories 790; Total Fat 30g (Saturated Fat 10g; Trans Fat 0g); Cholesterol 90mg; Sodium 1160mg; Total Carbohydrate 100g (Dietary Fiber 4g); Protein 30g **Exchanges:** 4 Starch, 2½ Other Carbohydrate, ½ Vegetable, 2½ Lean Meat, 4 Fat **Carbohydrate Choices:** 6½

## Savory Success Tips

If you have time in advance, cook some wild rice to use in place of the brown rice.

Cooked fresh or frozen green beans are a tasty side dish to serve with this turkey pot pie.

# Patchwork Turkey Pot Pie

**6 servings** • **PREP TIME: 15 Minutes** • **START TO FINISH: 1 Hour 35 Minutes**

2 cups diced cooked turkey breast

2 cups refrigerated cooked diced potatoes with onions (from 20-oz bag)

2 cups frozen mixed vegetables, thawed

1 jar (4.5 oz) sliced mushrooms, drained

½ cup sour cream

1 jar (12 oz) turkey gravy

¼ teaspoon dried sage leaves

1 Pillsbury refrigerated pie crust, softened as directed on box

**1** Heat oven to 375°F. Spray 3-quart casserole with cooking spray.

**2** In large bowl, mix turkey, potatoes, mixed vegetables, mushrooms, sour cream, gravy and sage. Spoon mixture into casserole.

**3** Unroll pie crust on work surface. Cut into 1½-inch-wide strips, then cut in opposite direction, making 1½-inch-square pieces (not all will be perfectly square). Starting with rounded-edge pieces around edge of casserole, cover top of turkey mixture with pie crust pieces, overlapping each piece.

**4** Bake 1 hour 15 minutes to 1 hour 20 minutes or until crust is golden brown and edges are bubbly.

**1 Serving:** Calories 390; Total Fat 18g (Saturated Fat 7g; Trans Fat 0g); Cholesterol 60mg; Sodium 760mg; Total Carbohydrate 40g (Dietary Fiber 4g); Protein 19g **Exchanges:** 2 Starch, ½ Other Carbohydrate, 1 Vegetable, 1½ Very Lean Meat, 3 Fat **Carbohydrate Choices:** 2½

## Savory Success Tip

Substitute 2 cups diced rotisserie or cooked chicken for the turkey and a 12-ounce jar of chicken gravy for the turkey gravy.

# Jack-O'-Lantern Sloppy Joe Pie

**4 servings** • **PREP TIME: 50 Minutes** • **START TO FINISH: 50 Minutes**

1   Pillsbury refrigerated pie crust, softened as directed on box

1½   lb bulk turkey sausage

1   medium onion, chopped (½ cup)

1   cup frozen corn, thawed

1   cup chunky-style salsa

½   cup chili sauce

2   tablespoons packed brown sugar

1   can (4.5 oz) chopped green chiles

2   tablespoons chopped fresh cilantro, if desired

**1**   Heat oven to 450°F. Unroll pie crust on ungreased cookie sheet. With sharp knife, cut jack-o'-lantern face from crust. If desired, place cutouts on crust to decorate, securing each with small amount of water.

**2**   Bake 9 to 11 minutes or until crust is light golden brown.

**3**   Meanwhile, in 10-inch nonstick skillet, cook sausage and onion over medium-high heat 8 to 10 minutes, stirring frequently, until sausage is no longer pink. Stir in remaining ingredients except cilantro. Heat to boiling. Reduce heat to medium-low; simmer uncovered 8 to 10 minutes, stirring occasionally, until corn is cooked and sauce is desired consistency.

**4**   Stir cilantro into sausage mixture. Carefully place warm baked crust over turkey mixture in skillet.

**1 Serving:** Calories 690; Total Fat 35g (Saturated Fat 11g; Trans Fat 0.5g); Cholesterol 105mg; Sodium 2690mg; Total Carbohydrate 61g (Dietary Fiber 5g); Protein 32g **Exchanges:** 2 Starch, 2 Other Carbohydrate, 3½ Medium-Fat Meat, 3 Fat **Carbohydrate Choices:** 4

## Savory Success Tip

Pork sausage can be used in place of the turkey sausage, but be sure to drain it well before adding the remaining ingredients.

# Rustic Meat and Potato Pie

**8 servings** • **PREP TIME: 35 Minutes** • **START TO FINISH: 1 Hour 45 Minutes**

1 box Pillsbury refrigerated pie crusts, softened as directed on box

1 lb lean (at least 80%) ground beef

1 tablespoon finely chopped garlic

2 teaspoons vegetable oil

2 cups sliced carrots

2 cups refrigerated cooked diced potatoes with onions (from 20-oz bag)

½ cup cooked real bacon pieces (from 3-oz jar)

¾ teaspoon dried thyme leaves

¾ teaspoon pepper

2 cups beef broth

5 tablespoons cornstarch

1 egg

1 tablespoon water

**1** Heat oven to 425°F. Make pie crusts as directed on box for Two-Crust Pie using 9-inch glass pie plate.

**2** In 12-inch skillet, cook beef and garlic over medium-high heat 5 to 7 minutes, stirring occasionally, until beef is thoroughly cooked; drain. Transfer beef mixture to large bowl. In same skillet, heat oil over medium heat. Cook carrots in oil 3 to 4 minutes, stirring occasionally, until crisp-tender. Add carrots, potatoes, bacon, thyme and pepper to beef mixture.

**3** In small bowl, mix broth and cornstarch with whisk; pour into skillet. Heat to boiling over medium heat; cook about 2 minutes or until thickened. Pour over beef and vegetables; stir to combine. Spoon mixture into crust-lined plate.

**4** Top with second crust; seal and flute. Cut slits in several places in top crust. In small bowl, beat egg and water. Brush over top crust.

**5** Bake 15 minutes. Reduce oven temperature to 375°F. Bake 40 to 45 minutes longer or until crust is browned, placing sheet of foil over entire crust during last 20 minutes. Let stand 10 minutes before serving.

**1 Serving:** Calories 470; Total Fat 25g (Saturated Fat 9g; Trans Fat 1g); Cholesterol 75mg; Sodium 890mg; Total Carbohydrate 45g (Dietary Fiber 2g); Protein 17g **Exchanges:** 3 Starch, ½ Vegetable, 1 Medium-Fat Meat, 3½ Fat **Carbohydrate Choices:** 3

# Deep-Dish Ground Beef Pot Pies

**4 pot pies • PREP TIME: 25 Minutes • START TO FINISH: 1 Hour**

## FILLING

- 1 lb lean (at least 80%) ground beef
- 1 medium onion, chopped (½ cup)
- 2 cups diced unpeeled russet potatoes
- 2 cups frozen mixed vegetables
- 1 can (14.5 oz) diced tomatoes with basil, garlic and oregano, undrained
- 1 jar (12 oz) beef gravy
- ⅛ teaspoon pepper

## CRUST

- 1 Pillsbury refrigerated pie crust, softened as directed on box
- 1 egg white, beaten
- 1 to 2 tablespoons finely chopped fresh parsley

**1** Heat oven to 425°F. Spray 4 (2-cup) individual ovenproof bowls with cooking spray. Place in 15×10×1-inch pan.

**2** In 12-inch nonstick skillet or 4-quart Dutch oven, cook beef and onion over medium-high heat 5 to 7 minutes, stirring occasionally, until beef is thoroughly cooked; drain. Stir in potatoes, frozen vegetables, tomatoes, gravy and pepper. Reduce heat to medium-low. Cover; cook 8 to 10 minutes, stirring occasionally, until potatoes are almost tender.

**3** Meanwhile, unroll pie crust on work surface. With 5-inch round cutter, cut 4 rounds from crust.

**4** Spoon beef mixture evenly into bowls. Place crusts over beef mixture; seal to edges of bowls. Cut slits in several places in crusts. Brush with egg white; sprinkle with parsley.

**5** Bake 30 to 35 minutes or until crusts are golden brown.

**1 Pot Pie:** Calories 490; Total Fat 23g (Saturated Fat 9g; Trans Fat 1g); Cholesterol 75mg; Sodium 1100mg; Total Carbohydrate 43g (Dietary Fiber 4g); Protein 28g **Exchanges:** 1½ Starch, 1 Other Carbohydrate, 1 Vegetable, 3 Medium-Fat Meat, 1½ Fat **Carbohydrate Choices:** 3

## Savory Success Tip

**To make one large pot pie, spoon beef mixture into sprayed 2-quart casserole. Cover mixture with uncut pie crust; seal edge against inside of casserole. Continue as directed above.**

# Ground Beef Pot Pie

**6 servings** • **PREP TIME: 20 Minutes** • **START TO FINISH: 1 Hour 5 Minutes**

1  box Pillsbury refrigerated pie crusts, softened as directed on box

1  lb lean (at least 80%) ground beef

1  medium onion, chopped (½ cup)

1  teaspoon garlic salt

½  teaspoon pepper

3  tablespoons cornstarch

3  cups frozen southern-style diced hash brown potatoes (from 32-oz bag), thawed

3  medium carrots, sliced (1½ cups)

1  jar (12 oz) beef gravy

**1** Heat oven to 450°F. Make pie crusts as directed on box for Two-Crust Pie using 9-inch glass pie plate.

**2** In 12-inch skillet, cook beef, onion, garlic salt and pepper over medium-high heat 5 to 7 minutes, stirring occasionally, until beef is thoroughly cooked; drain. Stir cornstarch into beef mixture until blended. Stir in potatoes, carrots and gravy. Cook 5 to 6 minutes over medium-high heat, stirring frequently, until hot.

**3** Spoon beef mixture into crust-lined plate. Top with second crust; seal edge and flute. Cut slits in several places in top crust; cover crust edge with pie shield ring or strips of foil to prevent excessive browning.

**4** Bake 35 to 40 minutes or until crust is golden brown. Let stand 5 minutes before serving.

**1 Serving:** Calories 530; Total Fat 26g (Saturated Fat 11g; Trans Fat 0.5g); Cholesterol 55mg; Sodium 920mg; Total Carbohydrate 55g (Dietary Fiber 3g); Protein 19g **Exchanges:** 3½ Starch, ½ Vegetable, 1 Medium-Fat Meat, 3½ Fat **Carbohydrate Choices:** 3½

## Savory Success Tip

**Use your own blend of spices, if you prefer. For example, seasoned salt, Italian seasoning or grilling herbs work well to flavor meat and potato dishes like this one.**

# Southeast Asian Samosa Pot Pie

6 servings • PREP TIME: 45 Minutes • START TO FINISH: 1 Hour 35 Minutes

## FILLING

1¼   cups diced red potatoes (about ½ lb)
1   lb lean (at least 80%) ground beef
1   large onion, chopped (1 cup)
2   large cloves garlic, finely chopped
2   tablespoons curry powder
2   teaspoons ground cumin
1   teaspoon ground ginger
¼   to ½ teaspoon crushed red pepper flakes
¾   cup beef broth
2   tablespoons cornstarch
½   teaspoon salt
¾   cup frozen sweet peas, thawed
¼   cup chopped fresh cilantro

## CRUST

Two-Crust Pastry (page 8) or 1 box Pillsbury refrigerated pie crusts, softened as directed on box

## CUCUMBER YOGURT SAUCE, IF DESIRED

½   cup plain fat-free yogurt
¼   cup finely chopped peeled cucumber
2   tablespoons chopped fresh mint leaves

**1**   In small saucepan, place potatoes and enough water to cover. Heat to boiling over medium-high heat; reduce heat to medium-low. Cook uncovered 10 minutes or until tender. Drain; set aside.

**2**   Meanwhile, in 10-inch nonstick skillet, cook beef over medium-high heat 5 minutes. Add onion. Reduce heat to medium. Cook 3 minutes longer, stirring occasionally, until beef is thoroughly cooked and onion is tender; drain. Add garlic, curry powder, cumin, ginger and pepper flakes; cook and stir 30 seconds.

**3**   In small bowl, mix broth, cornstarch and salt with whisk. Add to beef mixture. Heat to boiling over medium heat; reduce heat. Simmer 1 minute or until broth is slightly thickened. Remove from heat. Stir in potatoes, peas and cilantro; cool while preparing crust.

**4**   Heat oven to 400°F. Place 1 pastry round or pie crust in 9-inch glass pie plate. Spoon filling into pastry-lined plate. Cover with second pastry or crust; seal and flute. Cut 6 slits in top crust.

**5**   Bake 20 minutes. Cover crust edge with pie crust shield ring or strips of foil to prevent excessive browning. Bake 15 to 20 minutes longer or until crust is golden brown. Let stand 10 minutes before serving.

**6**   Meanwhile, in small bowl, stir together sauce ingredients. Serve pie with sauce.

**1 Serving:** Calories 550; Total Fat 32g (Saturated Fat 9g; Trans Fat 1g); Cholesterol 45mg; Sodium 750mg; Total Carbohydrate 44g (Dietary Fiber 3g); Protein 19g **Exchanges:** 2½ Starch, 1 Vegetable, 1½ Medium-Fat Meat, 4½ Fat **Carbohydrate Choices:** 3

## Savory Success Tip

To save time, substitute 1¼ cups refrigerated cooked diced potatoes (from 20-ounce bag) and skip step 1.

# Chili Pot Pie

**5 servings (1 cup each)** • **PREP TIME: 15 Minutes** • **START TO FINISH: 35 Minutes**

1   lb lean (at least 80%) ground beef

1   large onion, chopped (1 cup)

1   medium green bell pepper, chopped (1 cup)

1   cup sliced fresh mushrooms

2   teaspoons chili powder

1   can (15 oz) black beans, drained, rinsed

1   can (15 oz) pizza sauce

1   can (10¾ oz) condensed Cheddar cheese soup

1   can (10.2 oz) large refrigerated flaky biscuits

½   cup shredded Cheddar cheese (2 oz)

**1**  Heat oven to 375°F. In 12-inch nonstick skillet, cook beef and onion over medium-high heat 5 to 7 minutes, stirring occasionally, until beef is thoroughly cooked; drain.

**2**  Stir in remaining ingredients except biscuits and cheese. Cook about 5 minutes, stirring occasionally, until hot and bubbly. Spoon mixture into ungreased 2½-quart casserole.

**3**  Separate dough into 5 biscuits. Cut each biscuit in half crosswise; place biscuit pieces, cut side down, around edge of beef mixture. Sprinkle with cheese.

**4**  Bake 15 to 20 minutes or until biscuits are golden brown and no longer doughy on bottom.

**1 Serving:** Calories 630; Total Fat 29g (Saturated Fat 11g; Trans Fat 5g); Cholesterol 75mg; Sodium 1600mg; Total Carbohydrate 60g (Dietary Fiber 11g); Protein 34g **Exchanges:** 2½ Starch, 1 Other Carbohydrate, 1 Vegetable, 3½ Medium-Fat Meat, 2 Fat **Carbohydrate Choices:** 4

## Savory Success Tip

Try a different type of beans, such as kidney or pinto, in place of the black beans and Monterey Jack cheese instead of Cheddar would be a delicious change of flavor, too.

# Cheeseburger Pot Pie

**6 servings** • **PREP TIME: 20 Minutes** • **START TO FINISH: 40 Minutes**

1½  lb lean (at least 80%) ground beef
1  small onion, chopped (¼ cup)
¾  cup ketchup
2  tablespoons chopped dill pickle, if desired
⅛  teaspoon pepper
1  cup shredded sharp Cheddar cheese (4 oz)
1  Pillsbury refrigerated pie crust, softened as directed on box

**1** Heat oven to 450°F. In 10-inch skillet, cook beef and onion over medium-high heat 5 to 7 minutes, stirring occasionally, until beef is thoroughly cooked; drain. Reduce heat to medium. Stir in ketchup, pickle and pepper; cook 2 to 3 minutes or until thoroughly heated.

**2** In ungreased 9-inch glass pie plate, spread hot beef mixture. Sprinkle with cheese. Unroll pie crust over beef mixture; seal edge and flute. Cut slits in several places in top crust.

**3** Bake 13 to 20 minutes or until crust is golden brown and filling is bubbly. During last 10 minutes of baking, cover crust edge with strips of foil to prevent excessive browning.

**1 Serving:** Calories 460; Total Fat 28g (Saturated Fat 12g; Trans Fat 1g); Cholesterol 95mg; Sodium 650mg; Total Carbohydrate 26g (Dietary Fiber 0g); Protein 25g **Exchanges:** 1½ Starch, 3 Medium-Fat Meat, 2½ Fat **Carbohydrate Choices:** 2

## Savory Success Tips

For milder flavor, use an American-Cheddar cheese blend instead of the sharp Cheddar.

Ground turkey can easily be substituted for the ground beef.

# Muffin Tin Taco Pies

6 servings (2 pies each) • PREP TIME: 30 Minutes • START TO FINISH: 1 Hour 15 Minutes

## CRUST

Two-Crust Pastry (page 8)
or 1 box Pillsbury refrigerated
pie crusts, softened as directed
on box

1 egg white

½ teaspoon ground cumin

## FILLING

1 lb lean (at least 80%) ground
beef

1 medium onion, finely chopped
(¾ cup)

1 package (1 oz) 40% less-
sodium taco seasoning mix

½ cup chunky-style salsa

⅓ cup water

1 cup shredded Mexican cheese
blend (4 oz)

¼ cup chopped fresh cilantro

## TOPPINGS, IF DESIRED

Sour cream

Salsa

Sliced jalapeño chiles

Sliced ripe olives

Shredded lettuce

Chopped avocado

Chopped tomato

**1** Heat oven to 400°F. On floured surface with floured rolling pin, roll each pastry or pie crust to 12-inch round. Cut 6 (4-inch) rounds from each crust. Firmly press rounds in bottoms and up sides of 12 ungreased regular-size muffin cups. In small bowl, beat egg white and cumin with whisk until frothy. Generously brush mixture over insides of each pastry-lined cup.

**2** In 10-inch nonstick skillet, cook beef over medium-high heat 5 minutes. Add onion. Reduce heat to medium. Cook 3 minutes longer, stirring occasionally, until beef is thoroughly cooked and onion is tender; drain. Stir in taco seasoning mix, salsa and water. Cook over medium heat 5 minutes, stirring occasionally, until slightly thickened. Spoon hot beef mixture evenly into muffin cups.

**3** Bake 30 to 35 minutes or until crust edges are golden brown. Sprinkle tops of pies with cheese. Bake 2 to 3 minutes longer or until cheese is melted. Let stand 5 minutes before serving. Sprinkle with cilantro. Serve with toppings of choice.

**1 Serving:** Calories 590; Total Fat 37g (Saturated Fat 13g; Trans Fat 1g); Cholesterol 65mg; Sodium 1020mg; Total Carbohydrate 40g (Dietary Fiber 1g); Protein 23g **Exchanges:** 2½ Starch, 1½ Medium-Fat Meat, ½ High-Fat Meat, 5 Fat **Carbohydrate Choices:** 2½

## Sweet Success Tip

Brushing the pastry with an egg white before adding the filling helps seal the crust, keeping the dough crisp and flaky. It's particularly useful with a moist filling like this one.

# Impossibly Easy Mini Blue Cheeseburger Pies

6 servings (2 mini pies each) • PREP TIME: 15 Minutes • START TO FINISH: 1 Hour 5 Minutes

## BURGER MIXTURE

- 1 lb lean (at least 80%) ground beef
- 1 large onion, chopped (1 cup)
- ½ cup crumbled blue cheese (2 oz)
- 2 teaspoons Worcestershire sauce

## BAKING MIXTURE

- ½ cup Original Bisquick mix
- ½ cup milk
- 2 eggs

## TOPPING

- 6 tablespoons French-fried onions (from 2.8-oz can)

**1** Heat oven to 375°F. Spray 12 regular-size muffin cups with cooking spray.

**2** In 10-inch skillet, cook beef and onion over medium-high heat 5 to 7 minutes, stirring occasionally, until beef is thoroughly cooked; drain. Cool 5 minutes; stir in cheese and Worcestershire sauce.

**3** In medium bowl, stir baking mixture ingredients with whisk or fork until blended. Spoon slightly less than 1 tablespoon baking mixture into each muffin cup. Top each with about ¼ cup burger mixture and 1 tablespoon baking mixture.

**4** Bake 10 minutes. Sprinkle evenly with French-fried onions. Bake 15 to 20 minutes longer or until toothpick inserted in center comes out clean and tops are golden brown. Cool 5 minutes. With thin knife, loosen sides of pies from pan; remove from pan and place top side up on cooling rack. Cool 10 minutes longer before serving.

**1 Serving:** Calories 280; Total Fat 17g (Saturated Fat 7g; Trans Fat 1.5g); Cholesterol 120mg; Sodium 390mg; Total Carbohydrate 12g (Dietary Fiber 0g); Protein 19g **Exchanges:** ½ Starch, ½ Vegetable, 2½ Lean Meat, 2 Fat **Carbohydrate Choices:** 1

# Impossibly Easy Mini Cheeseburger Pies

**6 servings (2 mini pies each)** · **PREP TIME: 15 Minutes** · **START TO FINISH: 1 Hour 5 Minutes**

## BURGER MIXTURE

- 1 lb lean (at least 80%) ground beef
- 1 large onion, chopped (1 cup)
- 1 tablespoon Worcestershire sauce
- 1 teaspoon garlic salt
- 1 cup shredded Cheddar cheese (4 oz)

## BAKING MIXTURE

- ½ cup Original Bisquick mix
- ½ cup milk
- 2 eggs

## GARNISHES, IF DESIRED

- 12 mini kosher dill pickles
- 1 medium tomato, chopped
  Ketchup and mustard

**1** Heat oven to 375°F. Spray 12 regular-size muffin cups with cooking spray.

**2** In 10-inch skillet, cook beef and onion over medium-high heat 5 to 7 minutes, stirring occasionally, until thoroughly cooked; drain. Cool 5 minutes; stir in Worcestershire sauce, garlic salt and cheese.

**3** In medium bowl, stir baking mixture ingredients with whisk or fork until blended. Spoon slightly less than 1 tablespoon baking mixture into each muffin cup. Top each with about ¼ cup burger mixture and 1 tablespoon baking mixture.

**4** Bake about 30 minutes or until toothpick inserted in center comes out clean and tops are golden brown. Cool 5 minutes. With thin knife, loosen sides of muffins from pan; remove from pan and place top side up on cooling rack. Cool 10 minutes longer. Serve with pickles, tomato, ketchup and mustard.

**1 Serving:** Calories 290; Total Fat 18g (Saturated Fat 8g; Trans Fat 1g); Cholesterol 130mg; Sodium 500mg; Total Carbohydrate 11g (Dietary Fiber 0g); Protein 21g **Exchanges:** ½ Starch, 2 Lean Meat, ½ Medium-Fat Meat, ½ High-Fat Meat, 1 Fat **Carbohydrate Choices:** 1

# Impossibly Easy Mini Greek Burger Pies

**6 servings (2 mini pies each)** • **PREP TIME: 15 Minutes** • **START TO FINISH: 1 Hour 5 Minutes**

### BURGER MIXTURE

| | |
|---|---|
| 1 | lb lean (at least 80%) ground beef or ground lamb |
| 1 | large onion, chopped (1 cup) |
| ¼ | teaspoon crushed red pepper flakes |
| ½ | cup diced roasted red bell peppers (from 7.25-oz jar) |
| ½ | cup crumbled feta cheese (2 oz) |

### BAKING MIXTURE

| | |
|---|---|
| ½ | cup Original Bisquick mix |
| ½ | cup milk |
| 2 | eggs |

**1** Heat oven to 375°F. Spray 12 regular-size muffin cups with cooking spray.

**2** In 10-inch skillet, cook beef and onion over medium-high heat 5 to 7 minutes, stirring occasionally, until beef is thoroughly cooked; drain. Cool 5 minutes; stir in pepper flakes, roasted peppers and cheese.

**3** In medium bowl, stir baking mixture ingredients with whisk or fork until blended. Spoon slightly less than 1 tablespoon baking mixture into each muffin cup. Top each with about ¼ cup burger mixture and 1 tablespoon baking mixture.

**4** Bake 25 to 30 minutes or until toothpick inserted in center comes out clean and tops are golden brown. Cool 5 minutes. With thin knife, loosen sides of pies from pan; remove from pan and place top side up on cooling rack. Cool 10 minutes longer before serving.

**1 Serving:** Calories 270; Total Fat 15g (Saturated Fat 6g; Trans Fat 1g); Cholesterol 125mg; Sodium 350mg; Total Carbohydrate 13g (Dietary Fiber 0g); Protein 19g **Exchanges:** ½ Starch, ½ Vegetable, 2½ Lean Meat, 1½ Fat **Carbohydrate Choices:** 1

# Caramelized Onion–Beef Pastries

**8 servings** • **PREP TIME: 1 Hour** • **START TO FINISH: 1 Hour 25 Minutes**

2 tablespoons butter

2 cups sliced onions

3 cloves garlic, finely chopped

1 lb lean (at least 80%) ground beef

½ cup beef broth

⅓ cup chili sauce

1 teaspoon dried thyme leaves

½ teaspoon pepper

¼ teaspoon salt

¾ cup refrigerated cooked diced potatoes with onions (from 20-oz bag)

½ cup frozen mixed vegetables, thawed

2 boxes Pillsbury refrigerated pie crusts, softened as directed on box

**1** In 10-inch nonstick skillet, melt butter over medium heat. Cook onions in butter 10 minutes, stirring occasionally. Reduce heat to medium-low; cook 10 minutes longer, stirring occasionally, until golden brown. Add garlic; cook and stir 30 seconds. Remove from heat.

**2** Meanwhile, in another 10-inch skillet, cook beef over medium-high heat 5 to 7 minutes, stirring occasionally, until thoroughly cooked; drain. Stir in broth, chili sauce, thyme, pepper and salt. Heat to boiling over medium heat. Cook 2 to 3 minutes, stirring occasionally, until slightly thickened. Transfer mixture to large bowl. Stir in caramelized onions, potatoes and mixed vegetables. Place in refrigerator while preparing crust.

**3** Heat oven to 425°F. Unroll 1 pie crust on lightly floured surface. Fold sides of crust toward center; lightly press crust together to form rectangle, brushing off excess flour. Fold bottom and top of crust toward center to create smaller rectangle; lightly press together. Rotate rectangle a quarter turn so center seam is facing vertically in front of you. Roll crust to 16×6-inch rectangle, straightening ends as you roll. Cut crosswise to form 4 (6×4-inch) pieces. Repeat with remaining 3 pie crusts for a total of 16 pieces.

**4** Place 8 of the pie crust pieces on 2 large ungreased cookie sheets. Top evenly with meat mixture, leaving ½-inch border around edges. Roll 8 remaining pie crust pieces slightly larger (about 6½×5½ inches); place over filling. Fold edges under as you would a two-crust pie; press together to seal and flute. Cut 3 slits in top of each pie.

**5** Bake 20 to 25 minutes or until golden brown. Serve warm.

**1 Serving:** Calories 600; Total Fat 34g (Saturated Fat 15g; Trans Fat 1g); Cholesterol 55mg; Sodium 910mg; Total Carbohydrate 59g (Dietary Fiber 2g); Protein 14g **Exchanges:** 3 Starch, ½ Other Carbohydrate, 1 Vegetable, ½ Medium-Fat Meat, 6 Fat **Carbohydrate Choices:** 4

## Savory Success Tip

Uncooked pastries may be frozen up to 2 months. Bake directly from the freezer at 425°F for 15 minutes. Reduce oven temperature to 375°F; bake 15 to 20 minutes longer or until crust is golden brown and filling is hot.

# Empanada Grande

**3 servings** • **PREP TIME: 15 Minutes** • **START TO FINISH: 45 Minutes**

1 box Pillsbury refrigerated pie crusts, softened as directed on box

1 egg

4 oz smoked chorizo sausage links or kielbasa, casing removed, coarsely chopped (about 1 cup)

¾ cup frozen country-style shredded hash brown potatoes (from 30-oz bag), thawed

⅓ cup frozen sweet peas, thawed

1 small onion, chopped (¼ cup)

¼ teaspoon salt

**1** Heat oven to 400°F. Unroll pie crust on ungreased large cookie sheet.

**2** In large bowl, beat egg thoroughly; reserve 1 tablespoon in small bowl. Add remaining ingredients to egg in large bowl; mix well.

**3** Spoon chorizo mixture evenly onto half of crust to within ½ inch of edge. Brush edge of crust with reserved beaten egg. Fold crust over filling; press edges with fork to seal. Cut several slits in top of crust. Brush top with beaten egg.

**4** Bake 25 to 30 minutes or until golden brown. Cut into wedges to serve.

**1 Serving:** Calories 510; Total Fat 31g (Saturated Fat 12g; Trans Fat 0g); Cholesterol 40mg; Sodium 1030mg; Total Carbohydrate 46g (Dietary Fiber 2g); Protein 13g **Exchanges:** 3 Starch, ½ High-Fat Meat, 5 Fat **Carbohydrate Choices:** 3

## Savory Success Tips

Turnovers like these originated in Latin America. Family-size turnovers are called *empanada gallega*. Appetizer-size turnovers are *empanaditas*.

Thaw hash browns in a flash by placing them on a microwavable plate and microwave uncovered on Medium (50%) for 1 minute.

# Beef Empanadas

6 servings • PREP TIME: 20 Minutes • START TO FINISH: 45 Minutes

1   lb lean (at least 80%) ground beef

1   medium onion, chopped (½ cup)

½   teaspoon chili powder

¼   teaspoon salt

1   can (14.5 oz) diced tomatoes with mild green chiles, well drained

1   box Pillsbury refrigerated pie crusts, softened as directed on box

½   cup shredded Monterey Jack cheese (2 oz)

1   egg, beaten

**1**   Heat oven to 400°F. In 12-inch skillet, cook beef and onion over medium-high heat 5 to 7 minutes, stirring occasionally, until beef is thoroughly cooked; drain. Stir in chili powder, salt and tomatoes. Remove from heat.

**2**   Unroll pie crusts on ungreased large cookie sheet. Spoon about 2 cups beef mixture onto half of each crust, spreading to within ½ inch of edge. Top each with ¼ cup cheese.

**3**   Brush edge of each crust with beaten egg. Fold untopped half of each crust over filling; press edge with fork to seal. Cut slits in several places in top of each; brush with beaten egg.

**4**   Bake 20 to 25 minutes or until golden brown. Cut into wedges to serve.

**1 Serving:** Calories 510; Total Fat 31g (Saturated Fat 12g; Trans Fat 1g); Cholesterol 100mg; Sodium 690mg; Total Carbohydrate 39g (Dietary Fiber 2g); Protein 20g **Exchanges:** 2½ Starch, 2 Medium-Fat Meat, 4 Fat **Carbohydrate Choices:** 2½

## Savory Success Tip

If you like cilantro, chop 2 tablespoons and add it to the empanada filling with the tomatoes.

# Cornbread-Topped Sausage Pie

**6 servings** · **PREP TIME: 20 Minutes** · **START TO FINISH: 55 Minutes**

## SAUSAGE MIXTURE

- 1 lb bulk Italian sausage
- 1 medium onion, chopped (½ cup)
- 1 small bell pepper (any color), chopped
- 2 cloves garlic, finely chopped
- 1 can (15 oz) tomato sauce
- 1 box (9 oz) frozen corn, thawed
- 1 jar (4.5 oz) sliced mushrooms, drained

## CORNBREAD TOPPING

- ⅔ cup cornmeal
- ⅓ cup all-purpose flour
- 1 tablespoon sugar
- 2 teaspoons baking powder
- ¼ teaspoon sugar
- ½ cup milk
- 2 tablespoons vegetable oil
- 1 egg
- ¼ cup shredded pepper Jack cheese (1 oz)

**1** Heat oven to 400°F. In 10-inch skillet, cook sausage, onion, bell pepper and garlic over medium heat 8 to 10 minutes, stirring occasionally, until sausage is no longer pink; drain. Stir in tomato sauce, corn and mushrooms. Heat to boiling; remove from heat.

**2** In medium bowl, stir all topping ingredients except cheese. Beat vigorously with spoon 30 seconds. Stir in cheese.

**3** Spoon sausage mixture into ungreased 2-quart casserole. Pour topping over hot sausage mixture, spreading evenly.

**4** Bake uncovered 20 to 25 minutes or until topping is golden brown.

**1 Serving:** Calories 430; Total Fat 22g (Saturated Fat 7g; Trans Fat 0g); Cholesterol 85mg; Sodium 1320mg; Total Carbohydrate 39g (Dietary Fiber 4g); Protein 19g **Exchanges:** 2 Starch, 2 Vegetable, 1 High-Fat Meat, 2½ Fat **Carbohydrate Choices:** 2½

# Impossibly Easy Mini Breakfast Sausage Pies

**6 servings (2 mini pies each) • PREP TIME: 15 Minutes • START TO FINISH: 1 Hour 5 Minutes**

## SAUSAGE MIXTURE

¾  lb bulk pork breakfast sausage

1  medium onion, chopped (½ cup)

1  can (4 oz) mushrooms pieces and stems, drained

½  teaspoon salt

3  tablespoons chopped fresh sage leaves

1  cup shredded Cheddar cheese (4 oz)

## BAKING MIXTURE

½  cup Original Bisquick mix

½  cup milk

2  eggs

**1**  Heat oven to 375°F. Spray 12 regular-size muffin cups with cooking spray.

**2**  In 10-inch skillet, cook sausage and onion over medium-high heat 5 to 7 minutes, stirring occasionally, until sausage is no longer pink; drain. Cool 5 minutes; stir in mushrooms, salt, sage and cheese.

**3**  In medium bowl, stir baking mixture ingredients with whisk or fork until blended. Spoon slightly less than 1 tablespoon baking mixture into each muffin cup. Top each with about ¼ cup sausage mixture and 1 tablespoon baking mixture.

**4**  Bake about 30 minutes or until toothpick inserted in center comes out clean and tops are golden brown. Cool 5 minutes. With thin knife, loosen sides of pies from pan; remove from pan and place top side up on cooling rack. Cool 10 minutes longer before serving.

**1 Serving:** Calories 250; Total Fat 17g (Saturated Fat 8g; Trans Fat 0.5g); Cholesterol 105mg; Sodium 920mg; Total Carbohydrate 10g (Dietary Fiber 1g); Protein 14g **Exchanges:** ½ Starch, ½ Vegetable, 1½ High-Fat Meat, 1 Fat **Carbohydrate Choices:** ½

# Bangers and Mash Hand Pies

**14 mini pies** · **PREP TIME: 35 Minutes** · **START TO FINISH: 50 Minutes**

### POTATO FILLING

- ⅔ cup hot water
- 1 tablespoon butter
- ¼ teaspoon salt
- ⅔ cup plain mashed potato mix (dry)
- 2 tablespoons milk
- 1 tablespoon chopped fresh parsley, if desired

### MEAT FILLING

- ½ lb bulk pork sausage
- ¼ cup chopped onion
- 1 tablespoon dry brown gravy mix (from 0.75-oz package)
- ⅓ cup water

### CRUST

- 2 boxes Pillsbury refrigerated pie crusts, softened as directed on box
- 1 egg, beaten

**1** Heat oven to 425°F. In 1-quart saucepan, heat ⅔ cup hot water, butter and salt to boiling. Remove from heat. Stir in potato mix, milk and parsley just until moistened. Let stand about 1 minute or until liquid is absorbed. Whip with fork until smooth; set aside.

**2** In 8-inch skillet, cook sausage and onion over medium heat about 5 minutes, stirring occasionally, until sausage is no longer pink; drain, if necessary. In small bowl, mix gravy mix and ⅓ cup water. Add to skillet. Simmer until mixture thickens, stirring constantly. Set aside to cool.

**3** Unroll pie crusts on work surface. With 3½-inch round cutter, cut 7 rounds from each crust. Spoon about 1 tablespoon mashed potatoes in center of each of 14 rounds; press to flatten slightly. Top each with about 1 tablespoon meat mixture. Brush edges of pastry with water. Place remaining pastry rounds on top; pinch edges to seal.

**4** Place pies on ungreased cookie sheets. Using sharp knife, cut 3 slits in top of each pastry. Brush with beaten egg.

**5** Bake 9 to 12 minutes or until golden brown.

**1 Mini Pie:** Calories 80; Total Fat 5g (Saturated Fat 2g; Trans Fat 0g); Cholesterol 25mg; Sodium 160mg; Total Carbohydrate 7g (Dietary Fiber 0g); Protein 2g **Exchanges:** ½ Starch, 1 Fat **Carbohydrate Choices:** ½

## Savory Success Tip

The British pub food bangers and mash is a funny name for a relatively simple dish. It's just sausage and mashed potatoes, and here it's given a modern twist in the form of a hearty hand pie.

# Lasagna Pasta Pies

**8 pies · PREP TIME: 20 Minutes · START TO FINISH: 55 Minutes**

1 cup uncooked rotini pasta (3 oz)
1 lb bulk Italian pork sausage
1½ cups tomato pasta sauce
¾ cup ricotta cheese
1 can (16.3 oz) large refrigerated buttermilk biscuits
1 cup shredded mozzarella cheese (4 oz)

**1** Heat oven to 350°F. Cook and drain pasta as directed on package, using minimum cook time.

**2** Meanwhile, in 10-inch skillet, cook sausage over medium-high heat 5 to 7 minutes, stirring occasionally, until no longer pink; drain. Stir in pasta sauce, ricotta cheese and cooked pasta; cook 1 minute.

**3** Separate dough into 8 biscuits; press each biscuit to 5½-inch round. Firmly press rounds in bottoms and up sides of 8 ungreased jumbo muffin cups, forming ¼-inch rim. Fill cups with sausage mixture; sprinkle with mozzarella cheese.

**4** Bake 28 to 32 minutes or until golden brown. Cool 1 minute; remove from pan.

**1 Pie:** Calories 550; Total Fat 23g (Saturated Fat 11g; Trans Fat 0g); Cholesterol 40mg; Sodium 1420mg; Total Carbohydrate 62g (Dietary Fiber 2g); Protein 22g **Exchanges:** 3 Starch, 1 Other Carbohydrate, 2 Medium-Fat Meat, 2 Fat **Carbohydrate Choices:** 4

# Impossibly Easy Mini Crab Cake Pies

**6 servings (2 mini pies each) • PREP TIME: 15 Minutes • START TO FINISH: 1 Hour 5 Minutes**

## CRAB MIXTURE

- 2 cans (6 oz) crabmeat, drained, flaked
- ½ teaspoon seafood seasoning
- 1 tablespoon vegetable oil
- 1 medium onion, chopped (½ cup)
- ½ cup chopped red bell pepper
- ½ cup chopped green bell pepper
- 1 cup shredded mozzarella cheese (4 oz)

## BAKING MIXTURE

- ½ cup Original Bisquick mix
- ½ cup milk
- 2 eggs

## AIOLI

- ½ cup mayonnaise
- ½ teaspoon seafood seasoning
- 1 tablespoon fresh lemon juice

**1** Heat oven to 375°F. Spray 12 regular-size muffin cups with cooking spray.

**2** In small bowl, mix crabmeat and ½ teaspoon seafood seasoning; set aside. In 10-inch skillet, heat oil over medium-high heat. Cook onion and bell peppers in oil 4 minutes, stirring frequently. Add crabmeat mixture; cook and stir until thoroughly heated. Cool 5 minutes; stir in cheese.

**3** In medium bowl, stir baking mixture ingredients with whisk or fork until blended. Spoon slightly less than 1 tablespoon baking mixture into each muffin cup. Top each with about ¼ cup crab mixture and 1 tablespoon baking mixture.

**4** Bake about 30 minutes or until toothpick inserted in center comes out clean and tops are golden brown. Cool 5 minutes. With thin knife, loosen sides of pies from pan; remove from pan and place top side up on cooling rack. Cool 10 minutes longer.

**5** Meanwhile, in small bowl, mix aioli ingredients. Serve each mini pie topped with generous tablespoon of aioli.

**1 Serving:** Calories 340; Total Fat 24g (Saturated Fat 6g; Trans Fat 0.5g); Cholesterol 120mg; Sodium 660mg; Total Carbohydrate 12g (Dietary Fiber 1g); Protein 16g **Exchanges:** ½ Starch, ½ Other Carbohydrate, 1½ Very Lean Meat, ½ Medium-Fat Meat, 4 Fat **Carbohydrate Choices:** 1

# Cheese-Crusted Pizza Pot Pies

**4 pot pies • PREP TIME: 40 Minutes • START TO FINISH: 1 Hour**

1 package (12 oz) pork sausage links, casings removed

⅔ cup chopped onion

⅔ cup finely chopped carrots

½ cup chopped green bell pepper

3 cloves garlic, finely chopped

1¼ cups marinara sauce

⅔ cup sliced pepperoni (from 8-oz package)

⅓ cup chopped pimiento-stuffed green olives

1 cup shredded Italian cheese blend (4 oz)

1 can (11 oz) refrigerated thin pizza crust

1 egg, slightly beaten

8 slices (1 oz each) part-skim mozzarella cheese

Fresh oregano sprigs, if desired

**1** Heat oven to 450°F. Spray bottoms, sides and rims of 4 (10-oz) individual baking dishes (ramekins) with cooking spray. Place in 15×10×1-inch pan.

**2** In 12-inch skillet, cook sausage, onion, carrots, bell pepper and garlic over medium heat 10 to 12 minutes, stirring occasionally, until sausage is thoroughly cooked; drain. Stir in marinara sauce, pepperoni and olives. Simmer 3 to 5 minutes or until thickened. Remove from heat; stir in cheese blend. Divide meat mixture evenly among baking dishes.

**3** Unroll dough on large cutting board. Cut in half lengthwise, then cut in half crosswise. Place 1 dough piece over meat mixture in each dish, overlapping rim. Brush with egg. Top each pot pie with 2 slices mozzarella cheese, overlapping slightly.

**4** Bake 16 to 20 minutes or until crust is brown. Garnish with oregano.

**1 Pot Pie:** Calories 860; Total Fat 49g (Saturated Fat 19g; Trans Fat 0.5g); Cholesterol 155mg; Sodium 2180mg; Total Carbohydrate 60g (Dietary Fiber 4g); Protein 42g **Exchanges:** 2½ Starch, 1 Other Carbohydrate, 1½ Vegetable, 2 Lean Meat, 2½ High-Fat Meat, 4½ Fat **Carbohydrate Choices:** 4

# Not-Your-Mother's Tuna Pot Pie

**5 servings** · **PREP TIME: 25 Minutes** · **START TO FINISH: 50 Minutes**

1 cup uncooked ditalini (short tubes) pasta (4 oz)

4 slices bacon

1 large onion, chopped (1 cup)

1 teaspoon dried thyme leaves

2 tablespoons all-purpose flour

1 cup chicken broth

⅔ cup milk

2 cups frozen crinkle-cut carrots, thawed, well drained

1 can (12 oz) solid white tuna in water, drained, flaked

1 can (7 oz) whole kernel corn, drained

2 tablespoons Dijon mustard

2 slices white bread

2 tablespoons butter, melted

**1** Heat oven to 375°F. Cook and drain pasta as directed on package, using minimum cook time.

**2** Meanwhile, in 12-inch nonstick skillet, cook bacon over medium-high heat until crisp. Using slotted spoon, remove bacon to paper towels; drain. Crumble bacon; set aside. Cook onion and thyme in bacon drippings over medium-high heat, stirring occasionally, until onion is golden brown. Stir in flour; cook and stir 1 minute.

**3** Stir in broth and milk; heat to boiling. Boil and stir until thickened. Stir in carrots, tuna, corn, mustard and cooked pasta; heat to boiling. Fold in bacon. Spoon into ungreased 2-quart casserole.

**4** In food processor, place bread. Cover; process, using quick on-and-off motions, to make bread crumbs. In small bowl, mix bread crumbs and melted butter. Sprinkle over tuna mixture.

**5** Bake uncovered 20 to 25 minutes or until mixture is bubbly and topping is golden brown.

**1 Serving:** Calories 380; Total Fat 11g (Saturated Fat 5g; Trans Fat 0g); Cholesterol 40mg; Sodium 940mg; Total Carbohydrate 43g (Dietary Fiber 4g); Protein 27g **Exchanges:** 2½ Starch, 1 Vegetable, 2½ Lean Meat, ½ Fat **Carbohydrate Choices:** 3

## Savory Success Tips

If you don't have sliced bacon on hand but you do have real bacon bits, you can cook the onion and thyme in 1 tablespoon olive oil, then just sprinkle the pot pie with about ¼ cup bacon bits before you add the bread crumbs.

Any small pasta shape can be used in this easy one-dish meal.

# Roasted Vegetable–Goat Cheese Crostata

6 servings  ·  PREP TIME: 30 Minutes  ·  START TO FINISH: 1 Hour 40 Minutes

1¼  cups thinly sliced fingerling potatoes

1¼  cups small fresh cauliflower florets

1  cup coarsely chopped red onion

1  cup cubed red bell pepper

½  cup diagonally sliced carrots

2  large cloves garlic, finely chopped

4½  teaspoons olive oil

¼  teaspoon salt

⅛  teaspoon pepper

½  cup whipping cream

1  egg

2  teaspoons chopped fresh tarragon or thyme leaves

⅛  teaspoon salt

⅛  teaspoon pepper

1  Pillsbury refrigerated pie crust, softened as directed on box

⅓  cup crumbled chèvre (goat) cheese

**1**  Heat oven to 450°F. In large bowl, toss potatoes, cauliflower, onion, bell pepper, carrots, garlic, oil, ¼ teaspoon salt and ⅛ teaspoon pepper. Arrange vegetables in single layer in 15×10×1-inch pan. Roast uncovered 20 minutes or until tender and lightly browned. Cool to room temperature, about 15 minutes. Reduce oven temperature to 425°F.

**2**  In small bowl, beat whipping cream, egg, tarragon, ⅛ teaspoon salt and ⅛ teaspoon pepper with whisk.

**3**  Line 15×10×1-inch pan with cooking parchment paper; place pie crust in center of pan. Spoon roasted vegetables into center of crust, leaving 1½-inch border around edge. Fold crust border over filling, pleating crust and pressing gently to seal. Carefully pour cream mixture over vegetables. Sprinkle with cheese.

**4**  Bake 25 to 30 minutes or until crust is browned and knife inserted in center comes out clean. Let stand 5 minutes before serving.

**1 Serving:** Calories 340; Total Fat 22g (Saturated Fat 10g; Trans Fat 0g); Cholesterol 70mg; Sodium 400mg; Total Carbohydrate 29g (Dietary Fiber 2g); Protein 6g **Exchanges:** 1 Starch, ½ Other Carbohydrate, 1½ Vegetable, 4½ Fat **Carbohydrate Choices:** 2

## Savory Success Tip
Change this recipe easily by substituting cubed Yukon Gold potatoes for the fingerlings or trying different vegetables such as eggplant, zucchini, mixed colors of bell peppers or yellow onion instead of red (using a total of 5 cups of vegetables). The roasting time may vary, so watch carefully.

# Southwestern Pot Pie

**4 servings • PREP TIME: 15 Minutes • START TO FINISH: 55 Minutes**

2   tablespoons vegetable oil

1   large onion, chopped (1 cup)

2   cups cubed peeled sweet potatoes or butternut squash

2   cups chunky-style salsa

½   cup water

¼   teaspoon ground cinnamon

1   can (15 to 16 oz) garbanzo beans or chickpeas, drained

1   cup frozen corn, thawed

1   pouch (6.5 oz) cornbread & muffin mix

½   cup milk

1   tablespoon roasted sunflower nuts, if desired

**1** In 4-quart Dutch oven or saucepan, heat 1 tablespoon of the oil over medium-high heat. Cook onion in oil about 5 minutes, stirring occasionally, until crisp-tender.

**2** Stir in sweet potatoes, salsa, water and cinnamon. Heat to boiling; reduce heat. Cover; simmer 20 to 25 minutes or until potatoes are tender. Stir in beans and corn.

**3** In medium bowl, mix cornbread mix, milk and remaining 1 tablespoon oil. Stir in nuts. Drop by large spoonfuls onto vegetable mixture. Cover; simmer about 15 minutes or until toothpick inserted in center of dumplings comes out clean.

**1 Serving:** Calories 590; Total Fat 16g (Saturated Fat 3g; Trans Fat 0.5g); Cholesterol 0mg; Sodium 1230mg; Total Carbohydrate 94g (Dietary Fiber 15g); Protein 17g **Exchanges:** 5 Starch, 1 Other Carbohydrate, 2½ Fat **Carbohydrate Choices:** 6

## Savory Success Tip

**If you like black beans, feel free to use them in place of the garbanzo beans.**

# Rice and Bean Burrito Pot Pie

**6 servings** • **PREP TIME: 20 Minutes** • **START TO FINISH: 1 Hour 10 Minutes**

1 tablespoon olive or vegetable oil

1 large onion, chopped (1 cup)

2 cloves garlic, finely chopped

1 jalapeño chile, seeded, finely chopped

2 large tomatoes, chopped (about 2 cups)

2 cans (15 oz each) Spanish rice with bell peppers and onions

1 cup shredded Monterey Jack cheese (4 oz)

1 can (15 oz) pinto beans, drained, rinsed

1 can (11 oz) refrigerated original breadsticks

½ cup sour cream

**1** Heat oven to 375°F. Spray 2-quart casserole or 11×7-inch (2-quart) glass baking dish with cooking spray.

**2** In 10-inch nonstick skillet, heat oil over medium-high heat. Cook onion in oil about 5 minutes, stirring occasionally, until golden brown. Stir in garlic and chile; cook 1 minute, stirring constantly. Stir in tomatoes; cook until thoroughly heated. Remove from heat.

**3** In medium bowl, mix rice and cheese; spread in bottom and ½ inch up sides of casserole. Spread beans evenly over rice mixture. Top with tomato mixture.

**4** Bake uncovered 20 minutes. Remove from oven. Unroll dough; separate into 12 strips. Twist 10 strips; carefully arrange crosswise in single layer over casserole. Stretch and twist remaining 2 strips; place lengthwise across other strips of dough.

**5** Bake 20 to 25 minutes longer or until breadsticks are golden brown. Let stand 5 minutes before serving. Serve with sour cream.

**1 Serving:** Calories 480; Total Fat 15g (Saturated Fat 8g; Trans Fat 0g); Cholesterol 30mg; Sodium 730mg; Total Carbohydrate 68g (Dietary Fiber 7g); Protein 17g **Exchanges:** 3 Starch, 1 Other Carbohydrate, 1 Vegetable, 1 Lean Meat, 2 Fat **Carbohydrate Choices:** 4½

## Savory Success Tip

This vegetarian pot pie is so hearty you won't miss the meat. But if you do, you can add 1 pound of ground beef. Cook with the onion until thoroughly cooked, then drain before stirring in the garlic and chile. Continue as directed—except use a 3-quart casserole.

# Impossibly Easy South-of-the-Border Mini Veggie Pies

**6 servings (2 mini pies each)** • **PREP TIME: 20 Minutes** • **START TO FINISH: 1 Hour 15 Minutes**

## VEGGIE MIXTURE

- 1 tablespoon vegetable oil
- 1 large onion, chopped (1 cup)
- 1 to 2 chipotle chiles in adobo sauce (from 7-oz can), chopped
- ½ cup frozen corn, thawed
- 2 cloves garlic, finely chopped
- ¼ teaspoon dried oregano leaves
- ½ teaspoon salt
- 1 tablespoon fresh lime juice
- 1 cup canned black beans, drained, rinsed
- ¼ cup fresh cilantro, chopped
- 1 cup shredded Cheddar cheese (4 oz)

## BAKING MIXTURE

- ½ cup Original Bisquick mix
- ½ cup milk
- 2 eggs

## GARNISHES, IF DESIRED

- 1 pint cherry or grape tomatoes, cut in half
- 1 avocado, pitted, peeled and chopped
- ½ cup sour cream

**1** Heat oven to 375°F. Spray 12 regular-size muffin cups with cooking spray.

**2** In 10-inch skillet, heat oil over medium-high heat. Add onion, chiles, corn and garlic; cook 5 minutes, stirring occasionally. Add oregano, salt, lime juice, beans and cilantro; stir until combined. Remove from heat. Cool 5 minutes; stir in cheese.

**3** In medium bowl, stir baking mixture ingredients with whisk or fork until blended. Spoon slightly less than 1 tablespoon baking mixture into each muffin cup. Top each with about ¼ cup veggie mixture and 1 tablespoon baking mixture.

**4** Bake 30 to 35 minutes or until toothpick inserted in center comes out clean and tops are golden brown. Cool 5 minutes. With thin knife, loosen sides of pies from pan; remove from pan and place top side up on cooling rack. Cool 10 minutes longer before serving. Garnish with tomatoes, avocado and sour cream.

**1 Serving:** Calories 350; Total Fat 22g (Saturated Fat 9g; Trans Fat 0.5g); Cholesterol 100mg; Sodium 650mg; Total Carbohydrate 27g (Dietary Fiber 6g); Protein 13g **Exchanges:** 1 Starch, ½ Other Carbohydrate, 1 Vegetable, ½ Very Lean Meat, ½ High-Fat Meat, 3½ Fat **Carbohydrate Choices:** 2

## Savory Success Tip

**If your family does not like spicy food, substitute the chipotle chiles with 1 teaspoon ground cumin instead.**

# Chili Mac Pasta Pies

**8 pies • PREP TIME: 20 Minutes • START TO FINISH: 55 Minutes**

1   box (7¼ oz) macaroni and
    cheese dinner

    Milk and butter called for
    on macaroni and cheese box

1   can (15 oz) chili

1½  cups shredded Cheddar cheese
    (6 oz)

1   can (16.3 oz) large refrigerated
    buttermilk biscuits

**1**   Heat oven to 350°F. Make macaroni and cheese as directed on box. Stir in chili and ½ cup of the Cheddar cheese; cook 1 minute.

**2**   Separate dough into 8 biscuits; press each biscuit to 5½-inch round. Firmly press rounds in bottoms and up sides of 8 ungreased jumbo muffin cups, forming ¼-inch rim. Fill cups with macaroni mixture; sprinkle evenly with remaining 1 cup cheese.

**3**   Bake 28 to 32 minutes or until golden brown. Cool 1 minute; remove from pan.

**1 Pie:** Calories 460; Total Fat 21g (Saturated Fat 10g; Trans Fat 4g); Cholesterol 40mg; Sodium 1140mg; Total Carbohydrate 52g (Dietary Fiber 2g); Protein 14g **Exchanges:** 3 Starch, ½ Other Carbohydrate, ½ Medium-Fat Meat, 3 Fat **Carbohydrate Choices:** 3½

# Veggie Lovers' Pot Pie

**8 servings** • **PREP TIME: 30 Minutes** • **START TO FINISH: 55 Minutes**

3 tablespoons butter

1 large russet potato (1 lb), peeled, cut into ½-inch pieces (about 2½ cups)

1 large onion, chopped (1 cup)

1 teaspoon dried thyme leaves

½ teaspoon salt

¼ teaspoon pepper

¼ cup all-purpose flour

1 can (14 oz) vegetable broth

1 bag (1 lb) frozen broccoli, cauliflower and carrots, thawed, well drained

¼ cup milk

3 tablespoons grated Parmesan cheese

1 can (8 oz) refrigerated garlic butter crescent dinner rolls

**1** Heat oven to 375°F. Spray 9½- or 10-inch glass deep-dish pie plate with cooking spray.

**2** In 12-inch nonstick skillet, melt butter over medium-high heat. Add potato, onion, thyme, salt and pepper; cook 10 to 12 minutes, stirring occasionally, until potato is lightly browned. Sprinkle with flour; cook 1 minute, stirring constantly. Stir in broth. Heat to boiling; reduce heat. Cover; simmer about 8 minutes, stirring occasionally, until potato is almost tender.

**3** Remove from heat. Stir in vegetables, milk and cheese. Spoon mixture into pie plate. Separate dough into 8 triangles. Starting at short side of each triangle, roll up triangle halfway. Carefully arrange over vegetable mixture with tips toward center; do not overlap.

**4** Place pie plate on cookie sheet with sides. Bake 20 to 25 minutes or until crust is golden brown.

**1 Serving:** Calories 230; Total Fat 12g (Saturated Fat 5g; Trans Fat 1.5g); Cholesterol 15mg; Sodium 690mg; Total Carbohydrate 25g (Dietary Fiber 3g); Protein 5g **Exchanges:** 1 Starch, ½ Other Carbohydrate, 1 Vegetable, 2 Fat **Carbohydrate Choices:** 1½

## Savory Success Tips

**This pot pie is very versatile and can be served as a side dish or meatless main dish**

**Quickly and easily thaw the frozen vegetables by placing them in a colander and running under warm water.**

# Potato-Onion-Bacon Slab Pie

**6 servings** • **PREP TIME: 35 Minutes** • **START TO FINISH: 1 Hour**

2   medium Yukon Gold potatoes (¾ lb), peeled, cut into ¼-inch slices
½   lb bacon, cut into ½-inch pieces
1½  cups chopped sweet onions
1   can (8 oz) refrigerated seamless dough sheet
4   oz Gruyère cheese, shredded (1 cup)
¼   cup sliced green onions
¼   cup whipping cream
1   egg
½   teaspoon pepper

**1** Heat oven to 375°F. Line 15×10×1-inch pan with cooking parchment paper. In medium saucepan, place potatoes and enough water to cover. Heat to boiling. Boil uncovered 5 to 8 minutes or just until tender; drain well.

**2** Meanwhile, in 10-inch nonstick skillet, cook bacon over medium-high heat about 8 minutes, stirring frequently, until crisp. Drain on paper towels. Reserve 1 to 2 tablespoons drippings in skillet. Cook sweet onions in bacon drippings over medium heat about 8 minutes, stirring occasionally, until softened and lightly browned.

**3** Remove dough sheet from can; unroll in pan. Gently stretch or roll dough to 14×8-inch rectangle. Layer potatoes, sweet onions, bacon, ½ cup of the cheese and the green onions on dough, leaving 2-inch border around edges. Fold up sides of dough to partially enclose filling, pleating as necessary and pressing to seal.

**4** In small bowl, beat whipping cream, egg and pepper with whisk until blended. Slowly pour over filling. Sprinkle with remaining ½ cup cheese.

**5** Bake 20 to 25 minutes or until crust is golden brown.

**1 Serving:** Calories 370; Total Fat 21g (Saturated Fat 10g; Trans Fat 0g); Cholesterol 75mg; Sodium 630mg; Total Carbohydrate 30g (Dietary Fiber 1g); Protein 14g **Exchanges:** 1½ Starch, 1 Vegetable, 1 High-Fat Meat, 2½ Fat **Carbohydrate Choices:** 2

## Savory Success Tip

To prepare this pie ahead of time, cook the potatoes, bacon and onions the day before and refrigerate. Assemble the pie up to 2 hours before baking; cover and refrigerate. Add 3 to 5 minutes to the bake time, if necessary, to ensure the filling is thoroughly heated.

# Ham and Swiss Breakfast Hand Pies

4 pies • PREP TIME: 25 Minutes • START TO FINISH: 45 Minutes

1 box Pillsbury refrigerated pie crusts, softened as directed on box

3 oz thinly sliced deli ham, chopped (¾ cup)

4 teaspoons chopped fresh chives or green onion tops

1 cup shredded Swiss cheese (4 oz)

**1** Heat oven to 425°F. Unroll 1 pie crust on lightly floured surface. Fold sides of crust toward center; lightly press crust together to form rectangle, brushing off excess flour. Fold bottom and top of crust toward center to create smaller rectangle; lightly press together. Rotate rectangle a quarter turn so center seam is facing vertically in front of you. Roll crust to 16×6-inch rectangle, straightening ends as you roll. Cut crosswise to form 4 (6×4-inch) pieces. Repeat with second pie crust for a total of 8 pieces.

**2** Place 4 of the pie crust pieces on ungreased cookie sheet. Top evenly with ham, leaving ½-inch border around edges; sprinkle with chives and cheese. Moisten crust edges with water. Place 4 remaining pie crust pieces over filling; press edges with fork to seal. Using fork, gently poke 3 holes in top of each pie.

**3** Bake 20 minutes or until golden brown. Serve warm.

**1 Pie:** Calories 560; Total Fat 33g (Saturated Fat 15g; Trans Fat 0g); Cholesterol 50mg; Sodium 830mg; Total Carbohydrate 50g (Dietary Fiber 0g); Protein 15g **Exchanges:** 1½ Starch, 2 Other Carbohydrate, ½ Lean Meat, 1 High-Fat Meat, 4½ Fat **Carbohydrate Choices:** 3

## Savory Success Tips

Add a little chopped fresh spinach, 1 to 2 tablespoons, to each pie or change the meat from ham to cooked breakfast sausage, Italian sausage or bacon.

Pies can be made ahead, covered and refrigerated overnight. Bake as directed in the recipe.

# Cheesy Bacon-Tomato Pie

**6 servings** · **PREP TIME: 25 Minutes** · **START TO FINISH: 55 Minutes**

1 Pillsbury refrigerated pie crust, softened as directed on box

8 slices bacon, cut into ½-inch pieces

1 large sweet onion, chopped (1 cup)

2 medium tomatoes, chopped (1½ cups)

¼ cup chopped fresh basil leaves

¼ cup chopped fresh dill weed

½ cup reduced-fat mayonnaise

3 eggs

¼ teaspoon pepper

1 cup shredded Swiss cheese (4 oz)

**1** Heat oven to 450°F. Place pie crust in 9-inch glass pie plate as directed on box for One-Crust Filled Pie. Bake 6 to 7 minutes or until pale brown. Cool crust 15 minutes. Reduce oven temperature to 375°F.

**2** Meanwhile, in 10-inch nonstick skillet, cook bacon over medium-high heat about 8 minutes, stirring frequently, until crisp; drain on paper towels. Drain all but 1 teaspoon bacon drippings from skillet. Cook onion in bacon drippings over medium heat about 10 minutes, stirring occasionally, until softened and lightly browned.

**3** Spoon onion into partially baked crust; sprinkle with tomatoes. Top with basil, dill and bacon. In small bowl, mix mayonnaise, eggs and pepper with whisk. Pour over ingredients in crust. Sprinkle with cheese.

**4** Bake 25 to 30 minutes or lightly browned and set. (Knife inserted in center will come out moist but clean.)

**1 Serving:** Calories 390; Total Fat 27g (Saturated Fat 10g; Trans Fat 0g); Cholesterol 135mg; Sodium 620mg; Total Carbohydrate 23g (Dietary Fiber 1g); Protein 14g **Exchanges:** ½ Starch, ½ Other Carbohydrate, 1 Vegetable, ½ Lean Meat, 1 High-Fat Meat, 3½ Fat **Carbohydrate Choices:** 1½

## Savory Success Tips

If using tomatoes that are extra-juicy, seed the tomatoes before chopping. Slice each tomato crosswise in half and gently squeeze each half to remove the seeds and juice.

Other fresh herbs can be used in this recipe. Try tarragon, chives, chervil or mint in addition to the basil and dill.

# Quiche Lorraine

**8 servings** · **PREP TIME: 25 Minutes** · **START TO FINISH: 1 Hour 40 Minutes**

One-Crust Pastry (page 7) or 1 Pillsbury refrigerated pie crust, softened as directed on box

8 slices bacon, chopped

1 small onion, chopped (⅓ cup)

4 eggs

2 cups whipping cream or half-and-half

¼ teaspoon salt

¼ teaspoon black pepper

⅛ teaspoon ground red pepper (cayenne)

1 cup shredded Swiss or Gruyère cheese (4 oz)

**1** Heat oven to 425°F. Place pastry round or pie crust in 9-inch quiche dish or glass pie plate. Bake as directed for Partially Baked One-Crust Pie (page 9). Reduce oven temperature to 325°F.

**2** Meanwhile, in 10-inch skillet, cook bacon over medium heat, stirring occasionally, until crisp. Remove bacon with slotted spoon; drain on paper towels. Drain all but 2 teaspoons bacon drippings from skillet. Cook onion in bacon drippings over medium heat 3 to 5 minutes, stirring occasionally, until light golden brown. Set aside.

**3** In large bowl, beat eggs slightly with fork or whisk. Beat in whipping cream, salt, black pepper and red pepper. Sprinkle bacon, onion and cheese into partially baked crust. Gently pour egg mixture over ingredients in crust.

**4** Bake 45 to 50 minutes or until knife inserted in center comes out clean. Let stand 10 minutes before cutting.

**1 Serving:** Calories 620; Total Fat 52g (Saturated Fat 25g; Trans Fat 3g); Cholesterol 255mg; Sodium 580mg; Total Carbohydrate 20g (Dietary Fiber 0g); Protein 17g **Exchanges:** 1 Starch, 1 Vegetable, 1½ High-Fat Meat, 8 Fat **Carbohydrate Choices:** 1

**Seafood Quiche** Substitute 1 cup chopped cooked crabmeat (patted dry), imitation crabmeat, or cooked shrimp or salmon for the bacon. Substitute ⅓ cup finely chopped green onions for the onion; increase salt to ½ teaspoon.

**Spinach Quiche** Substitute 1 box (9 ounces) frozen chopped spinach, thawed and squeezed to drain, for the bacon. Sprinkle over onion and cheese.

## Savory Success Tip
**Baking the crust before adding the filling helps to keep it firm and flaky.**

# Canadian Bacon, Asparagus and Potato Quiche

8 servings • PREP TIME: 20 Minutes • START TO FINISH: 1 Hour 30 Minutes

One-Crust Pastry (page 7)
or 1 Pillsbury refrigerated pie
crust, softened as directed
on box

4 eggs
1 cup milk
½ teaspoon dried marjoram leaves
¼ teaspoon salt
1 cup frozen country-style shredded hash brown potatoes (from 30-oz bag), thawed
1 cup ½-inch pieces fresh asparagus
1 cup diced Canadian bacon
6 oz Havarti cheese, shredded (1½ cups)

**1** Heat oven to 425°F. Place pastry round or pie crust in 9-inch quiche dish or glass pie plate. Bake as directed for Partially Baked One-Crust Pie (page 9). Reduce oven temperature to 375°F.

**2** In medium bowl, beat eggs, milk, marjoram and salt with fork or whisk until well blended. Layer potatoes, asparagus, Canadian bacon and cheese in partially baked crust. Gently pour egg mixture over ingredients in crust.

**3** Bake 45 to 50 minutes or until knife inserted in center comes out clean. Let stand 5 minutes before cutting.

**1 Serving:** Calories 290; Total Fat 19g (Saturated Fat 8g; Trans Fat 2g); Cholesterol 140mg; Sodium 640mg; Total Carbohydrate 15g (Dietary Fiber 1g); Protein 15g **Exchanges:** 1 Starch, 2 High-Fat Meat, ½ Fat **Carbohydrate Choices:** 1

## Savory Success Tip
Substitute diced cooked ham or turkey ham for the Canadian bacon and Swiss cheese for the Havarti.

# Leek Quiche

**6 servings** · **PREP TIME:** 25 Minutes · **START TO FINISH:** 1 Hour 25 Minutes

1 Pillsbury refrigerated pie crust, softened as directed on box

2 tablespoons butter

2 medium leeks, cut in half lengthwise, then cut into ½-inch slices (about 4 cups)

3 eggs

1 cup milk

1 cup shredded Swiss cheese (4 oz)

½ teaspoon salt

¼ teaspoon pepper

⅛ teaspoon ground nutmeg

Fresh oregano sprig, if desired

**1** Heat oven to 400°F. Place pie crust in 9-inch glass pie plate as directed on box for One-Crust Filled Pie. Bake about 8 minutes or until very lightly browned.

**2** Meanwhile, in 12-inch skillet, melt butter over medium heat. Cook leeks in butter 7 to 9 minutes, stirring frequently, until tender but not brown. Remove from heat; set aside.

**3** In medium bowl, beat eggs with whisk. Stir in milk, cheese, salt, pepper and nutmeg until blended. Stir in leeks. Pour mixture into partially baked crust.

**4** Bake 10 minutes. Cover crust edge with strips of foil to prevent excessive browning. Reduce oven temperature to 300°F; bake 20 to 25 minutes longer or until knife inserted in center comes out clean. Let stand 15 minutes before cutting. Garnish with oregano.

**1 Serving:** Calories 320; Total Fat 20g (Saturated Fat 10g; Trans Fat 0g); Cholesterol 140mg; Sodium 490mg; Total Carbohydrate 23g (Dietary Fiber 0g); Protein 11g **Exchanges:** 1½ Starch, ½ Vegetable, ½ Medium-Fat Meat, ½ High-Fat Meat, 2½ Fat **Carbohydrate Choices:** 1½

## Savory Success Tip

Leeks look like giant green onions and are related to both onions and garlic. Choose leeks that are firm and brightly colored with an unblemished white bulb portion. Small leeks will be more tender than large ones. Be sure to wash leeks thoroughly because there is often sand between the layers.

# Metric Conversion Guide

## Volume

| U.S. UNITS | CANADIAN METRIC | AUSTRALIAN METRIC |
|---|---|---|
| ¼ teaspoon | 1 mL | 1 ml |
| ½ teaspoon | 2 mL | 2 ml |
| 1 teaspoon | 5 mL | 5 ml |
| 1 tablespoon | 15 mL | 20 ml |
| ¼ cup | 50 mL | 60 ml |
| ⅓ cup | 75 mL | 80 ml |
| ½ cup | 125 mL | 125 ml |
| ⅔ cup | 150 mL | 170 ml |
| ¾ cup | 175 mL | 190 ml |
| 1 cup | 250 mL | 250 ml |
| 1 quart | 1 liter | 1 liter |
| 1½ quarts | 1.5 liters | 1.5 liters |
| 2 quarts | 2 liters | 2 liters |
| 2½ quarts | 2.5 liters | 2.5 liters |
| 3 quarts | 3 liters | 3 liters |
| 4 quarts | 4 liters | 4 liters |

## Weight

| U.S. UNITS | CANADIAN METRIC | AUSTRALIAN METRIC |
|---|---|---|
| 1 ounce | 30 grams | 30 grams |
| 2 ounces | 55 grams | 60 grams |
| 3 ounces | 85 grams | 90 grams |
| 4 ounces (¼ pound) | 115 grams | 125 grams |
| 8 ounces (½ pound) | 225 grams | 225 grams |
| 16 ounces (1 pound) | 455 grams | 500 grams |
| 1 pound | 455 grams | 0.5 kilogram |

## Measurements

| INCHES | CENTIMETERS |
|---|---|
| 1 | 2.5 |
| 2 | 5.0 |
| 3 | 7.5 |
| 4 | 10.0 |
| 5 | 12.5 |
| 6 | 15.0 |
| 7 | 17.5 |
| 8 | 20.5 |
| 9 | 23.0 |
| 10 | 25.5 |
| 11 | 28.0 |
| 12 | 30.5 |
| 13 | 33.0 |

## Temperatures

| FAHRENHEIT | CELSIUS |
|---|---|
| 32° | 0° |
| 212° | 100° |
| 250° | 120° |
| 275° | 140° |
| 300° | 150° |
| 325° | 160° |
| 350° | 180° |
| 375° | 190° |
| 400° | 200° |
| 425° | 220° |
| 450° | 230° |
| 475° | 240° |
| 500° | 260° |

**Note:** The recipes in this cookbook have not been developed or tested using metric measures. When converting recipes to metric, some variations in quality may be noted.

# index

Page numbers in *italics* indicate illustrations

## A

ABC (Almond Bing Cherry) Pie, 42
Aioli, 304
Almond(s)
    ABC (Almond Bing Cherry) Pie, 42
    -Cherry Wedding Pies, Individual, 144, *145*
    Crumb Pie, Apple-Raspberry, 16, *17*
    -Pear Pie, 214, *215*
    -Raspberry Pie, Starstruck, 44, *45*
    in Summer's Delight Pie, 58
    in Sweet Cherry Pie, Amaretto, 40, *41*
Amaretto
    Cherry Pie, Sweet, 40, *41*
    Peach Tart, 196, *197*
    Truffle Sauce, White, 194, *195*

Apple
    -Blackberry Pie, 18
    -Blueberry-Peach Pie, 53
    -Blueberry Pie with Strawberry Sauce, 19
    -Butterscotch Cream Cheese Pie, 106
    -Caramel-Ginger Crostata, 208, *209*
    Caramel-Marshmallow Tarts, 134
    -Caramel-Pear Praline Pie, 22, *23*
    Caramel Pie, 210
    -Caramel-Toffee Pie with Pecans, 20, *21*
    Cheesecake Pie, 27
    -Cherry Mini Wedding Pies, 142, *143*
    Cider-Bourbon Sauce, Apple-Ginger Tart with, 204, *205*
    Dumplings, 32, *33*
    -Orange Juice Pie, 26
    -Pear Praline Pie, 24, *25*

    Pie, Classic, 14
    Pie Cupcakes, Spice Jumbo, 136
    Pie, French, 14
    -Raspberry Crumb Pie, 16, *17*
    RazApple Pie, Nutty, 15
    Slab Pie, 28, *29*
    Slab Pie, -Pomegranate, 30, *31*
    -Sour Cream Pie, 206, *207*
    Tart, Easy, 174, *175*
    Tart, -Ginger, with Cider Bourbon Sauce, 204, *205*
    Tart, Walnut, Maple-, 176
    Turnovers, Harvest, 135
Apricot
    -Cranberry Tart, Jeweled, *202–203*, 242, *243*
    Pie, 64
    Pie, Gingered, *12–13*, 70, *71*
Asparagus, Canadian Bacon and Potato Quiche, 324

## Recipe Testing and Calculating Nutrition Information

### RECIPE TESTING:

- Large eggs and 2% milk were used unless otherwise indicated.

- Fat-free, low-fat, low-sodium or lite products were not used unless indicated.

- No nonstick cookware and bakeware were used unless otherwise indicated. No dark-colored, black or insulated bakeware was used.

- When a pan is specified, a metal pan was used; a baking dish or pie plate means ovenproof glass was used.

- An electric hand mixer was used for mixing only when mixer speeds are specified.

### CALCULATING NUTRITION:

- The first ingredient was used wherever a choice is given, such as ⅓ cup sour cream or plain yogurt.

- The first amount was used wherever a range is given, such as 3- to 3½-pound whole chicken.

- The first serving number was used wherever a range is given, such as 4 to 6 servings.

- "If desired" ingredients were not included.

- Only the amount of a marinade or frying oil that is absorbed was included.

# B

Bacon
- Canadian, Asparagus and Potato Quiche, 324
- Chicken Pot Pies, Mini, 266, *267*
- -Potato-Onion Slab Pie, 318, *319*
- Quiche Lorraine, 322, *323*
- -Tomato Pie, Cheesy, 320, *321*

Baking methods, pie crust, 9
Baking methods, pies/tarts, 6

Banana
- Bananas Foster Pie, 88, *89*
- Cream Pie, 85
- Cream Pie, Chocolate-, 85
- Cream Pie, Macadamia Nut-, 90
- Cream Pie, Macadamia Nut-Chocolate-, 90
- -Dulce de Leche Pie, 86, *87*

Bangers and Mash Hand Pies, 300, *301*
Bean and Rice Burrito Pot Pie, 311

Beef
- Cheeseburger Pies, Mini Blue, Impossibly Easy, 286, *287*
- Cheeseburger Pies, Mini, Impossibly Easy, 288, *289*
- Cheeseburger Pot Pie, 283
- Chili Pot Pie, 282
- Empanadas, 296
- Greek Burger Pies, Mini, Impossibly Easy, 290, *291*
- Ground Beef Pot Pie, 279
- Ground Beef Pot Pie, Deep-Dish, 278
- Meat and Potato Pie, Rustic, 276, *277*
- -Onion Pastries, Caramelized, 292, *293*
- Samosa Pot Pie, Southeast Asian, 280, *281*
- Taco Pies, Muffin Tin, *252–253*, 284, *285*

Berry Pie(s). *See also specific berries*
- Cheesecake Squares, -Lemon, 154, *155*
- -Cherry Sweetheart, 48
- Custard, Fresh Berry, 92, *93*
- Ice Cream, 130, *131*
- Pizza, Fruit, 201
- Raz-Black-Blue, 54
- Rhu-Berry, 59
- Slab, Fresh Berry, 96, *97*
- Wedding, Mini, 142, *143*
- Wild Berry, 55

Berry Tart(s). *See also specific berries*
- -Cherry-Plum, Merry, 194, *195*
- Crumble, Mixed, 182, *183*
- Fruit Tart, Fresh, The Ultimate, 192
- Three-Berry, Creamy, 191

Biscuits
- Chicken Pot Pie Bubble Bake, 265
- Chicken Pot Pies, Bacon, Mini, 266, *267*
- Chicken Pot Pie, Skillet, 264
- Chili Mac Pasta Pies, 314
- Chili Pot Pie, 282
- Lasagna Pasta Pies, 302, *303*

Bisquick
- Cheeseburger Pies, Mini Blue, Impossibly Easy, 286, *287*
- Cheeseburger Pies, Mini, Impossibly Easy, 288, *289*
- Chicken Pies, Mini Thai, Impossibly Easy, 270, *271*
- Crab Cake Pies, Mini, Impossibly Easy, 304, *305*
- Greek Burger Pies, Mini, Impossibly Easy, 290, *291*
- Sausage Pies, Mini Breakfast, Impossibly Easy, 298, *299*
- Veggie Pies, Mini, Impossibly Easy South-of-the-Border, 312, *313*

Bittersweet Chocolate Pecan Pie, 231

Blackberry(ies)
- -Apple Pie, 18
- in Berry Pie, Wild, 55
- Cheesecake Squares, Berry-Lemon, 154, *155*
- Raz-Black-Blue Pie, 54
- Tart, Creamy Three-Berry, 191

Blueberry(ies)
- -Apple-Peach Pie, 53
- -Apple Pie with Strawberry Sauce, 19
- Cheesecake Pie, Fresh, 94, *95*
- Cheesecake Squares, Berry-Lemon, 154, *155*
- -Cherry Pie, 49
- Crumble Tart, Mixed Berry, 182, *183*
- in Fruit Pizza, 201
- -Lemon Cream Cheese Pie, 106
- Lemon Ice Cream Pie, -Topped, 122
- -Mango Hand Pies, 152, *153*
- Orange Ice Cream Pie, -Topped, 122
- -Peach Pie, 50
- Pie, 50, *51*
- Pie, Fresh, 52
- Raz-Black-Blue Pie, 54
- Rhu-Berry Pie, 59
- Slab Pie, Fresh, 96, *97*
- Swirl Pie, Crunchy Crust, 91
- Tart, Creamy Three-Berry, 191
- Tart, -Lemon, 179
- Wedding Pies, -Ginger, Individual, 144, *145*
- Wild Berry Pie, 55

Blue Cheeseburger Pies, Mini, Impossibly Easy, 286, *287*
Bourbon-Chocolate-Pecan Mini Pies, 156, *157*
Bourbon-Cider Sauce, Apple-Ginger Tart with, 204, *205*
Browned Butter Pecan Pie, 228
Brownie Pie, Fudgy, with Caramel Sauce, 232, *233*
Burrito Pot Pie, Rice and Bean, 311
Buster Sundae Pie, 129
Butter Crust, 7, 8
Buttermilk Pastry, Easy, 11

Butterscotch
- Cream Cheese-Apple Pie, 106
- Cream Pie, 85
- -Pumpkin Cream Tart, 220, *221*

# C

Café Latte Pie, 111
Canadian Bacon, Asparagus and Potato Quiche, 324

Caramel
- -Apple-Ginger Crostata, 208, *209*
- Apple Pie, 210
- -Chocolate Pie Supreme, 82, *83*
- Cream Pie, 84
- Dulce de Leche-Banana Pie, 86, *87*
- Pear-Apple Praline Pie, 22, *23*

Sauce, 218
Sauce, Fudgy Brownie Pie with, 232, *233*
-Toffee-Apple Pie with Pecans, 20, *21*
Turtle Cheesecake Tartlets, 234
Caramelized Onion-Beef Pastries, 292, *293*
Cashew
    -Chocolate-Cranberry Tart, 238, *239*
    -Chocolate Pie, 79
    Salted, -Bittersweet Chocolate Tart, 236, *237*
Chai Cream Pie, 112, *113*
Cheeseburger Pies, Mini Blue, Impossibly Easy, 286, *287*
Cheeseburger Pot Pie, 283
Cheesecake
    Apple Cheesecake Pie, 27
    Berry-Lemon Cheesecake Squares, 154, *155*
    Blueberry Cheesecake Pie, Fresh, 94, *95*
    Turtle Cheesecake Tartlets, 234
Cheese-Crusted Pizza Pot Pies, 306
Cheesy Bacon-Tomato Pie, 320, *321*
Cherry(ies)
    ABC (Almond Bing Cherry) Pie, 42
    Amaretto Sweet Cherry Pie, 40, *41*
    -Apple Mini Wedding Pies, 142, *143*
    -Berry Sweetheart Pie, 48
    -Blueberry Pie, 49
    -Chocolate Cream Cheese Pie, 106
    Heart-Shaped Pies, -Filled, 140, *141*
    Pie, 39
    Pie, Quick, 39
    Pie, Sparkling, 43
    -Plum-Berry Tart, Merry, 194, *195*
    -Red Raspberry Pie, 47
    -Strawberry Pie, 46
    in Summer's Delight Pie, 58
    Wedding Pies, -Almond, Individual, 144, *145*
Chicken Pie(s)
    Mediterranean Chicken Bake, 263
    Mini Thai, Impossibly Easy, 270, *271*
    Moroccan, 260, *261*

Chicken Pot Pie(s)
    Bubble Bake, 265
    with Flaky Crust, 256, *257*
    French Onion-, 272
    Individual, 254, *255*
    Lattice, Herbed, 258, *259*
    Mini, 268, *269*
    Mini Bacon, 266, *267*
    Skillet, 264
    Souvlaki, 262
Chili Mac Pasta Pies, 314
Chili Pot Pie, 282
Choco-Coco-Nut Mini Ice Cream Pies, 168
Chocolate
    -Banana Cream Pie, 85
    -Banana Cream Pie, Macadamia Nut, 90
    Bottom Pie, Rich, with Hazelnut Crust, 80, *81*
    -Bourbon-Pecan Mini Pies, 156, *157*
    Brownie Pie, Fudgy, with Caramel Sauce, 232, *233*
    -Caramel Pie Supreme, 82, *83*
    -Cashew-Cranberry Tart, 238, *239*
    -Cashew Pie, 79
    -Coconut Jumbo Pie Cupcakes, 137
    Cookie Crumb Crust, 12, 111, 124, 128
    -Cranberry Tart, 193
    Cream Cheese-Cherry Pie, 106
    Cream Pie, 85
    French Silk Pie, Classic, 76, *77*
    French Silk Pie, Mocha, 76, *77*
    German Chocolate Pie, 78
    Ice Cream Pies, Mini, Choco-Coco-Nut, 168
    -Macadamia Tart, 240
    -Peanut Butter Sauce, 124
    Pecan Pie, Bittersweet Chocolate, 231
    Raspberry Pie, White Chocolate-, 244, *245*
    Raspberry Pie Pops, White Chocolate-, 147
    Raspberry Tart, White and Dark Chocolate, 190
    S'mores Hand Pies, 166, *167*

Tart, Bittersweet, -Salted Cashew, 236, *237*
Chocolate Chip(s)
    Cookie-Stuffed Pies, 160, *161*
    -Pecan Pie, Spiced, 229
    in Turtle Cheesecake Tartlets, 234
Chocolate Curls, 82
Cider-Bourbon Sauce, Apple-Ginger Tart with, 204, *205*
Cinnamon Graham Cracker Crust, 191
Classic Apple Pie, 14
Classic French Silk Pie, 76, *77*
Cocktail Pie(s)
    Mai Tai, 116, *117*
    Sangria, 120, *121*
    Strawberry Daiquiri, 118, *119*
    Vodka Lemonade, 114
Coconut
    -Chocolate Jumbo Pie Cupcakes, 137
    Cream Pie, 85
    in German Chocolate Pie, 78
    Mai Tai Cocktail Pie, 116, *117*
    in Mango-Pineapple with Macadamia Lattice Crust, 72, *73*
    in Peach-Rhubarb Pie, 62, *63*
    Piña Colada Tart, 200
    in Pineapple, Mango and Cream Pie, Tropical, 98
Coffee
    Café Latte Pie, 111
    French Silk Pie, Mocha, 76, *77*
    Ice Cream Pie, 128
    Ice Cream Pie, "Jamocha," 126, *127*
Cookie Crumb Crust
    Chocolate, 12, 111, 123, 128
    Gingersnap, 12, 218
    Vanilla, 12, 130
Cookie-Stuffed Pies
    Chocolate Chip, 160, *161*
    Peanut Butter Cup, 159
    Peanut Butter and Jelly, 158
Cooling pies/tarts, 6
Cornbread-Topped Sausage Pie, 297
Country Rhubarb Crostata, 199
Crab Cake Pies, Mini, Impossibly Easy, 304, *305*
Crab, in Seafood Quiche, 322

Cranberry(ies)
-Apricot Tart, Jeweled, *202–203*, 242, *243*
in Cherry-Plum-Berry Tart, Merry, 194, *195*
-Chocolate-Cashew Tart, 238, *239*
-Chocolate Tart, 193
Mousse Mini Tarts, 246, *247*
-Raisin Maple Nut Pie, 241
Cream Cheese. *See also* Cheesecake
in Bananas Foster Pie, 88, *89*
in Berry Slab Pie, Fresh, 96, *97*
in Berry Tart, Creamy Three-Berry, 191
in Blueberry-Lemon Tart, 179
Butterscotch-Apple Pie, 106
in Caramel-Chocolate Pie Supreme, 82, *83*
Chocolate-Cherry Pie, 106
in Cranberry-Apricot Tart, Jeweled, *202–203*, 242, *243*
in Fruit Pizza, 201
Lemon-Blueberry Pie, 106
in Peach Tart, Amaretto, 196, *197*
in Pineapple, Mango and Cream Pie, Tropical, 98
in Pineapple-Lemon Layered Pie, 99
Pumpkin-Butterscotch Cream Tart, 220, *221*
Pumpkin Cheese Tart, 218
in S'mores Hand Pies, 166, *167*
in Strawberries and Cream Tart, 186, *187*
in Strawberry Marshmallow Pie, 108, *109*
in Strawberry Pie, Fresh, 57
in Strawberry Pretzel Pie, 110
Cream Pie(s)
Banana, 85
Banana, Chocolate-, 85
Banana, Macadamia Nut-, 90
Banana, Macadamia Nut-Chocolate-, 90
Butterscotch, 85
Café Latte, 111
Caramel, 84
Caramel-Chocolate, Supreme, 82, *83*

Chai, 112, *113*
Chocolate, 85
Chocolate-Cashew, 79
Coconut, 85
Dulce de Leche-Banana, 86, *87*
French Silk, Classic, 76, *77*
French Silk, Mocha, 76
German Chocolate, 78
Grasshopper, 111
Irish Cream, 111
Pear, 212, *213*
Tropical Pineapple, Mango and, 98
White Chocolate-Raspberry, 244, *245*
Cream Tart(s)
Berry, Three-, Creamy, 191
Blueberry-Lemon, 179
Cranberry-Chocolate, 193
Fruit, Fresh, The Ultimate, 192
Lemon Mascarpone, 100, *101*
Piña Colada, 200
Pumpkin-Butterscotch, 220, *221*
Raspberry-Lemon Meringue, 188, *189*
Raspberry, White and Dark Chocolate, 190
Strawberries and, 186, *187*
Creamy Three-Berry Tart, 191
Crostata
Caramel-Apple-Ginger, 208, *209*
Nectarine-Plum, 180, *181*
Pear, Fresh, 177
Rhubarb, Country, 199
Vegetable, Roasted, -Goat Cheese, 308, *309*
Crumb, Crumble
Apple Pie, Sour Cream-, 206, *207*
Apple-Raspberry Pie, 16, *17*
Berry Tart, Mixed, 182, *183*
Blueberry-Apple-Peach Pie, 53
Peach Pie, 66, *67*
Peach Wedding Pies, Mini, 142, *143*
Pear Pie, Dutch, 38
Sweet Potato Pie Squares, Streusel-Topped, 225
Crunchy Crust Blueberry Swirl Pie, 91
Crust. *See* Cookie Crumb Crust; Pie Crust; Pie Pastry

Cucumber Yogurt Sauce, 280
Cupcakes. *See* Pie Cupcakes, Jumbo
Custard
Berry Custard Pie, Fresh, 92, *93*
Pear Custard Pie, Elegant, 34, *35*
Rhubarb Custard Tart, 198
Cutouts, decorative, 9
Cutting pies/tarts, 6

**D**
Daiquiri Cocktail Pie, Strawberry, 118, *119*
Deep-Dish Ground Beef Pot Pies, 278
Dulce de Leche-Banana Pie, 86, *87*
Dumplings, Apple, 32, *33*
Dutch Pear Pie, 38

**E**
Easy Apple Tart, 174, *175*
Easy Lemonade Pie, 123
Egg Glaze, 49
Elegant Pear Custard Pie, 34, *35*
Empanada Grande, 294, *295*
Empanadas, Beef, 296

**F**
Fluted pie crust edge, 10
Forked pie crust edge, 10
Freezing pie pastry/filled pies, 6
French Apple Pie, 14
French Onion-Chicken Pot Pies, 272
French Silk Pie, Classic, 76, *77*
French Silk Pie, Mocha, 76, *77*
Fresh Berry Custard Pie, 92, *93*
Fresh Berry Slab Pie, 96, *97*
Fresh Blueberry Pie, 52
Fresh Pear Crostata, 177
Fresh Strawberry Pie, 57
Fresh Strawberry Tarts, 178
Frozen Pies. *See also* Ice Cream Pie(s)
Mai Tai Cocktail, 116, *117*
Sangria Cocktail, 120, *121*
Strawberry Daiquiri Cocktail, 118, *119*
Vodka Lemonade Cocktail, 114, *115*
Fruit Pie(s). See also Berry Pie(s); *specific fruits and berries*
Pizza, Fruit, 201
Summer's Delight, 58

Fruit Tart(s). See also Berry Tart(s); *specific fruits and berries*
    The Ultimate Fresh, 192
Fudgy Brownie Pie with Caramel Sauce, 232, *233*

**G**
German Chocolate Pie, 78
Ginger(ed)
    -Apple Tart with Cider Bourbon Sauce, 204, *205*
    Apricot Pie, *12–13*, 70, *71*
    -Blueberry Wedding Pies, Individual, 144, *145*
    -Caramel-Apple Crostata, 208, *209*
    -Lemon Curd Petite Pies, *132–133*, 162, *163*
    Pear Pie, Spiced, 36, *37*
Gingersnap Cookie Crumb Crust, 11, 218
Glaze, for baked pie crust, 10
Glaze, Egg, 49
Goat Cheese-Roasted Vegetable Crostata, 308, *309*
Golden Pecan Pie, 230
Graham Cracker Crust, 11
Graham Cracker Crust, Cinnamon, 191
Grape Pie, 56
Grasshopper Pie, 111
Greek Burger Pies, Mini, Impossibly Easy, 290, *291*
Ground Beef Pot Pie, 279

**H**
Ham and Swiss Breakfast Hand Pies, 318, *319*
Hand Pies
    Bangers and Mash, 300, *301*
    Blueberry-Mango, 152, *153*
    Ham and Swiss Breakfast, 318, *319*
    S'mores, 166, *167*
Harvest Turkey Pot Pie, 273
Hazelnut Crust, Rich Chocolate Bottom Pie with, 80, *81*
Heart-Shaped Cherry-Filled Pies, 140, *141*
Herbed Chicken Lattice Pot Pie, 258, *259*
Herringbone pie crust edge, 10

Holiday Pies
    Almond-Pear, 214, *215*
    Apple, Caramel, 210
    Apple, Sour Cream-, 206, *207*
    Brownie, Fudgy, with Caramel Sauce, 232, *233*
    Cranberry-Raisin Maple Nut, 241
    Ice Cream, Peppermint Cookie, 250, *251*
    Pear Cream, 212, *213*
    Pecan, 226, *227*
    Pecan, Bittersweet Chocolate, 231
    Pecan, Browned Butter, 228
    Pecan, Chocolate Chip-, Spiced, 229
    Pecan, Golden, 230
    Pecan, Kentucky, 226
    Pumpkin, 216, *217*
    Pumpkin Meringue, 219
    Pumpkin, Pecan-, 224
    Pumpkin, Praline, 216
    Sweet Potato, Roasted, 222, *223*
    Sweet Potato Squares, Streusel-Topped, 225
    White Chocolate-Raspberry, 244, *245*
Holiday Tarts
    Apple-Ginger, with Cider Bourbon Sauce, 204, *205*
    Caramel-Apple-Ginger Crostata, 208, *209*
    Chocolate, Bittersweet, -Salted Cashew, 236, *237*
    Chocolate-Cashew-Cranberry, 238, *239*
    Chocolate-Macadamia, 240
    Cranberry-Apricot, Jeweled, *202–203*, 242, *243*
    Cranberry Mousse Mini, 246, *247*
    Peppermint Candy, 249
    Pomegranate Tartlets, 248
    Pumpkin-Butterscotch Cream, 220, *221*
    Pumpkin Cheese, 218
    Turtle Cheesecake Tartlets, 234

**I**
Ice Cream Pie(s)
    Berry, 130, *131*
    Buster Sundae, 129
    Choco-Coco-Nut, Mini, 168

    Coffee, 128
    "Jamocha," 126, *127*
    Lemon, Blueberry-Topped, 122
    Lemonade, Easy, 123
    Lime Cooler, Mini, 169
    Orange, Blueberry-Topped, 122
    Orange Dream, Mini, 170, *171*
    Peanut Butter, 124, *125*
    Peppermint Cookie, 250, *251*
Impossibly Easy Mini Blue Cheeseburger Pies, 286, *287*
Impossibly Easy Mini Breakfast Sausage Pies, 298, *299*
Impossibly Easy Mini Cheeseburger Pies, 288, *289*
Impossibly Easy Mini Crab Cake Pies, 304, *305*
Impossibly Easy Mini Greek Burger Pies, 290, *291*
Impossibly Easy Mini Pumpkin Pies, 172, *173*
Impossibly Easy Mini Thai Chicken Pies, 270, *271*
Impossibly Easy South-of-the-Border Mini Veggie Pies, 312, *313*
Individual Chicken Pot Pies, 254, *255*
Irish Cream Pie, 111

**J**
Jack-O'-Lantern Sloppy Joe Pie, 275
"Jamocha" Ice Cream Pie, 126, *127*
Jeweled Apricot-Cranberry Tart, *202–203*, 242, *243*

**K**
Kentucky Pecan Pie, 226
Key Lime Pie, 104, *105*
Kiwi, in Fruit Pizza, 201

**L**
Lamb, in Mini Greek Burger Pies, Impossibly Easy, 290, *291*
Lasagna Pasta Pies, 302, *303*
Lattice-Top Crusts
    Classic, 10
    Easy, 10
    Macadamia, Mango-Pineapple Pie with, 72, *73*
Leek Quiche, 325

Lemon
  -Blueberry Tart, 179
  Cheesecake Squares, Berry-,
    154, *155*
  Cream Cheese-Blueberry Pie, 106
  Curd-Ginger Petite Pies, *132–133*,
    162, *163*
  Curd Jumbo Pie Cupcakes, 164, *165*
  Ice Cream Pie, Blueberry-Topped, 122
  Mascarpone Tart, 100, *101*
  Meringue Pie, 102, *103*
  Meringue Tart, Raspberry-, 188, *189*
  -Pineapple Layered Pie, 99
Lemonade Pie, Easy, 123
Lemonade Vodka Cocktail Pie, 114, *115*
Lime Cooler Ice Cream Pies, Mini, 169
Lime, Key Lime Pie, 104, *105*

## M

Macadamia (Nut)
  -Banana Cream Pie, 90
  -Chocolate-Banana Cream Pie, 90
  -Chocolate Tart, 240
  Lattice Crust, Mango-Pineapple Pie
    with, 72, *73*
Mac Pasta Pies, Chili, 314
Mai Tai Cocktail Pie, 116, *117*
Mango
  -Blueberry Hand Pies, 152, *153*
  Mai Tai Cocktail Pie, 116, *117*
  Pineapple, and Cream Pie, Tropical, 98
  -Pineapple Pie with Macadamia
    Lattice Crust, 72, *73*
Maple-Apple Walnut Tart, 176
Maple Nut Cranberry-Raisin Pie, 241
Marshmallow(s)
  -Caramel Apple Tarts, 134
  in Chai Cream Pie, 112, *113*
  in Grasshopper Pie, 111
  S'mores Hand Pies, 166, *167*
  Strawberry Pie, 108, *109*
Mascarpone Lemon Tart, 100, *101*
Meat and Potato Pie, Rustic, 276, *277*
Mediterranean Chicken Bake, 263
Meringue
  Lemon Meringue Pie, 102, *103*
  Lemon Meringue Tart, Raspberry-,
    188, *189*

Pumpkin Meringue Pie, 219
  in Sour Cream-Raisin Pie, 107
Merry Cherry-Plum-Berry Tart, 194, *195*
Mini Pies. *See also* Hand Pies; Pie
    Cupcakes, Jumbo; Turnovers;
    Wedding Pies, Mini
  Bourbon-Chocolate-Pecan, 156, *157*
  Cheeseburger, Blue, Impossibly
    Easy, 286, *287*
  Cheeseburger, Impossibly Easy,
    288, *289*
  Cheesecake Squares, Berry-Lemon,
    154, *155*
  Cherry-Filled Heart-Shaped, 140, *141*
  Chicken, Thai, Impossibly Easy,
    270, *271*
  Chicken Pot Pies, 268, *269*
  Chicken Pot Pies, Bacon, 266, *267*
  Cookie-Stuffed, Chocolate Chip,
    160, *161*
  Cookie-Stuffed, Peanut Butter Cup,
    159
  Cookie-Stuffed, Peanut Butter and
    Jelly, 158
  Crab Cake, Impossibly Easy,
    304, *305*
  Crusts/Shells, Baked Individual, 9
  Greek Burger, Impossibly Easy,
    290, *291*
  Ice Cream, Choco-Coco-Nut, 168
  Ice Cream, Lime Cooler, 169
  Ice Cream, Orange Dream, 170, *171*
  Lemon Curd, Ginger-, Petite,
    *132–133*, 162, *163*
  Pie Poppers, 146
  Pumpkin, Impossibly Easy, 172, *173*
  Raspberry-White Chocolate Pie
    Pops, 147
  Sausage, Breakfast, Impossibly
    Easy, 298, *299*
  Strawberry-Rhubarb, 150, *151*
  Strawberry-Rhubarb Pie Pops,
    148, *149*
  Veggie, South-of-the-Border,
    Impossibly Easy, 312, *313*
Mini Tarts
  Caramel Apple-Marshmallow, 134
  Cranberry Mousse, 246, *247*

Pastry, Baked Individual, 9
Pear Tartlets, 138, *139*
Peppermint Candy, 249
Pomegranate Tartlets, 248
Turtle Cheesecake Tartlets, 234
Mixed Berry Crumble Tart, 182, *183*
Mixed Pluot Tart, 184, *185*
Mocha French Silk Pie, 76, *77*
Moroccan Chicken Pie, 260, *261*
Muffin Tin Taco Pies, *252–253*, 284, *285*

## N

Nectarine-Plum Crostata, 180, *181*
Nectarines, in Summer's Delight Pie, 58
Not-Your-Mother's Tuna Pot Pie, 307
Nut(s). *See also specific nuts*
  Crunchy Crust Blueberry Swirl Pie, 91
  Crust, Easy, 11
  Maple, Cranberry-Raisin Pie, 241
  RazApple Pie, Nutty, 15
Nutty RazApple Pie, 15

## O

One-Crust Pie Pastry, 7
Onion
  -Beef Pastries, Caramelized, 292, *293*
  French Onion-Chicken Pot Pies, 272
  -Potato-Bacon Slab Pie, 318, *319*
Orange
  Apple Pie, Orange Juice-, 26
  Ice Cream Pie, Blueberry-Topped, 122
  Ice Cream Pies, Mini Orange Dream,
    170, *171*
  Pecan Pie, 230

## P

Pastry. *See* Phyllo; Pie Pastry; Puff
    Pastry; Tart Pastry
Pastry, Press-in-the-Pan, 11
Patchwork Turkey Pot Pie, 274
Peach(es)
  Amaretto Tart, 196, *197*
  -Blueberry-Apple Pie, 53
  -Blueberry Pie, 50
  -Cinnamon Wedding Pies,
    Individual, 144, *145*
  Crumble Pie, 66, *67*
  Crumble Wedding Pies, Mini, 142, *143*

Pie, 64, *65*
Plum Peachy Pie, 69
-Rhubarb Pie, 62, *63*
Slab Pie, 68
in Summer's Delight Pie, 58
Peanut Butter
-Chocolate Sauce, 124
Cup Cookie-Stuffed Pies, 159
Ice Cream Pie, 124, *125*
and Jelly Cookie-Stuffed Pies, 158
Pear
-Almond Pie, 214, *215*
-Apple Praline Pie, 24, *25*
Caramel-Apple Praline Pie, 22, *23*
Cream Pie, 212, *213*
Crostata, Fresh, 177
Custard Pie, Elegant, 34, *35*
Pie, Dutch, 38
Pie, Spiced Gingered, 36, *37*
Tartlets, 138, *139*
Pecan(s). *See also* Praline
-Bourbon-Chocolate Mini Pies, 156, *157*
Caramel-Toffee-Apple Pie with, 20, *21*
in German Chocolate Pie, 78
in Peach-Rhubarb Pie, 62, *63*
Pie, 226, *227*
Pie, Bittersweet Chocolate, 231
Pie, Browned Butter, 228
Pie, -Chocolate Chip, Spiced, 229
Pie, Golden, 230
Pie, Kentucky, 226
Pie, Orange, 230
-Pumpkin Pie, 224
Peppermint Candy Tarts, 249
Peppermint Cookie Ice Cream Pie, 250, *251*
Petite Pies and Tarts. *See* Mini Pies; Mini Tarts
Phyllo
Apple Dumplings, Lighter, 32
Chicken Bake, Mediterranean, 263
Chicken Pie, Moroccan, 260, *261*
Pie(s). *See* Berry Pie(s); Cream Pie(s); Frozen Pies; Fruit Pie(s); Holiday Pies; Mini Pies; Savory Pies

Pie Crust. *See also* Cookie Crumb Crust; Pie Pastry
Crunchy, Blueberry Swirl Pie, 91
cutouts, decorative, 9
edges, decorative, 10
Graham Cracker, 11, 191
Hazelnut, 80, *81*
lattice-top, 10
Macadamia Lattice, 72, *73*
Nut, Easy, 11
Pillsbury refrigerated, 211, 235
Pie Cupcakes, Jumbo
Apple Spice, 136
Chocolate-Coconut, 137
Lemon Curd, 164, *165*
Pie Pastry. *See also* Phyllo; Puff Pastry; Pie Crust
Baked, Glaze for, 10
baking, 6
Butter Crust, 7, 8
Buttermilk, Easy, 11
food processor method, 8
freezing, 6
One-Crust, 7
One-Crust, Baked, 9
One-Crust, Partially Baked, 9
Press in the Pan, 11
tips for, 150
top crust treatments, 52
Two-Crust, 8
Pie plates, 6
Pie Poppers, 146
Pie Pops, Raspberry-White Chocolate, 147
Pie Pops, Strawberry-Rhubarb, 148, *149*
Pie Squares, Cheesecake, Berry-Lemon, 154, *155*
Pie Squares, Sweet Potato, Streusel-Topped, 225
Pillsbury refrigerated pie crust, 211, 235
Piña Colada Tart, 200
Pinched pie crust edge, 10
Pineapple
-Lemon Layered Pie, 99
Mango and Cream Pie, Tropical, 98
-Mango Pie with Macadamia Lattice Crust, 72, *73*

Piña Colada Tart, 200
Pizza, Fruit, 201
Pizza Pot Pies, Cheese-Crusted, 306
Plum
-Cherry-Berry Tart, Merry, 194, *195*
-Nectarine Crostata, 180, *181*
Peachy Pie, 69
Pluot Tart, Mixed, 184, *185*
Pomegranate-Apple Slab Pie, 30, *31*
Pomegranate Tartlets, 248
Potato(es)
Bangers and Mash Hand Pies, 300, *301*
Canadian Bacon and Asparagus Quiche, 324
and Meat Pie, Rustic, 276, *277*
-Onion-Bacon Slab Pie, 318, *319*
Samosa Pot Pie, Southeast Asian, 280, *281*
Pot Pie(s). *See also* Chicken Pot Pie(s)
Cheeseburger, 283
Chili, 282
Ground Beef, 279
Ground Beef, Deep-Dish, 278
Pizza, Cheese-Crusted, 306
Rice and Bean Burrito, 311
Samosa, Southeast Asian, 280, *281*
Southwestern, 310
Tuna, Not-Your-Mother's, 307
Turkey, Harvest, 273
Turkey, Patchwork, 274
Veggie Lovers', 315
Praline
Apple-Pear Pie, 24, *25*
Pear Caramel-Apple Pie, 22, *23*
Pumpkin Pie, 216
Press-in-the-Pan Pastry, 11
Press-in-the-Pan Tart Pastry, 11
Pretzel Strawberry Pie, 110
Puff Pastry
Chicken Pot Pie with Flaky Crust, 256, *257*
Chicken Pot Pies, Individual, 254, *255*
Pear Tartlets, 138, *139*
Pumpkin
-Butterscotch Cream Tart, 220, *221*
Cheese Tart, 218

Pumpkin (continued)
  Meringue Pie, 219
  Mini Pies, Impossibly Easy, 172, *173*
  -Pecan Pie, 224
  Pie, 216, *217*
  Praline Pie, 216

## Q

Quiche
  Canadian Bacon, Asparagus and
    Potato, 324
  Leek, 325
  Lorraine, 322, *323*
  Seafood, 322
  Spinach, 322
Quick Cherry Pie, 39
Quick Rhubarb Pie, 60

## R

Raisin-Cranberry Maple Nut Pie, 241
Raisin-Sour Cream Pie, 107
Raspberry(ies)
  -Almond Pie, Starstruck, 44, *45*
  -Apple Crumb Pie, 16, *17*
  Cheesecake Squares, Berry-Lemon,
    154, *155*
  Cherry-Berry Sweetheart Pie, 48
  Cherry-Red Raspberry Pie, 47
  Chocolate Tart, White and Dark
    Chocolate, 190
  Crumble Tart, Mixed Berry, 182, *183*
  Ice Cream Pie, Berry, 130, *131*
  -Lemon Meringue Tart, 188, *189*
  RazApple Pie, Nutty, 15
  Raz-Black-Blue Pie, 54
  Sangria Cocktail Pie, 120, *121*
  Slab Pie, Fresh Berry, 96, *97*
  Tart, Creamy Three-Berry, 191
  -White Chocolate Pie, 244, *245*
  -White Chocolate Pie Pops, 147
RazApple Pie, Nutty, 15
Raz-Black-Blue Pie, 54
Refrigerated pie crust, Pillsbury,
  211, 235
Rhubarb
  Crostata, Country, 199
  Custard Tart, 198
  -Peach Pie, 62, *63*
  Pie, 60, *61*

Pie, Quick, 60
Rhu-Berry Pie, 59
-Strawberry Mini Pies, 150, *151*
-Strawberry Pie, 60
-Strawberry Pie Pops, 148, *149*
Rhu-Berry Pie, 59
Rice and Bean Burrito Pot Pie, 311
Rich Chocolate Bottom Pie with
  Hazelnut Crust, 80, *81*
Roasted Sweet Potato Pie, 222, *223*
Roasted Vegetable-Goat Cheese
  Crostata, 308, *309*
Rope pie crust edge, 10
Rum
  in Mai Tai Cocktail Pie, 116, *117*
  in Piña Colada Tart, 200
  in Strawberry Daiquiri Cocktail Pie,
    118, *119*
Rustic Meat and Potato Pie, 276, *277*

## S

Salted Cashew-Bittersweet Chocolate
  Tart, 236, *237*
Samosa Pot Pie, Southeast Asian,
  280, *281*
Sangria Cocktail Pie, 120, *121*
Sauce(s)
  Aioli, 304
  Amaretto Truffle, White, 194, *195*
  Caramel, 218
  Caramel, Fudgy Brownie Pie with,
    232, *233*
  Chocolate-Peanut Butter, 124
  Cider-Bourbon, Apple-Ginger Tart
    with, 204, *205*
  Cucumber Yogurt, 280
  Strawberry, Apple-Blueberry Pie
    with, 19
Sausage
  Bangers and Mash Hand Pies,
    300, *301*
  Breakfast Sausage Mini Pies,
    Impossibly Easy, 298, *299*
  Cornbread-Topped Sausage Pie, 297
  Empanada Grande, 294, *295*
  in Lasagna Pasta Pies, 302, *303*
  Pizza Pot Pies, Cheese-Crusted, 306
  Sloppy Joe Pie, Jack-O'-Lantern, 275

Savory Pies. *See also* Chicken Pot
    Pie(s); Pot Pie(s); Quiche
  Bacon-Tomato, Cheesy, 320, *321*
  Bangers and Mash Hand Pies,
    300, *301*
  Cheeseburger, Mini Blue, Impossibly
    Easy, 286, *287*
  Cheeseburger, Mini, Impossibly
    Easy, 288, *289*
  Chicken Bake, Mediterranean, 263
  Chicken, Mini Thai, Impossibly Easy,
    270, *271*
  Chicken, Moroccan, 260, *261*
  Chili Mac Pasta, 314
  Crab Cake, Mini, Impossibly Easy,
    304, *305*
  Empanada Grande, 294, *295*
  Empanadas, Beef, 296
  Greek Burger, Mini, Impossibly Easy,
    290, *291*
  Ham and Swiss Breakfast Hand
    Pies, 318, *319*
  Lasagna Pasta, 302, *303*
  Meat and Potato, Rustic, 276, *277*
  Onion-Beef Pastries, Caramelized,
    292, *293*
  Potato-Onion-Bacon Slab Pie,
    318, *319*
  Sausage, Breakfast, Mini,
    Impossibly Easy, 298, *299*
  Sausage, Cornbread-Topped, 297
  Sloppy Joe, Jack-O'-Lantern, 275
  Taco, Muffin Tin, *252–253*, 284, *285*
  Vegetable, Roasted, -Goat Cheese
    Crostata, 308–309
  Veggie, Mini, Impossibly Easy
    South-of-the-Border, 312, *313*
Scalloped pie crust edge, 10
Seafood
  Crab Cake Pies, Mini, Impossibly
    Easy, 304, *305*
  Quiche, 322
  Tuna Pot Pie, Not-Your-Mother's, 307
Sherbet
  Lemon Ice Cream Pie, Blueberry-
    Topped, 122
  Orange Dream Mini Ice Cream Pies,
    170, *171*

Orange Ice Cream Pie, Blueberry-Topped, 122
Sangria Cocktail Pie, 120, *121*
Vodka Lemonade Cocktail Pie, 114
Skillet Chicken Pot Pie, 264
Slab Pie(s)
  Apple, 28, *29*
  Apple-Pomegranate, 30, *31*
  Berry, Fresh, 96, *97*
  Peach, 68
  Potato-Onion-Bacon, 318, *319*
Sloppy Joe Pie, Jack-O'-Lantern, 275
S'mores Hand Pies, 166, *167*
Sorbet, in Mai Tai Cocktail Pie, 116, *117*
Sorbet, in Strawberry Daiquiri Cocktail Pie, 118, *119*
Sour Cream-Apple Pie, 206, *207*
Sour Cream-Raisin Pie, 107
Southeast Asian Samosa Pot Pie, 280, *281*
Southwestern Pot Pie, 310
Souvlaki Pot Pie, Chicken, 262
Sparkling Cherry Pie, 43
Spiced Chocolate Chip-Pecan Pie, 229
Spiced Gingered Pear Pie, 36, *37*
Spinach Quiche, 322
Starstruck Raspberry-Almond Pie, 44, *45*
Storing pies/tarts, 6
Strawberry(ies)
  -Cherry Pie, 46
  Crumble Tart, Mixed Berry, 182, *183*
  Daiquiri Cocktail Pie, 118, *119*
  in Fruit Pizza, 201
  Marshmallow Pie, 108, *109*
  Pie, Fresh, 57
  Pretzel Pie, 110
  -Rhubarb Mini Pies, 150, *151*
  -Rhubarb Pie, 60
  -Rhubarb Pie Pops, 148, *149*
  Sauce, Apple-Blueberry Pie with, 19
  Slab Pie, Fresh Berry, 96, *97*
  Tart, and Cream, 186, *187*
  Tarts, Fresh, 178
  Wild Berry Pie, 55

Streusel-Topped Sweet Potato Pie Squares, 225
Summer's Delight Pie, 58
Sundae Pie, Buster, 129
Sweetened Whipped Cream, 80
Sweet Potato Pie, Roasted, 222, *223*
Sweet Potato Pie Squares, Streusel-Topped, 225
Swiss and Ham Breakfast Hand Pies, 318, *319*

**T**
Taco Pies, Muffin Tin, *252–253*, 284, *285*
Tart(s). *See* Berry Tart(s); Cream Tart(s); Crostata; Fruit Tart(s); Holiday Tarts
Tartlets. *See* Mini Tarts
Tart Pastry. *See also* Pie Pastry
  Baked Individual, 9
  baking, 6
  Press-in-the-Pan, 11
  Shells, 249
Thai Chicken Pies, Mini, Impossibly Easy, 270, *271*
Three-in-One Mini Wedding Pies, 142, *143*
Toffee-Caramel-Apple Pie with Pecans, 20, *21*
Tomato-Bacon Pie, Cheesy, 320, *321*
Tropical Pineapple, Mango and Cream Pie, 98
Tuna Pot Pie, Not-Your-Mother's, 307
Turkey
  Pot Pie, Harvest, 273
  Pot Pie, Patchwork, 274
  Sloppy Joe Pie, Jack-O'-Lantern, 275
Turnovers
  Apple Harvest, 135
  Empanada Grande, 294, *295*
  Empanadas, Beef, 296
Turtle Cheesecake Tartlets, 234
Two-Crust Pie Pastry, 8

**U–V**
Ultimate Fresh Fruit Tart, The, 192

Vanilla Cookie Crumb Crust, 11, 130
Vegetable(s). *See also specific vegetables*
  Pies, Mini Veggie, Impossibly Easy South-of-the-Border, 312, *313*
  Pot Pie, Southwestern, 310
  Pot Pie, Veggie Lovers', 315
  Roasted, -Goat Cheese Crostata, 308, *309*
Veggie Lovers' Pot Pie, 315
Vodka Lemonade Cocktail Pie, 114

**W**
Walnut Apple-Maple Tart, 176
Walnuts, in Maple Nut Cranberry-Raisin Pie, 241
Wedding Pies, Mini
  Apple-Cherry, 142, *143*
  Berry, 142, *143*
  Blueberry-Ginger, Individual, 144, *145*
  Cherry-Almond, Individual, 144, *145*
  Peach-Cinnamon, Individual, 144, *145*
  Peach Crumble, 142, *143*
Whipped Cream, Sweetened, 80
White Chocolate-Raspberry Pie, 244, *245*
White Chocolate-Raspberry Pie Pops, 147
White and Dark Chocolate Raspberry Tart, 190
Wild Berry Pie, 55

**Y**
Yogurt
  in Berry Slab Pie, Fresh, 96, *97*
  in Blueberry-Lemon Tart, 179
  Cucumber Sauce, 280
  in Mai Tai Cocktail Pie, 116, *117*
  in Sangria Cocktail Pie, 120, *121*
  in Vodka Lemonade Cocktail Pie, 114